RESEARCHERS AND
THEIR 'SUBJECTS'

This book is dedicated to all those who take part in research

RESEARCHERS AND THEIR 'SUBJECTS'

Ethics, power, knowledge and consent

Edited by Marie Smyth and Emma Williamson

First published in Great Britain in October 2004 by

The Policy Press
University of Bristol
Fourth Floor
Beacon House
Queen's Road
Bristol BS8 1QU
UK

Tel +44 (0)117 331 4054
Fax +44 (0)117 331 4093
e-mail tpp-info@bristol.ac.uk
www.policypress.org.uk

© Marie Smyth and Emma Williamson 2004

British Library Cataloguing in Publication Data
A catalogue record for this book is available from the British Library.

Library of Congress Cataloging-in-Publication Data
A catalog record for this book has been requested.

ISBN 1 86134 514 3 paperback

A hardcover version of this book is also available

Marie Smyth is Head of Research and Communication for Criminal Justice Inspection Northern Ireland and Chair of Research Ethics Committee 1 for Northern Ireland and **Emma Williamson** is a Research Fellow in the Centre for Ethics in Medicine, University of Bristol, UK.

Cover design by Qube Design Associates, Bristol.
Front cover: the image was created by George Row using original photographs. See http://veryireland.com/rats/ for details.
Printed and bound in Great Britain by Hobbs the Printers Ltd, Southampton.

Contents

Notes on contributors

Hilary Abrahams is a Research Associate in the Domestic Violence Research Group, University of Bristol. She is currently working on an evaluation of supported housing for vulnerable groups of people, including women escaping domestic violence, for the Safer Communities Supported Housing Fund.

Pat Anderson works for the NHS as a Patient Involvement Facilitator, project managing the National Patient Surveys. Prior to this Pat worked as a Research Associate in the School for Policy Studies at the University of Bristol. Her research interests include parenting, the role of the family in society and the PPI agenda.

Richard Ashcroft is Leverhulme Senior Lecturer in Medical Ethics and Head of the Medical Ethics Unit at Imperial College London. A philosopher by training, he has published widely in medical ethics and the ethics of medical research in particular.

Ailsa Cameron is a Research Fellow in the Centre for Health and Social Care, at the School for Policy Studies, University of Bristol. Her main areas of research interest are changing professional roles and joint working between health and social care agencies. Ailsa is also a member of an NHS research ethics committee.

Trudy Goodenough is a Research Associate in the Centre for Ethics in Medicine, University of Bristol, and worked on the Ethical Protection in Epidemiology Genetics (EPEG) Project from 2001-03. She currently organises the Centre's programme of training for ethics committee members. Trudy is a qualified nurse and midwife, and has a PhD in developmental psychology.

Stacey Gramlich is a Researcher who worked from 1999-2002 on the Swindon People First Project about direct payments. Swindon People First is an organisation run by people with learning difficulties, and all the researchers were people with learning difficulties. Stacey, along with Swindon People First colleagues, has published on a range of issues relating to the experiences of people with learning difficulties.

Gill Hague, Senior Research Fellow, is Co-Founder and current Director of the Domestic Violence Research Group (to be relaunched September 2004 as the Violence Against Women Research Group), School for Policy Studies, University of Bristol.

John Henderson is a Senior Lecturer at the University of Bristol and a Consultant Paediatrician in Paediatric Respiratory Disease at Bristol Royal Hospital for Children. He qualified at the University of Manchester in 1981 and trained in Paediatrics and Paediatric Respiratory Medicine in Manchester, London, Bristol and Perth, Western Australia. His research interests include the epidemiology of respiratory disorders in children, particularly in early life exposures and the development of asthma.

Julie Kent is Reader in Sociology in the Faculty of Economics and Social Science at the University of the West of England. In addition to work on the Ethical Protection in Epidemiology Genetics (EPEG) Project described in Chapter Three, her current research is focused on issues relating to the innovation and regulation of human implant technologies and tissue-engineered medical products. She has also published work on participatory research methods, the sociology of childbirth and reproduction, and women in social research.

Naomi Kent works at the Care Network in Bath and North East Somerset where she is the coordinator of the Carers Together consultation programme. Previously she was a Research Fellow at the School for Policy Studies, University of Bristol, working on the Economic and Social Research Council (ESRC)- funded pilot project looking at 'Significant Life Events in Old Age', researching the relationship between ageing and dying.

Liz Lloyd is a Lecturer in Community Care in the School for Policy Studies at the University of Bristol. A gerontologist, she has particular interest in the study of ageing, care and dependency and related ethical and political dilemmas. Liz's recent research has been primarily focused on end of life care in old age.

Melanie McCarry is Economic and Social Research Council (ESRC) Post-Doctoral Research Fellow in the area of male violence, young people and gender constructions (masculinity) in the Domestic Violence Research Group at the School for Policy Studies, University of Bristol.

Ellen Malos is a Senior Research Fellow in the University of Bristol. She has along history of activism in the women's movement and Women's Aid. She was a founder member, with Gill Hague, of the Domestic Violence Research Group within the School for Policy Studies in the University of Bristol.

Sarah Nelson is a writer and a Research Fellow in Sociology at the University of Edinburgh. She was formerly a social work journalist. She is author of *Incest: Fact and myth* (Stramullion, 1982/87) and has published widely on topics relating to child sexual abuse, including investigative interviewing of children, physical and psychological effects of childhood sexual abuse, community prevention of childhood sexual abuse, organised abuse and feminist approaches to abuse issues.

Vicky Nicholls is the UK Project Coordinator for the Strategies for Living Project. At the time of writing she was responsible for overseeing the Project and managing the team. Vicky had previously worked as Research Support Worker in the first phase of Strategies for Living, and prior to that in a range of voluntary sector organisations including the Greater London Association of Community Health Councils and South East Mind.

Neil Palmer is a Researcher who has worked on a number of projects developed by the Bristol Self-Advocacy Research Group. Neil has been involved in a number of projects looking at disability and discrimination. With other members of the Bristol Group, he gained a diploma from the Open University for his work on the project he describes in the current book.

Jean Rafferty has been a freelance writer for over 20 years and is the author of two books on sport. She is currently holder of a journalist's fellowship from the Joseph Rowntree Foundation to write *Disposable women*, a book on prostitution. She was shortlisted for Feature Writer of the Year in the 1997 British Press Awards for her work on ritual abuse and rape. In 1999 she won the National Daily category in the Travelex Travel Writing Awards for her 'inspired piece' on Buenos Aires. She has travelled widely for her journalism and has taught on various journalism workshops in developing countries as well as on Strathclyde University's postgraduate course in journalism studies.

Tais Silva was formerly a health psychologist in Brazil working with women survivors of sexual and domestic violence. She was also the coordinator of the first refuge for women survivors of domestic violence in Brazil. She has a Masters in Women's Studies from Lancaster University (1998-99) and has worked for the national and local health departments of Brazil, as a consultant on issues affecting women survivors of violence. Tais is currently studying for a PhD in the School for Policy Studies, at the University of Bristol. Her thesis is entitled 'The medicalisation of violence against women: tracing medical and psychological discourses on sexual and domestic violence in Brazil'.

Phil Scraton is Professor of Criminology in the Institute of Criminology and Criminal Justice, School of Law, Queen's University, Belfast. Until recently he was Professor and Director of the Centre for Studies in Crime and Social Justice at Edge Hill University College. His primary research includes the regulation and criminalisation of children and young people; controversial deaths and the state; the rights of the bereaved and survivors in the aftermath of disasters; the politics of truth and official inquiry; and critical analysis and its application.

Marie Smyth is Head of Research and Communication for Criminal Justice Inspection Northern Ireland and Chair of Research Ethics Committee 1 for Northern Ireland. She was Jennings Randolph Senior Fellow (2002-03) in the

United States Institute of Peace in Washington DC and founder of the Institute for Conflict Research (Belfast). She was on the academic staff of the University of Ulster for 20 years.

Tracey J. Stone was a Research Assistant and postgraduate student in the Centre for Ethics in Medicine, University of Bristol, from 1999 until 2004. During this time she was also seconded as a Research and Development Officer for the United Bristol's Health Trust. Tracey's PhD thesis examined the ethics of recruitment onto clinical trials and was awarded in 2004. She has published in this area and in relation to research governance and research ethics committees.

Beth Tarleton is a Research Fellow in the Norah Fry Research Centre, University of Bristol. Her interests include user consultation and involvement, the development of accessible information, the provision of services for disabled children and their families and services for individuals with autistic spectrum disorders. Beth joined the Norah Fry Research Centre in 1998 after completing her MPhil which looked at teachers' beliefs regarding children's special educational needs. Beth is a qualified primary school teacher and has been involved in supporting groups/activities for disabled children and adults for many years.

Rachel Waters worked for the Strategies for Living Project at the time of writing. She was the Research Training and Support Worker for the Project in Wales, supporting Wales-based projects. Rachel had previously worked as a drop-in centre worker at Newport Mind.

Val Williams is a Research Fellow who joined the Norah Fry Research Centre, University of Bristol, in January 1997. Her current research interests include discursive analysis of interaction, inclusive research and supporting people with learning difficulties to take a full role in the research process. She is also involved in communicating about research in accessible ways, and is especially keen to support the authorship of people with learning difficulties themselves. Val's previous careers were in support services in further and adult education, and in teaching.

Emma Williamson is a Research Fellow in the Centre for Ethics in Medicine, University of Bristol. Her doctoral thesis examined domestic violence and the response of the medical profession (1994-98, University of Derby). She has worked at the University of Bristol since 1998.

Sarah Wright was the Research Training and Support Worker for the Strategies for Living Project in England, supporting England-based projects. Sarah had previously worked in both research and administration roles and continues to work with the GOLD (Growing Older with Learning Disabilities) group, who focus on using drama as a form of self-advocacy.

Introduction

Emma Williamson and Marie Smyth

Why this book?

On 6 February 2002, the Academy of Learned Societies for the Social Sciences organised a seminar in London to examine the theme of 'Ethics and Research Guidelines' from a diversity of perspectives. The majority of participants and speakers at that event were social scientists with an interest in ethics and research. All of the major professional social scientific bodies were represented: the British Sociological Association, the Academy of Learned Societies for the Social Sciences, the Social Policy Association and the Social Research Association. The aim of that meeting was to discuss the consolidation of ethics guidance given to social scientists from the various bodies represented there.

What emerged more clearly than ever was the diversity of views and approaches among social scientists concerning ethical issues. Some delegates were concerned about external review, others about gate keeping. Others were concerned with the increased bureaucracy involved in ethical regulation and the possible impact that more stringent ethical review processes could have on social research. As many have realised, even greater diversity is apparent when social science research approaches and practice are juxtaposed with those in medicine or the physical sciences.

The editors of this book first met one another at that meeting. There, they participated in a lively discussion in which divergent views emerged and discovered a common interest in and concern for increasing the accountability of the researcher; in other words, improving the ethical quality of research by managing more effectively the power differentials between researchers and those they research. This book was conceived out of their subsequent discussions.

One particular shared concern was that the arrangements for ethical governance being discussed at that meeting took little or no account of research participants' views. Research into participants' views is rare, even within the health and medical ethics literature, although some research has been published on this topic alongside so-called 'grey' literature (Alderson, 2000, 2001; Ashcroft et al, 2003; Whong-Barr and Haimes, 2003; Williamson et al, 2004). In spite of this, there is still a lack of participant involvement in the consideration of research ethics. Indeed, little attention has been paid to the views of research participants on their role in and experience of research, and most writing on the subject is largely a by-product of research on other issues. While some might argue that the lack of literature in this area is not problematic per se, it becomes so when considering the notion of 'ethical protection'. This concept implies that there are individuals (potential research participants) in need of protection, and that there are ethical standards that will enable it to occur. This book, then, aims to redress the problem by considering how research participants perceive ethics and how such ethical protection can be afforded them. These issues are especially pressing in the light of recent scandals, such as Bristol (Kennedy, 2001) and Alder Hey Hospital (Redfern, 2001), which have occurred in the field of medicine, perhaps the most heavily governed of research areas. In these cases, the retention of organs for the purpose of research resulted in increased public awareness of ethical issues and widespread public concern about research and science (Wellcome Trust/MRC, 2000). In both instances, families were understandably angry that organs had been retained without their informed consent. The legal measures introduced in the wake of these scandals (such as the Human Tissue Bill) are intended to protect individuals by making it illegal to retain human tissue for the purpose of research without consent. Other legislation affects non-medical research. Beyond medicine, the current implementation of the EU Clinical Trials Directive has implications for researchers wanting to conduct any research involving human subjects irrespective of their discipline.

In the social sciences, discussions such as that conducted at the Academy of Learned Social Sciences meeting, have pointed to the current lack of ethical review in that field. While medicine has recently come under the most intense criticism as a result of various scandals, medical ethical review processes are in place, whereas ethical review in most social science and other research is patchy if not entirely absent. The introduction of comprehensive ethical review for all-human subject research may well uncover ethical problems in social science and other fields of research practice. As such, discussion about ethics in all research is particularly timely.

This book explores the relationship between researchers and participants across a number of different disciplines and from both perspectives. Although the exploration of these issues begins in a social science context, the book crosses the disciplinary boundaries that normally segregate discussion of research ethics, particularly between the social and natural sciences. This cross-disciplinary aspect of the discussion is a key aim of this book. Contributions from health, medicine, medical ethics and journalism, as well as from social policy, women's studies, and the mental health research arena, provide a diverse examination of the relationships that exist between researchers and those who participate in research. Comparison is possible, similarities across fields can be identified, and disparities in research governance considered. In addition, the viewpoints of participants, service-users and research advocates are presented alongside those of researchers themselves. By describing the relationship between the researcher and researched from these various standpoints, this book showcases research which challenges the traditional researcher–researched dichotomy, alongside standard research practice, thus offering the opportunity to compare the diverse perspectives.

How to use this book

Rather than trying to provide a comprehensive ethical framework for the protection of research participants, this book highlights the contradictions that exist in the application of ethics within individual projects, between projects, and across disciplines. By juxtaposing these views alongside the perspectives of other stakeholders, this book offers a survey of ethical dilemmas faced by both researchers and participants in the course of the research process. The book is divided into three distinct parts, and a synthesis of the analysis is presented in the conclusion.

Part One considers research and research ethics from the participant's perspective. It includes innovative approaches to research that break down the traditional researcher–researched divide as well as findings from research which sought the views of research participants. This includes 'patients' who were asked to participate in clinical trials (Chapter Two) as well as healthy children consented, by proxy, to participate in epidemiological research since their birth (Chapter Three). Both of these chapters describe the experience of research and decision making from the perspective of participants. They raise questions about consent, which are addressed briefly in this Introduction. Service-user research is also addressed in the chapter written by the Strategies for Living Project (Chapter One). This candid examination of the benefits and problems associated with service-user research raises a number of questions about power within the research relationship and ethical concerns that affect all those engaged in the research endeavour. Chapter Four includes the experiences of researcher advocates as well as 'career' researchers[1]. In particular, the chapter challenges the traditional view of research as something that provides a means to an end. In this account of a number of different studies, the way in which knowledge is produced is examined from the perspective of those whom that knowledge is intended to serve. The authors also question the notion of 'inclusion'.

Part Two includes two chapters that address different experiences of the ethical review/governance process. Both describe researchers' experiences of external ethical review through local research ethics committees (LRECs). By describing that process, additional concerns about what constitutes the subject of ethical protection (the individual participant, knowledge, wider society, and so on) are raised. In both cases, the research is concerned with service-users' views of medical services, health services and other services. As such, it is participants' positions as users of health provision that creates the need for external LREC review rather than the vulnerable nature of the individual respondents. As becomes clear in Part Three of this book, other researchers outside of health interact with these same 'vulnerable' individuals without having to undergo external ethical review. These researchers include academics and an investigative journalist whose work includes interviewing survivors of child sexual abuse, the subject also of Chapter Five. By describing the review process and the ethical considerations that researchers must address in the medical context, both chapters in Part Two raise ethical concerns beyond governance. These issues are further expanded within Part Three of the book.

Part Three, then, contains chapters by an investigative journalist, social scientists, an epidemiologist, and researcher activists. Ethical practice, it seems, cannot be considered outside of the knowledge paradigm. The methodological and epistemological approaches taken by researchers influence how the relationship between researchers and participants are acted out. The approach also determines how knowledge itself is constructed and utilised. Chapter Ten describes the complex negotiation between knowledge and power that faces researchers when dealing with those they research. This contrasts with Chapter Nine, where the relative methodological certainty evident in the medical research field presents a much less problematised concept of knowledge. The final chapter of the book (Chapter Eleven) reflects on the research relationship through the edited proceedings of a round table discussion among researchers. Here, these researchers discuss ethical issues within the academy; also, they reflect on the impact of their work, and discuss how ethical protection and the relationship that exists between researcher and researched underpins the production of knowledge from research.

What's in a name?

The title of this book – *Researchers and their 'subjects'* – is deliberately controversial. People who take part in research are known by so many names: subjects, cohorts, victims, participants, co-researchers, service-users, informants, experts, cases – to name but a few. Furthermore, some contributors to this volume, writing from a range of disciplinary and experiential perspectives, use these terms in different ways. For example, Chapter Nine, which addresses epidemiological research, refers to participants as both 'subjects' and 'cohorts'. Each contributor has used the terms prevalent in their fields, and through comparison of these usages we hope to provoke debate about how the language we use influences and reflects the research processes we adopt.

Language can provide an indication of the nature of the research relationship. It has implications for the way in which knowledge is constructed and for methodological approaches. Language use also provides important signposts to the values informing research practice. A wide variety of approaches to research and the terminology associated with each are presented in this book. For example, service-user-led research, such as that described by the Strategies for Living Project in Chapter One, uses the subjective perspectives of the researchers, who are also service-users, as a valuable knowledge resource throughout the research process. This approach contrasts with the use of more quantitative or 'objective' forms of data collection, which would be standard within medical research, for example, described in Chapter Nine.

For some, the term 'subject' implies subjugation and a lessening of the status and rights of people who participate in research. At the risk of offending or angering some readers, we have included the diversity of approaches, so that we can begin to examine how labels, and the power relationships that underlie them, operate in the research relationship. Contributors address the issue of the relationship between the researched population and researchers. Perhaps the clearest statement is made in Chapter Four by Stacey Gramlich, an advocate researcher:

> Researchers often try to include people with learning difficulties, but the real power lies with the non-disabled people. People don't always believe that research can be done by people with learning difficulties, but we have found our way of doing it, and it's worked for us.

Through the contributions of both researchers and participants, some of which showcase research that has focused specifically on participants' views of research itself, various perspectives are presented, and the diversity of relationships between researcher and research participants emerges. Indeed, as is evident in Chapters One, Four and Eight, this distinction between researcher and researched is by no means fixed. In these examples, the boundaries between the two are challenged and broken down in an effort to conduct research that will produce knowledge for those whose interests the research is intended to serve. These concerns are also evident in Chapter Ten, where, as an active researcher, Phil Scraton attempts to grapple with the dilemma of power and knowledge in his work with disempowered social groups.

The irony of embarking on the process of putting this book together is that contributing researchers (including the editors) have had to ask searching questions of themselves, chief among which includes whether they as researchers have a right to comment on others' lives when the 'subjects' of that same research have demonstrated an interest in and ability to conduct research on their own experiences independently of researchers. This raises a set of further issues. Do researchers generally perform socially useful tasks? What role do they play in improving our understanding of problematic social and societal issues, and how do they assist in addressing social problems? How can researchers give research power and skills away, and are they interested in doing so? Of course, there are no definitive answers to these questions, and the quest for such answers succeeds only in uncovering new questions. Why should researchers try to balance power in their relationships with those they research? Yet the reflections of researchers from a variety of perspectives offer some valuable insights for participants and researchers, irrespective of their discipline or experiences.

What is research?

Power and knowledge

The diversity of views represented in this collection raises the fundamental question about what 'research' actually is. Should the notion of research be confined to academic research? Does it include service evaluation? Is investigative journalism research? All of the contributors to this book consider themselves active in research, whether as participants, researchers, or within roles defined outside of this dichotomy. By considering the research relationship, all the chapters address the management of those relationships within a paradigm of knowledge construction. Each chapter deals with the issue of power in the research relationship to some extent, whether explicitly (Chapters Five, Eight and Ten) or implicitly (Chapters Two and Nine).

Key to the function of power within knowledge construction is the methodological and epistemological perspectives of the researchers. In Chapter One by the Strategies for Living Project, for example, the notion of objective knowledge construction is challenged. This is both a pragmatic and epistemological choice on the part of the research team. In Chapter Seven, Jean Rafferty, an investigative journalist, depicts a very different notion of 'truth' which prioritises the narrative story rather than objective fact. Both of these approaches are in contrast to the positivistic approach to epidemiological research set out in Chapter Nine. The methodological and epistemological stance of the various contributors might influence the outcome of ethical dilemmas. To conduct a randomised control trial, you would choose to consent participants without full knowledge of which treatment they were going to receive. Yet in spite of the differences between the ethical and methodological stances, there is a convergence in the types of questions which all of the researchers have identified. In this particular example, this relates to the nature of informed consent and how the rights of the individual are balanced alongside the benefits to society. Here, the methodological approach influences the value and beneficial effect of the research itself. This calls into question the current disparities in research governance across disciplinary boundaries. If there are fundamental questions about ethical protection, then why are some researchers required to evidence this and others not?

Research ethics

Put simply, the fundamental ethical concern in non-therapeutic research is how the rights of the individual, potential participant are balanced against the potential benefit of research to wider society[2]. Following the atrocities committed during the Second World War, the Declaration of Helsinki (1964) very clearly stated that non-therapeutic research could not be conducted without the informed consent of the individual, irrespective of the benefits to wider society. This championing of autonomy, as a form of ethical protection, resulted in a number of populations being excluded from potential research. This would include anybody deemed 'incompetent' to consent to research. This has since changed and has meant an increasing recognition that research is necessary. Within medical research at least, external review seeks to 'protect' potential participants by making decisions about potential risk and harm, and balancing the standpoints of wider society (often represented as the scientist) and the potential respondent. This change to the overtly autonomous and rights-based approach sees the introduction of utilitarian principles, that society must share the burden of research in order to maximise the potential benefits derived from it. At present, this approach has not overridden the need for autonomy, but works alongside it. Where ethical review takes place, it is the responsibility of the committee to balance such decisions. Where there is no ethical review process, such decisions are left to the individual researcher/journalist who may or may not have the ethical knowledge and training to make such decisions.

Non-therapeutic research and service evaluation: potential conflict

The majority of the contributions to this book focus on non-therapeutic research. (The exception is Chapter Two by Tracey J. Stone, where it is patients who have been requested to take part in a randomised clinical trial, within a therapeutic context, whose experiences are described and considered.) The distinction between therapeutic and non-therapeutic research is important in terms of both ethics and governance. Specifically, whether the participant of research will directly benefit from taking part in research is an important consideration for those making ethical judgements about research (such as LRECs). The prominence of autonomy as an ethical principle is paramount when participants are not likely to directly benefit from research inclusion, which in the case of non-therapeutic research is most likely. This significantly impacts on the inclusion of individuals who are not deemed competent to consent to non-therapeutic research such as older people with dementia (Chapter Six), children (Chapter Three), individuals with learning disabilities (Chapter Four) and individuals with mental health problems (Chapter Five) who may or may not be deemed competent to consent.

Sarah Nelson in Chapter Five describes in detail the status of research – therapeutic or non-therapeutic – that could be categorised as evaluating therapeutic services. Here, the parameters of therapeutic treatment, non-therapeutic research and service evaluation became blurred. It raises a question about the extent that non-therapeutic research into service evaluation impacts on the therapeutic service it seeks to evaluate. In Nelson's experience, the lack of distinction between the two jeopardised her research project. This issue recurs the discussion of the practice of investigative journalism by Jean Rafferty (Chapter Seven) and again by the Domestic Violence Research Group (Chapter Eleven), where the possible impact of research is considered. Other issues, such as potential harm and risk, and the extent to which the researcher is responsible for the subsequent therapeutic care of the participant, are also raised. Can any research participant taking part in potentially emotionally disturbing research ever be sufficiently informed to give truly informed consent? Both of these issues illustrate how the boundaries between so-called therapeutic and non-therapeutic research and service evaluation can be problematised.

Research governance

Good ethical practice and good research governance are synonymous and interdependent. Internationally recognised ethical principles for 'biomedical' research enshrined in the World Medical Association's (WMA) Declaration of Helsinki (1964) include informed consent, confidentiality, anonymity and protection from harm and exploitation for research subjects. These ethical principles are regulated in research in a number of different ways: through funders; peer review; advisory groups; publication peer review processes; and finally through an Ethics Committee process. Each of these processes has relative merits and problems (Kent et al, 2002). However, it is only the process of ethical review through the Ethics Committee system that is endorsed by government through the Research Governance Framework (Council of Europe, 2001).

Ethical review, usually conducted within medical and health research by an ethics committee, is intended to assess the merits of a proposal to conduct research and to set a standard for the ethical practice of researchers in carrying out research. Governed in the UK by the Centre Office for Research Ethics Committees (COREC), the purpose of Local and Multi-site Research Ethics Committees (LRECs and MRECs) is to review research proposals in order to:

> ... provide the independent advice to participants, researchers, funders, sponsors, employers, care organisations and professionals on the extent to which proposals for research studies comply with recognised ethical standards. (COREC, 2003)

Ethics Committees comprise medical staff, scientists, members of the public (lay representatives) and other interested parties. Their job is to consider applications in relation to the various stakeholders, funders, researchers, participants and wider society. They do so by scrutinising applications for their compliance with general ethical principles and the range of policies intended to protect human subjects (for example, MRC, 1993, 2000; Council of Europe, 1997; BIO, 1999). In addition, specific guidance exists which considers vulnerable subjects (MRC, 1993), the transfer of information (HUGO, 2000), and standards of research (WMA, 1964). These guidelines differ across national and international boundaries both in terms of their content and the way in which they are implemented. For UK purposes, the most important guidelines are now the Department of Health's Governance Arrangements for Research Ethics Committees and the European Clinical Trials Directive, which at the time of writing is still to be enacted into UK law (Council of Europe, 2001).

The impact of the directive is not yet known. Yet consultations have indicated that there is a potential problem of further overwhelming the already overburdened RECs. The role and responsibilities and the training needs of REC members may change with the proposed policy implementation. For example, should RECs be required to take quasi-legal responsibility for the decisions they make, REC members will need to ensure that they are adhering to current legislation. The new policy acknowledges the need for far more public involvement in the REC process. Ensuring that the composition of RECs contains a balance of professional, scientific and lay members is important in order to ensure that those who may have a vested interest in specific stakeholder perspectives (for example, scientists) do not control ethical decision making. It is this conflict, between individual autonomy and wider social benefits, which forms the basis of contradictions within the original declaration of Helsinki and the subsequent guidelines that have emerged. The adjudication of the ethical dilemmas inherent in the protection of the 'rights' of participants alongside safeguarding the interests of science creates the ground on which all researcher–researched relationships stand. According to COREC,

> (L)RECs are responsible for acting primarily in the interest of potential research participants and concerned communities, but they should also take into account the interests and needs of researchers who are trying to undertake research of a good quality. (COREC, 2003)

At present, COREC is responsible for reviewing a range of research areas, including:

- patients and users of the NHS (this includes all potential research participants recruited by virtue of the patient's or user's past or present treatment by, or use of, the NHS, as well as NHS patients treated under contracts with private sector institutions);
- individuals identified as potential research participants because of their status as relatives or carers of patients and users of the NHS (as defined above);
- access to data, organs or other bodily material of past and present NHS patients;
- fetal material and IVF involving NHS patients;
- the recently dead in NHS premises;
- the use of, or potential access to, NHS premises or facilities;
- NHS staff recruited as research participants by virtue of their professional role.

> If requested to do so, an NHS REC may also provide an opinion on the ethics of similar research studies not involving the categories listed above, carried out for example by private sector companies, the Medical Research Council (or other public sector organisations), charities or universities. (COREC, 2003)

The categories explicitly identified within the COREC guidance relate specifically to health and medical research. Its final paragraph, however, reflects increasing concerns about research conducted outside of the health or medical setting. By acknowledging that research which falls outside their original remit (the categories listed here), COREC raise, by implication, questions about the uniformity of research across different settings and concerns about its regulation.

Guidance for social scientists

Although not as rigorously governed as medical research, social research does adhere on the whole to the voluntary ethical guidelines produced by the various professional bodies. The British Sociological Association (BSA) has an approved statement of ethical principle[3]. These guidelines address professional integrity, relations with and responsibility towards research participants, and relations with and responsibilities towards sponsors and/or funders. While comprehensive in the issues they address (informed consent, ongoing consent, anonymity, covert research, and privacy), this statement suggests that:

> Although sociologists, like other researchers are committed to the advancement of knowledge, that goal does not, of itself, provide an entitlement to override the rights of others. Members must satisfy themselves that a study is necessary for the furtherance of knowledge before embarking upon it. (BSA, 2001)

The BSA statement, like that of the Social Research Association (SRA, 2003) is, on the whole, a positive statement of ethical intent. However, without an ethical review process, it need not carry any weight within individual projects, and relies on a process of self-regulation. The recent review of ethical guidelines conducted by the BSA and the SRA continues to highlight this (www.the-sra.org.uk/index2.htm, accessed November 2003). Membership of these organisations is voluntary and members do not have to sign up to this statement but are referred to it for guidance. The BSA statement (2001) begins:

> This statement is meant, primarily, to inform members' ethical judgements rather than to impose on them an external set of standards. The purpose is to make members aware of the ethical issues that may arise in their work, and to encourage them to educate themselves and their colleagues to behave ethically.

The reliance on self-regulation raises an important issue. What are the set of standards external to? Within medicine, ethical standards are seen to characterise the fiduciary relationship between doctors and patients and are expected to be transmitted via a process of professionalisation. Similarly, as the BSA statement implies, social scientists are expected to internalise a set of professional values that inform their actions as researchers. As it stands, this guidance, while extremely useful, does not constitute anything approaching the rigour that is offered by the process of ethical review. The Economic and Social Research

Council (ESRC) is also currently involved in a consultation exercise examining ethical review within the social sciences, one element of which is the review process[4].

One concern of contributors to this book, is whether guidance is sufficient in ensuring that research participants receive appropriate ethical protection. In order to make such a judgement, it is necessary to ascertain the significance of ethical protection to research participants. This is one of the areas explored in this book.

Journalism

The ethical review and guidance offered to journalists differs from that operating in medical, health, and social research. This differentiation only matters, however, if we believe that the research conducted by journalists is comparable to other types of research. As we hope we have illustrated by the inclusion of Chapter Seven, which describes in detail the type of research conducted by an investigative journalist, the content, structure, and subject of journalism and 'academic' research is often extremely similar despite differences in the purpose of such endeavours. As such, we believe it is relevant to question the guidelines to which different researchers adhere irrespective of their location within or outside of the academy. The National Union of Journalists (NUJ) does not have a specific ethical policy for its members, but does have a code of conduct (NUJ, 2003a). The first point of this code states that "a journalist has a duty to maintain the highest professional and ethical standards". The concept of ethics within this code is presented as taken for granted, and potential conflict between individual journalists' idea of what is ethical is not addressed. The NUJ approach also places emphasis on the importance of "freedom of the press" without consideration of potential conflicts between press freedom and individual rights. For example, a story written by a journalist, published in line with the principle of the press's right to freedom, could harm an individual. Does it make a difference who that individual is? Should the press's right to freedom always take precedence over an individual's rights to privacy and/or confidentiality and anonymity? The NUJ code does not offer any guidance on how journalists and editors should deal with such conflicts. Mike Jempson, of the organisation Presswise, supports this view. He "was critical of the NUJ who have not circulated the IFJ [International Federation of Journalists] guidelines to their members, despite the NUJ's affiliation to the IFJ and its presence at the conference where the guidelines were adopted" (NUJ, 2003b).

As with the NUJ within the UK, the IFJ, which represents 500,000 journalists worldwide (IFJ, 2003), offers a code that sees freedom of the press rather than the protection of parties investigated or represented by journalists as the core of ethical journalistic practice.

In *The virtuous journalist*, Klaidman and Beauchamp (1987) offer a useful insight into the particularities of the ethics governing the practice of journalism. Beauchamp, whose other work is in the area of medical ethics and principalism, is concerned with the principles of ethical conduct. With Klaidman, Beauchamp emphasises the importance of specific concepts such as reaching and maintaining trust; avoiding bias and harm; serving the public; escaping manipulation; and inviting criticism and accountability in ethical journalistic practice. Unlike medicine, where doctors take a Hippocratic Oath and are regulated by the British Medical Association and equivalent national bodies outside the UK, journalists are not accountable to the profession of journalism (Klaidman and Beauchamp, 1987, p 217). They do, however, posit specific journalistic accountability (above and beyond to the general public, readers and viewers) to subjects of stories, sources, supervisors and employers (Klaidman and Beauchamp, 1987, p 217). In this volume, our focus is on the accountability of journalists to the subjects of their stories.

There are varying degrees of regulation within medical research and social science research. For social scientists working within the medical or health fields, they are bound by the standard ethical review practice in medicine and health, whereas social scientists, working in other fields doing similar work but in different locations, are not required to undergo such processes. Differences in review procedures notwithstanding, the basic ethical principles are similar. These include (informed) consent of the participant; confidentiality; anonymity; and a balance of the principles of beneficence (best interests of the individual), with particular regard to the potential risks and benefits of the research. Klaidman and Beauchamp argue that such regulation should extend to the way journalists research in order to improve their accountability to the subject of a story:

> Subjects of stories are generally the parties most directly affected by their publication. Many will be unharmed by their moment in the spotlight, but others will be projected into the public eye in a manner harmful to their interests. Their private sorrows might be exploited; they might be defamed, made to suffer financial losses, or any number of other unpleasantnesses. There may be compelling reasons to cast a subject into the public eye against his or her will, even if risk to reputation, legal risk, or financial risk is inevitable; *but there should be effective measures to ensure accountability for risks imposed, even on subjects whose interests are damaged as a result of the legitimate pursuit of news.* (Klaidman and Beauchamp, 1987, p 218; emphasis added)

The authors point out that a study (Leigh, 1974) conducted as early as 1947 by the Commission on Freedom of the Press suggested that press freedom and accountability are synonymous, and that, without accountability, journalism cannot remain free. The 1947 study goes on to suggest that it is only through discipline exercised by journalists themselves, within the public domain, that such accountability will be achieved (Klaidman and Beauchamp, 1987, p 220). This is in line with the current guidance required of other researchers outside journalism, where peer review, ethical review, funding processes all influence and regulate the way in which research is conducted. As Jean Rafferty in Chapter Seven acknowledges, there may be some shifts in research, which bring journalism and academic research closer together. Indeed, the variety of contributions to this book illustrates this very point. The fundamental question relating to research governance arises: why do differences in ethical standards and priorities exist? If a journalist's priority is to get the story and present it to a wider audience, rather that concern and sensitivity about the rights of the individual interviewee, as Rafferty suggests, should this principle then also apply to academic researchers? At present, medical researchers are prohibited from taking such a stance as enshrined in internationally recognised guidance. Researchers may balance the potential risk to participants against wider social good, but no such mandate exists to prioritise social benefit. These considerations are addressed in a number of the chapters included in this book, most notably in Chapter Nine by John Henderson.

Ethical responsibility

The wider ethical or moral responsibilities of researchers go beyond the ethical guidance given within a governance framework. A more abstract and general notion of ethical or moral responsibility, it could be argued, cuts across the various disciplinary boundaries, and the differentiations between the governance provisions within them. There is an overarching set of ethical principles that apply by virtue of the common humanity of all of the practitioners and the human objects of their enquiries.

A number of key areas of concern arise out of the chapters contained in this book about the ethics of research, and in particular about the relationship between the researcher and participant. These include:

- how participants are recruited, informed, and enrolled or give consent to participation;
- the ethical principles that guide the researcher when designing a research project;
- the impact of the ethical review governance process on the researcher and participant;
- the (in)ability of researchers, with potentially competing interests, to make an objective judgement about the best interests of their potential or actual participants;
- the role and responsibilities of the consenting participant;
- the cognisance taken of the relative vulnerability of specific groups of participants within the ethical governance process of research (for example, dealing with those who have fiduciary relationships with vulnerable potential participants, or dealing with those who are legally deemed not to be competent to consent on their own behalf);
- the protection of vulnerable participants from any inappropriate attention from researchers.

Arising out of these questions, a central set of issues emerges, namely issues of autonomy and choice, particularly with regard to the participant's decision to participate or not in research; the obligations of non-maleficence (to do no harm) on researchers; issues of justice, and differing understandings of justice; and conflicts of interest, which are of particular concern for the researcher whose activities are not subject to any formal external ethical review process.

As the contributions to this book demonstrate, it is not always possible to resolve these ethical issues by referring to the available ethical guidance. The Declaration of Helsinki and the various ethical guidance documents produced since then contradict one another. The complexities of attempting to balance the rights of individual participants against the needs of wider society and science are difficult.

The ethical dilemmas that arise in research are often difficult to address, and it is these that researchers and participants have been asked to revisit, describe, and analyse in this book. By placing the views of participants alongside those of researchers, we hope this collection will demonstrate new and innovative ways in which researchers from a range of disciplines think about the ethics of the relationships they have with participants. By implication, we also hope that the dialogue started here through the comparison of different case studies and approaches will be useful for policy makers and those responsible for research governance. This is particularly important as various social science funding bodies begin to look seriously at the possibility of ethical review to enforce both ethical principles and the Clinical Trials Directive. We hope that this book goes some way to redressing the balance when it comes to who sets the research and research ethics agenda and imbalances in the relationships between all those who participate in research. Finally, we hope that the reflections of researchers presented here of their experiences of research will encourage and inspire other researchers to reflect similarly on their work.

Notes

[1] These terms are used descriptively and the problematic nature of differentiating between them is acknowledged.

[2] The difference between and implications of therapeutic and non-therapeutic research are addressed later.

[3] The British Psychology Association also has similar guidance. 'Ethics committees' were absent from an examination of the web pages of both the Policy Studies Association and Political Science Association. Members of these associations may well look to the British Sociological Association guidelines for advice.

[4] Further information and working papers are available from www.york.ac.uk/res/ref/documents.htm.

References

Alderson, P. (2000) *Young children's rights: Exploring beliefs, principles and practice*, London: Jessica Kingsley.

Alderson, P. (2001) 'Research by children', *International Journal of Social Research Methodology*, vol 4, no 2, pp 139-53.

Ashcroft, R., Goodenough, T., Williamson, E. and Kent, J. (2003) 'Children's consent to research participation: social context and personal experience invalidate fixed cutoff rules', *American Journal of Bioethics*, vol 3, no 4, pp 16-18.

BIO (Biotechnology Industry Organisation) (1999) *BIO Policy statement regarding the prohobition of discriminatory use of medical information*, www.bio.org

BSA (British Sociological Association) (2001) http://britsoc.co.uk

COREC (Centre Office for Research Ethics Committees) (2003) www.corec.org.uk (accessed 1 December).

Council of Europe (1997) *Convention for the protection of human rights and dignity of the human being with regard to the application of biology and medicine: Convention on human rights and biomedicine*, Strasbourg: Council of Europe.

Council of Europe (2001) *European Parliament and the Council of the European Union: Clinical Trial Directive*, 20/EC.

HUGO (2000) *Hugo statement on patenting of DNA sequences – in particular response to the European Biotechnology Directive*, www.gene.ucl.ac.uk/hugo/

IFJ (International Federation of Journalists) (2003) www.ifj.org (accessed 1 December).

Kennedy (2001) *The Bristol Royal Infirmary Inquiry*, London: DoH.

Kent, J., Williamson, E., Goodenough, T. and Ashcroft, R. (2002) 'Social science gets the ethics treatment: research governance and ethical review', *Sociological Research Online*, vol 7, issue 4, www.socresonline.org.uk/7/4/williamson.html

Klaidman, S. and Beauchamp, T.L. (1987) *The virtuous journalist*, Oxford: Oxford University Press.

Leigh, R.D. (ed) (1974) *A free and responsible press*, Chicago, IL: University of Chicago Press.

MRC (Medical Research Council) (1993) *The ethical conduct of research on children: Working party on research on children*, London: MRC.

MRC (2000) *Personal information in medical research*, London: MRC.

NUJ (2003a) www.nuj.org.uk/front/inner.php?docid=59 (accessed 6 November).

NUJ (2003b) www.nuj.org.uk/front/ inner.php?docid=423andPHPSESSID= 808460ccb328ad861692692b3a2e9ded (accessed 6 November).

Redfern, M. (2001) *The report of the Royal Liverpool Children's Inquiry*, London: DoH.

SRA (2003) www.the-sra.org.uk/Ethicals.htm (accessed 1 December).

Wellcome Trust/MRC (2000) *Public perceptions of the collection of human biological samples*, London: Wellcome Trust.

Whong-Barr, M. and Haimes, E. (2003) 'Why say no? Reasons for non-participation in the North Cumbria Community Genetics Project', *European Journal of Human Genetics*, vol 11, supplement I.

Williamson, E., Goodenough, T., Kent, J. and Ashcroft, R. (2004) 'Children's participation in genetic epidemiology: consent and control', in R. Tutton and O. Corrigan (eds) *Donating, collecting and exploiting human tissue*, London: Routledge.

WMA (World Medical Association) (1964) *Declaration of Helsinki*, Geneva: WMA.

Part One:
Participation and inclusion

Ethical considerations in service-user-led research: Strategies for Living Project

*Sarah Wright, Rachel Waters, Vicky Nicholls
and members of the Strategies for Living Project*

Introduction

The rationale for user-led research in mental health has been widely documented in recent years (see, for example, Beresford and Wallcraft, 1997; Faulkner and Layzell, 2000; Nicholls, 2001; Nicholls et al, 2003). Such work includes placing independent research that is designed and carried out by people with direct personal experience of mental or emotional distress in a framework of emancipatory research. It aims not only to increase the sum of knowledge, but also to alter the status quo, to influence and change relationships of power. It is more overt than traditional approaches about the politics of research; in fact, it aims to shift these. Such research recognises the effect of research on those taking part as well as its potential wider effects on the situations, dynamics and organisations that it is investigating.

In mental health, user-led research has developed in the context of a world where people using mental health services have traditionally been asked very personal questions by outside researchers (often academic or clinical researchers) without any influence on the sorts of questions that get asked or what happens to the information that they share with such researchers. In this sense, user-led research is about people with experience of distress – service-users or survivors[1] – taking control of their lives. This is the context in which the Strategies for Living Project based at the Mental Health Foundation has developed and grown.

The Strategies for Living Project

This chapter focuses on the experience of the second phase of this project: Strategies for Living Phase II. This phase attempted to implement a particular set of ethics. The ethical approach taken was built on the values of the programme: a person-centred approach; responsiveness to individual needs; a recognition of diversity; involving participants in the progress of the research; and the usual ethical considerations in research, including clarity of information and sensitivity to confidentiality, among others[2]. It is generally agreed that attention to ethics should be an integral part of all research processes. In Strategies for Living, there is a strong belief that sound research and sound ethics go hand in hand.

Strategies for Living is a programme of work addressing mental health services that aims to promote and encourage the development of service-user and survivor empowerment through supporting research, evaluation and information gathering. In Strategies for Living Phase II, 12 user-led research projects were supported across the UK, including:

- research into service-users' experiences of accessing the benefits system;
- the impact of the loss of work, and strategies for returning to work after ill-health;
- resources in the community for black women in Bradford;
- evaluation of the effects of Five Rhythms Dance;
- self-help groups for women who self-harm;
- coping strategies in a psychiatric hospital setting; leave from hospital for detained patients;
- a directory of advocacy projects;
- coping strategies of carers of people diagnosed with manic depression.

A number of key issues has emerged from the research that Strategies for Living has conducted and supported which typify the approach of the project. Service-users select the topics for research; they are members of the steering group; they design the research projects, and are, ideally, the researchers and interviewers on individual projects. Conducting user-led research in this context has also enabled the project to identify specific problems or additional needs that arise from this approach, for example, the ongoing training and support needs of researchers including peer support; recognition that the process of research is as important as the final product; sharing findings in relevant ways to relevant audiences (especially other service-users); informing services and service development; and informing participants about the results and any action.

Strategies for Living Phase II was made possible through a three-year grant from the Community Involvement funding stream of the Community Fund. The grant ran from October 2000 to September 2003. This followed a previous grant for three years in which Strategies for Living carried out its own in-depth study of people's personal ways of coping with mental distress. It also supported six user-led research projects.

The Strategies for Living Phase II project team comprised a UK programme coordinator, Vicky Nicholls; three research, support and training workers (RSTWs) who worked directly with researchers in each of the countries across the UK, Monica Griesbaum (Scotland and Northern Ireland), Rachel Waters (Wales) and Sarah Wright (England); and a project assistant, Stephanie Wells.

The programme's aims have been:

- to learn from and build on the experience of Strategies for Living Phase I;
- to build the capacity of service-users and survivors to explore their chosen strategies for living and coping with distress via research and information-gathering projects;
- to develop a UK network of community involvement in research and information-gathering projects;
- to enhance opportunities for service-users and survivors to feed concerns and ideas into the future development of local mental health services;
- to strengthen the infrastructure of local user-led mental health services;
- at an individual level, to enhance people's self-confidence and self-esteem; develop skills in an area that provides flexible ways of working (that is, capable of fitting in with periods of distress); and build relationships with others which enable people to contribute more to local communities;
- to raise awareness nationally of the value of user-led research, and of alternative strategies for dealing with distress.

Ethics training

Each RSTW spent a day training researchers on the topic of ethics. The selected researchers were all people who identified as experiencing mental distress and/or having used mental health services. The researchers based in England, Scotland, Northern Ireland and Wales had all submitted research proposals to Strategies for Living Phase II. Their projects were selected using criteria developed by Strategies for Living from Phase I and in consultation with other service-users, and the selection decisions were made by the Strategies for Living Advisory Committee[3]. In addition, ethical principles were present throughout the research training programme and the research support process.

Ethical considerations in research include: the research relationship; participation; transparency and honesty; consent; payment; safety; and confidentiality. Ethics committee processes are also a serious consideration. The following sections of this chapter outline in more detail the implications of each of these ethical considerations as they emerged within the Strategies for Living projects.

The research relationship

The work of Strategies for Living Phase II was composed of people with experience of mental distress developing the research topic and carrying out the research, supported by a team of people also with this identity. While some researchers would regard the 'biased' or 'subjective' perspective of those with experience of mental distress as problematic, or compromising the quality of the research, the Strategies for Living approach regards this as a valuable asset. Rather than seeing subjectivity as something negative in the research, the project acknowledged and embraced it.

It is this subjectivity together with an understanding of the user/survivor movement that equipped researchers within the Strategies for Living projects to investigate subjects they considered of relevance and importance to them.

The researchers' own experiences and closeness to the subject rendered them more likely to be able to build a positive relationship with the research participant, breaking down the power dynamics between researcher and the researched. Participants in the research often felt more able to trust a researcher that they perceived as having empathy because of their own self-knowledge about the experiences being investigated. (Many of the researchers reported that people opened up to them more because they had disclosed their experiences of and understandings about mental health issues.)

Although in some respects subjective experience can be positive, such disclosure within the research process can also raise additional methodological, and thus ethical, concerns which need to be considered. One of the difficulties faced by researchers was that they were, at times, so close to the subject of the research that they were incapable of the distance required in order to address the issues analytically. This difficulty was overcome by involving other people in the analysis and writing up of the research. The RSTWs worked with researchers on their analysis and included, within the training given to researchers, guidance on how to be systematic in the analysis process.

An additional concern was that there was potentially more risk of emotional harm for the researcher in this kind of research than in research where the researcher does not identify with the experiences being investigated. Researchers with experiences as service-users were at times more likely than those with 'distance' from the subject to feel distressed after conducting an interview, because of the resonance with the feelings and experiences described by interviewees. Several researchers described their experience thus; sometimes this was not directly after an interview but later on when re-reading the transcript or doing the analysis.

The RSTW ensured that someone was available for each researcher to talk to (or debrief) after each interview, should the researcher choose to do so. Where researchers were working with others in a team, they would usually arrange to talk to one of their co-researchers. However, when the researcher was working alone, the RSTW or another member of the Strategies for Living team would make themselves available for debriefing.

Sometimes researchers decided not to take advantage of the debriefing system which was put in place after the interview, but it emerged at a later time that they had found elements of the research experience distressing or difficult. In light of the evaluation of Strategies for Living Phase I, where this was identified as desirable, we asked about access to emotional support on the funding application forms of subsequent research and encouraged researchers to consider their own emotional needs throughout the research process. One or two projects did have access to local outside support beyond co-researchers, family or friends, but most did not pursue this.

One researcher found herself feeling vulnerable when interviewing a service-user who was concerned for her safety in her own home. The researcher described a situation where someone came to the door and the participant hid with her child behind some furniture, causing the researcher to do the same. The researcher said that at the time she just reacted in the same way as the interviewee, but afterwards this tapped into her own distress and feelings of vulnerability. It is important to recognise, therefore, that doing user-led research can raise distressing issues for researchers as well as having a positive impact on the research.

Boundaries between researchers and participants

Another difficulty for user/survivor researchers is the issue of emotional and physical distance (boundaries) between researchers and participants who might share some common experience. Some researchers described feeling a strong desire to help the people that they were interviewing, because they had experience in a particular area. This was illustrated by several researchers who described the time allocated for interviews as being too short because they ended up in long discussions about possible support or information they could give to the participant (Faulkner and Layzell, 2000). One researcher described feeling personally affected by an interview that they had carried out. The interviewee was clearly distressed about their situation, and the researcher felt that the coping strategies used by the interviewee were counterproductive. The researcher spent a lot of time talking with the participant but felt that the interviewee was unable to accept or use support. This left the researcher feeling distressed and frustrated.

Researchers were advised to give participants a list of organisations offering help in the area of concern as well as general telephone helplines so that participants could avail themselves of support if they felt distressed after the interview. This issue raises questions about the role of researchers, and service-user researchers in particular, and the limitations of that role. All researchers, whether service-users or not, have to address the issues of boundaries in their work.

It is important to think about boundaries between research and support roles. The project learned the importance of trying to maintain them, although researchers can and will sometimes be personally affected by their research.

Participation within the research projects

The level of participation of research participants is related to the power dynamics within the research. In training and supervision, the project encouraged researchers to try to involve participants as much as possible in their research, by ensuring that all the information given to participants was presented in an accessible form and that researchers were available to the participants for questions and comments. Interview and focus group transcripts were returned to interviewees for feedback on both the analysis and findings, either by post or in workshops. And finally, researchers were encouraged to disseminate their research reports to interviewees.

In order to demonstrate respect and the valuing of participants' time and experiences, the project recommended that participants were paid for their time, given information about support they might access if they found the interview or focus group distressing, and given the opportunity to have a copy of the final report.

Many if not all of the projects tried to do some of these things. Payment to participants was widely practiced, as was ensuring participants had plenty of information about what they could do immediately following interviews if they were feeling vulnerable.

However our theoretical aims were not always successful in practice. First, it takes a lot of time to build in good participation to a project; secondly, it is time-consuming to return transcripts and wait for responses; and, thirdly, it is even more time-consuming to incorporate comments from participants into findings and final reports.

Similarly, obtaining research participants' feedback on findings can be fraught with difficulties. It can be difficult to receive critical feedback from participants who feel the findings or write-up of the research do not reflect their experience. One of 12 Strategies for Living Phase II projects was The Dancing for Living Project. Here, people with experience of distress took part in a series of Five Rhythms Dance workshops[4]. This project held a reunion for participants to give their feedback on the findings. Some participants had hoped to see the research written up in a way that was more biased towards their personal experience of the dance. The researchers explained that the analysis process, and presentation of a balanced view, had come directly from the findings. It was important to remember that participants will have their own ideas based on their personal experiences of what they expect or want the research to look like.

The Strategies for Living Project strongly felt that, for the research to move forward, to become more emancipatory, participation and continued involvement of participants was vital. In terms of basic good practice, it was our intention to encourage researchers to attempt the methods of involving participants that we have just mentioned. Practical restraints sometimes made this difficult, but as the Dancing for Living example illustrates, it is important to include participant feedback, especially when participants might disagree with the way results are analysed and presented.

Transparency and honesty

The training programme was devised so that it would initially run concurrently with researchers beginning their research tasks and data collection. Our position was that all researchers carrying out research under a Strategies for Living banner, in particular undertaking interviews or facilitating focus groups, should have taken part in our training.

Within the research agreement, it was stipulated that researchers should discuss all research materials with the relevant RSTW before using them. This was reiterated in training and support sessions. However, this did not always happen in practice: sometimes, researchers got too caught up in their own desire to move forward in the research. A problem did arise in one project where the research team sent out a questionnaire without it having been agreed by the RSTW. The questionnaire was not as sensitive to certain issues as it should have been and as a result the project received a complaint from one of the recipients. Furthermore, the project had very few questionnaires returned.

These were lessons for us all. Despite our view that research was not some kind of mysterious process only to be done by those 'in the know', there are sensitive ways of conducting research, and these were skills that needed to be developed by those new to research.

Other examples of technical problems emerged in the research: equipment did not work; tapes ran out; recording quality was poor. To be ethically sound, it was felt that researchers should be honest with participants when things went well and especially when things went wrong. We were keen that researchers should explain to participants when a recording did not work, that they give the participant the opportunity to redo the interview, or to try to fill in gaps on their transcripts. These are problems which all researchers encounter, but which can have a much bigger impact on service-users inexperienced in the role of researchers. It is important, therefore, that all researchers are honest about the problems they encounter in research so that others, especially those new to research, can learn from them.

Consent

Issues of consent were discussed in training, and examples of consent forms shared. The ongoing nature of consent was discussed in training; for example, that research participants could withdraw at any point in the research process, including after having seen a transcript.

In one example, where the research project was based in a secure mental health setting, the researcher and support worker had planned to hold meetings with participants to go through all the information relating to all aspects of confidentiality and consent. They did this because not all of the participants could read and write, and they wanted to make sure that everyone felt respected and properly informed. However, in reality, problems arose:

- The secure unit where the research was based was not easily accessible by public transport, and so access for participants and researchers was difficult.
- Participants did not want to attend two sessions and preferred to get straight on with their interviews.

- Participants were also conscious that they were missing out on activities in the hospital by attending these meetings. In the end, these participants did give consent to being interviewed but it was hard to be sure of their levels of understanding of the full purpose of the research.

Again, this example of conducting research within a secure mental health setting highlights the practical problems that can influence the way in which researchers are able to approach the research process. It also illustrates how researchers can sometimes overestimate the importance of the research in the lives of participants. Again, this is not something unique to research conducted by service-users; however, it highlights an important difference which exists between the service-user and the service-user researcher.

Payments to participants

As already mentioned, the Strategies for Living Project encouraged researchers to pay participants for the time they spent in interviews and focus groups. This was considered important in terms of respecting and valuing people who agree to be involved in research.

However, the issue of payment did raise discussion. Some researchers were concerned that people might only take part because they were being paid and that this could introduce bias. The reality that people have a variety of motivations for taking part in research, whether paid or unpaid, was discussed. Having clear criteria for selecting participants ensured that the people involved were those who were most relevant for the study.

In the end, not all researchers did pay participants. One researcher who did not said that the people involved did not want to be paid; rather, it was enough to be telling their story and for that to be taken seriously. Another project did not pay participants. The Dancing for Living Project was evaluating people's experience of Five Rhythms Dance through a series of workshops. The project was expensive because it required hiring a qualified dance teacher. The researchers decided that, as the women involved as participants would be receiving dance instruction, they were getting something back for being involved. This did not deter people from participating in the project, as there was a waiting list of prospective dance and research participants.

This approach to research might appear unusual. However, it should be remembered that the various projects conducted in the second phase of the Strategies for Living Project were attempting to offer an alternative research approach. By embedding research within approaches to well-being (such as dance), traditional boundaries between services and research inevitably break down.

Researcher safety

Interview skills training for researchers was conducted over a two-day period. The training covered issues of safety for researchers and what to do if a research participant became abusive, threatening or violent during an interview. Researchers were advised to hold interviews in public buildings where possible. Some researchers were able to use local mental health organisations' offices to conduct interviews, but other researchers undertook interviews in participants' homes.

In these situations, we advised researchers to inform another member of their research team or their RSTW of the address they were going to, and the times that they would be there. If the interviewee's home was in an unfamiliar location or a place that was not perceived as safe, researchers were encouraged to use taxis to get to and from the address. Support workers also offered to telephone researchers at a certain time after the interview to check on their safety and to offer debriefing from the interview.

As with some of the issues previously raised, researcher safety is not something specific to service-user-led research. All researchers, at some time, are potentially vulnerable as a result of the research process. However, not all organisations responsible for research address the issue as thoroughly and practically as is demonstrated by the Strategies for Living Project.

Confidentiality and its limits

In this programme of work, confidentiality was an issue for researchers as well as participants. (This also relates to the previous section on safety.) For example, in order to maintain safety, it was sometimes necessary for a researcher to inform a Strategies for Living team member where they were going. It was made clear in training that participants should be informed that the limits of confidentiality extended to the team and not solely the interviewer.

Most researchers in the project were not working from within an organisational base. Many were working from their own homes, although sometimes with access to office space. When advertising for interviewees to telephone them in connection with their research, the researchers needed to decide which telephone numbers they should use. This raised a number of problems. For example, although it was practical to put their home numbers on advertising materials, this made some researchers feel very vulnerable.

There was not just an issue of home telephone numbers. Researchers who were looking at particularly sensitive issues, for example strategies for surviving domestic abuse, did not want their names to appear on the advertising materials.

Solutions to these dilemmas were found, namely that researchers purchased mobile phones from their research budget to be used for the projects and also used local organisations' numbers or the Strategies for Living telephone number, and researchers used pseudonyms.

In addition to problems arising in the researcher–participant interaction, service-user researchers also place themselves in a vulnerable position by identifying and advertising themselves as user/survivor researchers. By doing so, these researchers make a statement regarding their own personal background and experience. Strategies for Living addressed this issue by reflecting on the political nature of the term user-led research. Through its service-user research, Strategies for Living is trying to shift agendas and build new evidence on the kinds of services and supports that users of mental health services want and need. This evidence is coming from standpoint research in which the identity of the researcher is an explicit aspect of the research process. The benefits of this include participants feeling more able to talk openly, as discussed earlier in this chapter, and can help to lead to more genuinely user-centred mental health services. However, the honesty about personal experience of vulnerability can be costly to the researcher, partly because of the continued stigma that society attaches to mental health problems.

It could be argued that a potential conflict arises in relation to the costs of identification for the individual researcher and the benefits to the service-user population as a whole. This type of cost–benefit analysis appears to be particular to research in which the researcher chooses to expose a hidden aspect of identity that may cause them to feel vulnerable (such as sexuality and unseen disabilities). Within traditional research processes, power is described in terms of researchers benefiting from research and costs born by participants. In the case of service-users, this differentiation is broken down. For some of the Strategies for Living researchers, identifying publicly with a service-user label was difficult – indeed, one researcher withdrew.

Confidentiality and anonymity for participants

Each participant was asked to sign a consent form after having been given full information about the research and how their interview data would be used. However, difficulties arose in terms of anonymity in small qualitative studies where people might be recognised, due to their race or ethnicity, the location of the study, gender or other identifying features of their experiences. When using extracts from these studies, it was important that participants were not to be identified. It is possible to change some identifying details (such as removing names in extracts); however, too much change can sometimes result in the meaning of statements being altered. In some cases, research material had to be left out because of the danger that the person could be identified. Therefore, maintaining confidentiality can at times impact on the methodology of the project.

A further issue raised was whether researchers had an obligation, in certain circumstances, to break the confidentiality of the participants. For example, if an interviewee spoke about suicide in their interview, would a researcher be required to disclose this information? Researchers (and indeed the staff team) had a range of views about how to approach this dilemma. The particular issue of whether there was a moral obligation to intervene if someone revealed the intention to commit suicide, as opposed to talking about suicidal feelings, was discussed. Researchers were encouraged to talk to such participants in order to find out if they had any support networks. Researchers were also instructed to provide participants with a list of organisations that provide help and support to those with suicidal feelings. Another suggestion was that the researcher might follow up the interview with a telephone call. As was outlined earlier in relation to how researchers experienced the research process, this type of continued contact does raise questions about the boundaries of the relationship between researchers and participants. Researchers were not encouraged to break the participant's confidence without their permission. This would have meant breaking the agreement made with the participant who had entered the interview having understood the confidentiality and anonymity clause.

The law requires researchers (and other citizens) to break the confidence of the participant if they disclose having committed, or being about to commit, a crime such as child abuse. Participants were made aware of this prior to the interview.

Ethics committees

Two research teams supported by Strategies for Living Project Phase II were asked to submit their projects for consideration by independent research ethics committees. One of these was one of four supported projects in Wales; the other, one of four supported projects in Scotland. Ethics committee approval was required in projects where contact was being made with service-users via NHS services or where the setting for the research was under the responsibility of the NHS. (Applying for research ethics committee approval raised a number of concerns for the project which are also addressed in Chapters Five and Six in Part Two of this book.)

One of the two Strategies for Living supported projects did not get as far as the ethics committee. The prospect of applying to the ethics committee represented a significant barrier to the researcher and was one of the main reasons why this project was not completed.

The other project, which was looking at the system of leave for patients in a secure hospital in Wales, also required ethics committee approval. The experience of the RSTW was that it was initially difficult to find an appropriate ethics committee. A substantial amount of research had to be undertaken in relation to this. It was eventually through the Welsh Assembly website that the correct committee was identified and contacted.

The process of seeking ethics committee approval was daunting from the start. The project team felt that it was unlikely that committee members would be expecting, or be familiar with, the type of work the project proposed. We were concerned that the committee would not understand our approach to the research, seeing the involvement of a user researcher as a negative aspect causing bias, rather than as a positive aspect to be openly acknowledged and valued. We were also concerned that a medical model would be applied and that the methods we planned to use would be seen in a negative way.

Presenting a research project to an ethics committee for approval is an arduous task for even the most experienced of researchers. However, trying to get ethics committee approval for a qualitative user-led research project is even more complex. We experienced problems with the paperwork, as well as within our meetings with the committee. We also had doubts about whether the process would be particularly helpful to us. Ethical issues were already central to our planning process, but we felt that these were not necessarily the types of issues that the ethics committee would be concerned with. In many respects, the ethics committee process felt like a gate-keeping exercise and one which could potentially undermine the project's ability to continue and succeed.

Paperwork

The ethics committee forms were based on the assumption that the research was medical (for example, randomised control trials or drug testing). It was assumed that the lead researcher would be a medically trained doctor. In addition, assumptions were made about both the methodological approach and the potential risks that needed to be considered. There were a lot of questions that were irrelevant to our research and inversely not enough space given to describe the project and the possible risks that are specific to this type of research. In order to ensure that a fair representation of the project was given, it was necessary to attach several extra pages to the standard application form in order to explain our study properly.

We felt that many ethical issues relevant to user-led research were not explicitly addressed within the forms or in the subsequent meeting. For example, there was no consideration of power dimensions within the research project, particularly between researchers and participants. This was central to the object of our research, as well as our methodological approach. In medical research, which ethics committees are familiar with, the researcher is usually a professional and/or academic, and the participants are patients. The resulting power imbalance is accepted and not seen as needing to be challenged or reduced in any way. Another issue not tackled by the ethics committee was that of the possible consequences of the researcher having had similar experiences to the participants, for example, the researcher becoming distressed after or during the interviews. Again in medical research, it is not usual for the researcher to be open about any experiences they have had that may be similar to participants, and where this is acknowledged it is not seen as a central consideration as it is in user-led research.

Meeting the ethics committee

The project team were asked to present their research at an ethics committee meeting. The meeting itself was very formal: the room was laid out in a boardroom meeting style, and this felt very intimidating to the researchers present. Members of the committee referred to the RSTW as "Doctor", thus perpetuating the idea that there are certain people who do research automatically. The language used by the committee was formal, and slightly jargonistic. This was particularly evident in the first question, which was long and technical: how were we going to analyse the findings and would we be using a grounded theory approach? At the time of the meeting, the researcher had not completed the research training session on analysis and found the question difficult to answer in detail. The question, we felt, could have been asked in a much simpler way.

On the committee there were no service-user representatives; almost everyone involved were doctors, and the majority of non-medics were other professionals. We were also concerned that the decisions made by this committee might be influenced by their professional experiences. Many ethical issues that an ethics committee might address, confidentiality for example, will apply to many different types of research. However, the perspective from which these issues are considered can result in very different solutions and recommendations being proposed. The ethics committee in this example suggested we should keep our data in a locked drawer in the ward staff office, in the ward where the research participants lived. This would have meant that theoretically any member of staff would have access to the data. This raised a number of serious concerns for us. We felt that the committee failed to realise that one of the positive aspects of the project was that it gave participants the opportunity to talk to researchers who were completely independent of the hospital, without this information being passed on to staff. Asking that the data be maintained within a clinical setting, we felt, was based on an underlying belief that the 'doctor knows best' and that medical staff should have access to any information about patients.

Another consequence of the make up of the ethics committee was that it would have been easy for us to feel intimidated. The success of the project was, after all, dependent on them being positive about user-led research. We felt that the meeting could have been done in a much less intimidating way and yet still been as thorough. One way in which ethics committees could be made more accessible to all types of researchers is by having members with a range of experience and understanding, covering all types of research approaches (for example, action research, feminist research, user-led research, participatory research, and so on). This would result in a broader understanding within the committee of the value of a diversity of research approaches with differing values and principles. This understanding of the underlying principles could help lead to practical changes in committee procedures that reflect the principles of the research proposal being considered. For example, in user-led research in mental health, the values of accessibility, of recognising and valuing everybody's contributions, of empowerment, and of the importance of process, could be taken into account in the procedure for gaining ethical approval, as well as in the research itself.

The result for this particular project was approval by the ethics committee. This, we felt, was a huge achievement for the researchers involved and for the Strategies for Living Project. Despite differences in our research and that research normally considered by the ethics committee, we felt that they took our approach seriously and the committee could see the value, and potential difficulties, in conducting service-user-led research. The process itself also raised further questions about the research governance process and how it creates barriers to inclusion for service-users. The fears we had about how our research might be construed by such a committee, while not borne out in this situation, are supported by the experiences of other researchers (see Part Two of this book).

Ethical guidelines

At the outset of this project, the Mental Health Foundation did not have its own set of ethical guidelines (we now have these in place), which would have set minimum standards for good practice in terms of participation. We did refer to ethical guidance from the British Psychological Society and the British Sociological Association, although these were not always entirely suited to the sort of participatory research that we were supporting. We also referred to the ethical guidelines from the Association for Research in the Voluntary and Community Sector. However, since the start of this project, we have become proactive in on-going discussions and debates around ethics in user-led research with Consumers in NHS Research, the Joseph Rowntree Foundation and other survivor researchers[5].

Conclusions and recommendations

This chapter has described the ethical issues that arose during Phase II of the Strategies for Living Project. These ethical issues centred around participation, transparency and honesty, consent, payment, safety and confidentiality, ethics committee approval and methodology. Service-user-led research provides an opportunity to challenge the traditional relationships which exist between researchers and participants by giving service-users the tools and skills necessary to conduct research. By drawing on researchers' own experiences of services, they bring to a project such as this considerable added value, knowledge, and experiences that can inform the content and process of research. We wanted this research to be carried out with the highest standards of participation and ethics. Although we feel confident that we addressed ethical issues throughout the research process, it is also important to recognise the possible limitations of our approach and ethical practice.

Practical problems, such as time constraints, were a problem in a number of projects. While this is a problem faced by all researchers, it was especially important in our case to take into account that projects may be interrupted and run behind schedule since we were working with many individuals new to research. Researchers were volunteers and sometimes the work was interrupted due to other commitments or ill health. Due to the fact that researchers were also people who experience distress, it was also necessary to ensure that adequate support was given to them throughout the research process.

As a result of our experiences we would make the following recommendations and conclusions:

1. It is important to ensure that researchers are given a copy of the organisation's ethical guidelines at the start of the project and that there is a clear and shared understanding of the ethical governance of the project, including minimum expected standards regarding the research relationship. This has implications for both researchers and participants.
2. It is important to work through ethical issues with all researchers during training, including the issue of boundaries. By doing so, the responsibilities of both participants and researchers can be addressed.
3. Researchers should be provided with training about the potential conflicts that can arise between participatory and traditional approaches to research.
4. Researchers should also be provided with information on the role and structures of research ethics committees. The organisation should at least offer support to user researchers in taking a research proposal to an ethics committee, but ideally offer to do this on their behalf.

Finally, it is important to acknowledge that by including service-users in the research process, the various projects overseen by the Strategies for Living Project have been able to conduct participatory research that centres on the perspectives of service-users. As such, this type of research challenges traditional research relationships and offers alternative ways of producing valuable knowledge that serves people with mental health problems alongside wider society.

Notes

[1] Different people use the terms *survivor* and *service-user* rather differently. However, 'service-user' is usually used where the people to be involved in a project are using or have used mental health services. Sometimes in a research project, this means they have used the service in question. Different definitions of mental health services are sometimes used; for example, some people include in this secondary mental health services; some only acute services; others will include use of talking treatments and primary mental health care support. 'Survivor' is often intended as a broader term to include people who have experienced mental or emotional distress, whether or not they have used mental health services. However, 'survivor' may also be used politically to refer to people who have survived mental health services and/or treatments; people who are 'psychiatric system survivors'.

[2] For a full discussion of the ethical implications of user-led research in mental health, please refer to the *Guidelines for the ethical conduct of survivor research* (Faulkener, 2004: forthcoming).

[3] The Strategies for Living Advisory Committee is made up, in the majority, of people who experience mental distress and/or who have used mental health services.

[4] Five Rhythms Dance was developed by Gabrielle Roth. It involves moving dancers through five rhythms – flowing, staccato, chaos, lyrical and stillness – as they dance their feelings to the music. See Roth and Loudon (1989).

[5] Consumers in NHS Research (now called INVOLVE) have been consulting with a range of groups including survivors, service-users and carers on social care ethics and the format for new social care ethics committees with a view to informing the implementation of the Department of Health Social Care Research Governance Framework. The Joseph Rowntree Foundation is currently funding a project producing ethical guidelines for survivor research, led by Alison Faulkner.

References

Beresford, P. and Wallcraft, J. (1997) 'Psychiatric system survivors and emancipatory research: issues, overlaps and differences', in C. Barnes and G. Mercer (eds) *Doing disability research*, Leeds: Disability Press.

Faulkner, A. (2004: forthcoming) *Guidelines for the ethical conduct of survivor research*, Bristol/York: The Policy Press/Joseph Rowntree Foundation.

Faulkner, A. and Layzell, S. (2000) *Strategies for living*, London: Mental Health Foundation.

Nicholls, V. (2001) *Doing research ourselves*, London: Mental Health Foundation.

Nicholls, V., Wright, S., Waters, R. and Wells, S. (2003) *Surviving user-led research*, London: Mental Health Foundation.

Roth, G. and Loudon, J. (1989) *Maps to ecstasy: Teachings of an urban shamam* Novato, CA: New World Library.

TWO

Making the decision about enrolment in a randomised controlled trial

Tracey J. Stone

Introduction

This chapter describes the decision making of a purposively sampled group of oncology patients about taking part in a randomised controlled trial (RCT). The data presented here was gathered for a NHS-sponsored PhD project, one aim of which was to feed back to local clinical researchers and Research Ethics Committees in order to improve the process for future patients.

The chapter, therefore, is structured around the idea of choice, of exactly what participants understood their choices to be, and the extent to which they felt free to choose. This has associated implications for the ethical requirement of voluntariness in informed consent. Features of the process that they felt made the decision more or less difficult will be covered as will variances in attitudes to the risks contingent in research involvement and the way in which information about risk was used. The roles of self-interest and altruism in deciding whether to agree to take part in research were discussed, and are reported here.

Terminology

Various terms are used to describe people who agree to take part in medical research. 'Subject', 'respondent', 'participant' or 'patient', for example, and collective terms such as 'cohort' and 'control group', all of which are illustrative of researchers' attitudes towards the people they are researching. The small-scale study reported here was qualitative and largely inductive at both the data collection and analysis stages. Focus groups were used to encourage participant generated themes within the theoretical framework of the research. Furthermore, the viability of the study was highly dependent on the goodwill of those who were invited to take part. (Lack of direct benefit to participants who were or had recently been seriously ill meant that no telephone follow-up took place.) Those who did come to the discussions were explicitly encouraged to express their thoughts and recollections. In light of this, they were consistently referred to as 'participants', as this term adequately captures the sense of a respectful representation of individuality. However, the literature on the subject included only a small number of studies where similar conditions applied (Searight and Miller, 1996; Featherstone and Donovan, 1998; Snowdon et al, 1998; Ellis et al, 1999; Donovan et al, 2002). The majority were larger, often questionnaire surveys (Maslin, 1994; Sugarman et al, 1998) or administered questionnaires (Kemp et al, 1984). The people being researched were often referred to as 'participants' where, particularly in the surveys, they had little chance to influence the agenda. There is an implicit power imbalance between researcher and researched in the methodologies described, although this can be mediated somewhat by piloting questionnaires and incorporating contributions from people who are being researched. However, individuals who agree to take part in research are not *prima facie* participants. The methodology employed must allow scope for the 'subject' to actively participate, before they can be described as 'participants' in any meaningful way.

Informed consent and randomised controlled trials (RCTs)

Informed consent requirements for medical research generally (including clinical trials) are defined by professional ethical guidelines such as the Declaration of Helsinki (WMA, 2000), General Medical Council (2001), Council for International Organisations in Medical Science (CIOMS) (2002) and the European Clinical Trials Directive (European Parliament and the Council of the European Union, 2001). Valid, informed consent for research involving groups not defined as specifically 'vulnerable'[1] requires that the potential participant is legally competent, consents voluntarily in light of adequate understanding of sufficient information, and gives explicit permission for his or her enrolment in the project by signing a consent form (Beauchamp and Childress, 1994, pp 142-63). These requirements are the result of cumulative debate since the pronouncements of the Nuremberg Code in 1947 with the explicit aim of protecting the interests and autonomy of those who volunteer to be the human subjects of medical research. As statements premised upon normative moral values, these standards of practice in the recruitment of subjects assume a normatively rational response on the part of those making the decision. That is to say that legally competent individuals will identify their best interests regarding the proposition of involvement in research and choose to consent to involvement, or decline the option, after weighing the associated risks and benefits in relation to their self-defined goals. However, the possibility that some people may make the decision according to other priorities exists, with implications for the validity of the informed consent they may give, given the authority of the professional guidelines and (as of 2004) the law in this area. The relationship between individual researchers and individual subjects, and the quality of their communication, is the crucial variable in maintaining the validity of informed consent for research from which we all ultimately benefit.

For reasons of theoretical coherency, this project purposively recruited oncology patients who had made a decision about whether to be involved in a RCT, rather than studies using other methodologies. The positivist scientific method underlying the design of randomised controlled trials requires that there be genuine uncertainty within the medical community about the superiority of the trial treatment against standard treatment or placebo. This concept – termed 'clinical equipoise' – was first defined by Freedman (1987, pp 141-5). Clinical equipoise removes the ethical worry about individual doctors enrolling patients while suspecting that one trial arm is more efficacious than a comparator. Where genuine uncertainty exists within the medical community as a whole, the trial is ethically justified. Furthermore, randomisation removes the power of the doctor/researcher to choose the treatment that he or she feels is in the patient's best interest (without removing them from the trial). The implication of this is that the protection offered by a doctor acting on the principle of beneficence is removed and the patient considering trial entry must make an autonomous decision to give informed consent in the context of this new arrangement of the doctor's priorities. For informed consent to be valid, prospective participants for RCTs must therefore understand at least the practical implications of randomisation and equipoise in the trial, without necessarily being burdened with scientific explanations of these concepts. Local and multi-centre research ethics committees review research protocols to ensure that the random allocation of comparative treatments is explained clearly in lay terms in the patient's information (and also, more controversially, to consider whether clinical equipoise exists and if the randomisation procedure is valid).

> We now have a system in which there are two separate protections of the rights and interests of research subjects; subjects protect themselves through the informed consent process and they are further protected by the independent review. Normally, each of these protective processes is necessary for the licitness of research. (Brody, 2001, p 9)

It is worth noting that, while the second layer of protection afforded by 'independent review' includes scrutiny of informed consent documents and strategies, ethics review committees cannot know exactly what is said in these encounters or whether the dynamics of power, environment and circumstance endanger the validity of any informed consent granted. This chapter presents the experience of the informed consent process from the point of view of individuals who have been through the process, with illustrations of their reasoning in their own words.

Methodology

The research used a combination of three focus group interviews and two individual semi-structured interviews to gather data on participants' decision making about clinical trial entry. Conducting three focus groups allowed for triangulation in case any group proved to be particularly extreme in their response and interpersonal dynamics. The sampling and recruitment procedure was the same for the focus groups and the individual interviews. The initial research design did not include individual interviews; however, as two people were unable to attend to the group discussions, they agreed to meet individually. Given the relatively small number of participants, the contributions of these two people were valuable additions to the data and also improved the representativeness of the sample. The inclusion criteria were patients who had been approached for clinical trial entry and had either given informed consent to trial entry, declined trial participation or consented to trial participation and then been excluded before participation began. They had, or were in, remission from different cancers (colon, breast, prostate or testicular). The sample included both male and female adult participants who were mobile and generally well enough to participate in a group or individual discussion. The Local Research Ethics Committee gave approval for the study and the results were presented to both a local meeting and an annual national Multi-centre Research Ethics Committee conference. Thirteen patients (nine men, four women) of the 25 who had been approached agreed to take part in the research. Each focus group included participants that reflected the theoretical purpose of the sampling as far as possible. This was not possible in the third focus group because of the unforeseen withdrawal on health grounds of two of the participants. However, this shortfall in representation was compensated for by the inclusion of two in-depth, semi-structured interviews with participants who had the profiles lacking in the group. (Questions used for the focus group discussions and the individual interviews are listed in the Appendix included with this chapter.)

The initial hypothesis of this research was that people in this situation make decisions in a normatively rational way. Decision theory has the same premise and works to support and improve this. The development of a simple but useful decision tool for use as part of the informed consent process was, therefore, an initial objective of the study. To this end, decision theory questions were introduced to elicit individual utilities for four possible outcomes of trial participation. Participants were asked as a group to arrange in order of preference the four possible outcomes of the decision they faced. These were:

- consent to trial entry and health improves;
- consent to trial entry and health does not improve;
- decline trial entry and health improves;
- decline trial entry and health does not improve.

They were then asked to reach a mutually agreed value from one to 100 (where 100 was the best possible outcome and one was the worst imaginable). The expectation was that the process of negotiating an agreement (or failing to reach one) would elucidate aspects of their individual priorities and reasoning.

In fact, there was a considerable amount of negative feedback about these questions to the extent that it appeared to be causing enough frustration to damage the ambience of the groups. The reaction to the attempt to elicit individual utilities in the first individual interview similarly caused frustration and confusion. The participants found it difficult to see the point of it or to abstract from the close discussion of their real life experiences to a hypothetical scenario. As they seemed to think the exercise invalid because of its abstract nature, there was a perceptible danger of generating the feeling that their earnestly related experiences were trivialised by the introduction of hypothetical abstractions on the same subject. Attempts to explain the concept of individual utilities only seemed to confound this. Therefore, I abandoned this exercise before it was completed in the third focus group and did not introduce it in the second individual interview where the participant was tired towards the end and seemed especially vulnerable to confusion. This inevitably introduced some methodological inconsistency; however, I was concerned that the participants should leave the group and the individual interviews feeling that the exercise had been worthwhile, not only for their own satisfaction but also to avoid any negative attitudes to similar research in the future. This methodological inconsistency is not sufficient to invalidate the research. Attempting this exercise did in fact generate some interesting comments on individual attitudes to research, risk and personal experience. These were coded for in the analysis across the whole data set. Moreover, this unexpected response was an example of the value of qualitative research in offering opportunities for surprises and new insights contributed by the participants. The failed attempt to arrive at expected utility values was the point at which the research took an unanticipated turn. Prior assumptions about instrumentally rational reasoning in this context were contradicted and the search for an explanation eventually uncovered a much more interesting thesis.

The data were analysed using thematic content analysis; specifically, the 'constant comparison' method to code individual comments from the participants against coding categories. The analysis was theory and data driven, in that an initial set of codes was derived to meet the theoretical purposes of the research. These were then added to by categories of interest that arose directly from the data. The initial set of codes was additionally informed by the results of reviewing the literature on patient motivation and decision making about involvement in medical research.

Findings

A number of themes arose from the coding process. While there is insufficient space to include them all here, comments relating to the concept of choice and specifically voluntariness and freedom of choice are presented. More or less difficulty in making the decision, and factors that influenced this are reported, as are findings on attitudes to risk information. The roles of altruism and self-interest and tensions between these concepts are discussed and each of the themes is illustrated with direct quotations from the participants (all names are pseudonyms).

The concept of choice

The first part of the analysis investigated how participants in medical research responded to being offered the choice of trial participation; how they conceptualised that choice; and how they approached it. This described the patients' initial reactions to the idea of being involved in research, and implications these reactions may have had on their approach to, and management of, the decision.

The most common response of participants on being asked to recall their first reactions to the prospect of clinical trial entry was to incorporate it into the story of the diagnosis and treatment of their illness as a whole. In relation to the aims of this book, this raises the question of whether therapeutic research in health is different from other forms of non-therapeutic research. The assimilation of research specific processes into the wider narrative of illness or identity may also occur in other fields.

In this project, Sally saw trial participation as another unpleasant thing that, like chemotherapy, "had to be done". For these people, deciding about clinical trial participation was only one aspect of having cancer. The recruitment interviews, trial interventions and monitoring took place in the same setting as diagnostic and treatment consultations. Some participants found the shift from a fiduciary relationship (that is, a relationship based on unequal power and an implicit contract of trust between the parties) where the doctor guided treatment decisions, to deciding for him or herself about research participation, very unsettling. In one case, this extended to asking the recruiting doctor for an explicit recommendation. Others took the introduction of the prospect of trial participation by a doctor they respected and trusted as an implicit recommendation. It is a feature of respect for the autonomy of persons that one may autonomously ask someone else to make the decision. However, autonomously handing over the task of choosing does not release the decision owner from responsibility for that outcome. The implication of this for informed consent for medical research is that, where theoretical risks develop into material effects (for example, if the trial protocol is unpleasant, onerous or confusing), the research doctor who 'recommended' the trial may be the focus of disappointment, hurt or feelings of betrayal. This occurred with one participant who telephoned after finishing the trial to complain about his treatment.

However, there are also wider lessons which can be learned about how potential research participants make choices, balance costs and benefits, and relate to the aims and objectives of the research team. As such, the data presented here is of importance to all researchers who conduct research with 'human subjects'. A number of different strategies for dealing with the situation of choice arose. Two patients were clear about the demarcation of trial and treatment. Adrian and Jeremy avoided the burden of worrying about the decision by choosing to decline trial entry relatively quickly. It appeared to them to involve too much inconvenience for something that they felt at first glance to be against their best interests. Having to make a choice can itself be a burden, as Bob describes.

> "My first reaction was [animated, distressed voice] 'Oh no ... totally ... now I've got testicular cancer, and I've got to make a CHOICE'. So that was my first, err, more, WHY have I got to make a choice? That was the first reaction." (*Bob*)

Being required to choose increased the difficulty of coping with the disease and Bob seems to have experienced the withdrawal of beneficent authority as abandonment. In addition, he had to find the emotional strength to deal with a complex decision in an unfamiliar and frightening situation. The prospect of trial participation introduced uncertainty about an issue of serious personal consequences, at a time when the confidence of experts was a source of much needed emotional support. It is clear that Bob felt that being required to take responsibility for such an important decision was unfair[2]. In contrast, Michael used his considerable experience of decision making in business as a model for this situation. Jeremy's response to Michael's comments that "It's like buying a fridge", suggests the 'postmodern-consumer' approach to choice described by Alderson and Goodey (1998). The choice is seen as a matter of facts and a weighing of risks and benefits. In this model, the individual is an expert in choosing between the many options on offer in a consumer driven society.

> "So I said 'Yes, I would be interested depending upon what the drug was and what the effect was' ... talked to the research nurse about it and let me, let's go from there. So as far as I was concerned I was happy enough to be offered and see what was involved.... You go through this [green form], you discuss it till you're blue in the face, you get everybody involved, and I was using other doctors.... I'm saying, 'Ok, what's the facts, what's the, when have you got to make your mind up, who's got the information?' – get as much as you can and make your mind up." (*Michael*)

> "It's like buying a fridge, isn't it!" [Laughter all round] (*Jeremy*)

The laughter around the table confirmed the irony of this statement rather than the endorsement of it. To reduce the decision to that of consumer choice ignores the complicating effect of the emotional investment that the decision required, the scale of which became evident as the discussion progressed.

For some, the importance of maintaining a positive attitude in dealing with the disease extended to trial entry as an expression of this. One implication of this was that some participants discounted negative factors about the trial, such as side effects, and overestimated the chances of personal benefit. Maintaining a positive attitude had symbolic significance for some, as a way of defining oneself as a strong person in the face of adversity and being offered this choice was a chance to express moral strength, among other things. One participant, on the contrary, was pleased to have an understanding of the uncertainties involved, being realistic about the options available was important to her, even if this resulted in her feeling that the difficulty of the choice was 'overwhelming'.

Voluntariness and freedom of choice

Most of the participants were clear that participation in the trial was voluntary in the sense envisaged by the 'professional' view of informed consent (outlined earlier in this chapter). However, the degree to which informed consent was substantively voluntary varied (Hewlett, 1996): one participant was unaware that standard treatment was an available alternative, while two others asked for and received a direct recommendation to join the trail from their recruiting doctor. However, the option to withdraw from the trial was well understood and often quoted. For example:

> "Yes, I was going to say.... They also said, didn't they, that if you were in the trial and, em, didn't want to go ahead, you know, you wouldn't be any less thought of, your treatment would be just the same, it wouldn't be detrimental to you at all in any way. And so, you weren't pressurised with these things, were you?" (*Sally*)

Felicity was less certain and appears to have been swept along by the process. Her daughter remembered the facts of the interview differently, but even on Felicity's version of events, meaningful voluntary consent was undermined by the recommendation to participate.

> "Well, I've been thinking actually, and I said to my daughter, but she denied it, that I was just told I was going to be on one. But she said, 'We have decided it would be a good thing for you to be on one, but you have the option'.... And it was quite a shock when it's fait accompli, when you're actually in X and it's suddenly presented to you and I think I would have coped. Well it was only that one day I didn't cope." (*Felicity*)

This example illustrates the importance of research ethics training for researchers and others who recruit patients for medical research. Felicity was aware of the requirement of signing a consent form but was convinced that others had already made the decision about her participation. Whatever the exact words of the clinician were, this was clearly her impression. Her decision cannot have been truly voluntary (Felicity suffered emotional harm by being back in the hospital for a pre-trial x-ray), therefore, or even substantively so, despite her signature on the form. Respect for patient autonomy in informed consent for research is important precisely because of the uncertainty of the risks and benefits involved. Moreover, trial specific treatments – that is, any procedure that is not for the primary purpose of managing the patient's condition – are not permitted in the professional ethical guidelines for clinical research[3]

(although controversially, this may be routine practice where time between diagnosis and starting treatment in a trial is short).

In line with his avoidance of dealing with the uncertain benefit of trial entry, Arthur saw the option to decline entry as dependent upon the process of being adequately informed, rather than as a choice based on accepting the risks involved in testing a new treatment.

> "No I didn't really [feel pressured]. I don't think you would.... If I'd felt
> that it wasn't explained to me properly, I didn't get enough information,
> then I could have opted out." (*Arthur*)

The reported restrictions on choice arose from perceptions of the severity of their illness. In response to Arthur describing his prognosis of having between two to five years to live as a justification for seizing the option of trial entry, Bob said:

> "I think it's just circumstances, you know? I mean, I think if you're sort of,
> if you're limited to the choices that you take, then you tend to go for the
> trial." (*Bob*)

However, Bob's words express an opinion that having a frightening prognosis – in envisioning one's own imminent death – pushes people towards participating in trials. There is a suggestion that trial participation provides at least the solace of hope and perhaps even survival. Essentially, the more life threatening the situation, the greater the emotional need for apparent certainty by inflating the prospect of saving one's life through participation in research. The influence of health status as limiting choice, as described here, does not mean that Arthur's decision was not voluntary in the sense envisaged by the professionally instituted standards of informed consent that were defined earlier. He understood that he was under no obligation to enrol in the trial. It is an example of the 'substantially voluntary' informed consent described by Hewlett (1996); that is to say, influenced by emotional concerns that cannot be removed from the scenario. As such, emotions play an important role in the consent process, as well as in the risks/benefits analysis. The potential for emotional harm cuts across all areas of research, be it therapeutic medical research, or other non-therapeutic research in health (see Chapter Five of this book), social science (Chapters Eight and Eleven), or journalism (Chapter Seven).

While most of the participants understood, on one level, that taking part in a clinical trial was voluntary, and furthermore that their explicit and written permission was required, the choice itself was limited in other ways. Self-protective persons rejected the trial because the decision itself was onerous, it prolonged and intensified their (and other peoples) idea of them as 'cancer patients' and because it involved inconvenience additional to that imposed by the illness itself. In some cases, the choice is restricted by loyalty to loved ones who may be keen that the patient grasps the chance of participation or avoids the uncertainty involved by declining. Voluntariness in this choice situation is not therefore the relatively straightforward absence of pressure to consent from recruiting doctors. Other factors, such as physical and emotional pain or gratitude, can make some decisions to consent less than wholly voluntary. Subjective influences cannot be eradicated, and it may be damaging and dangerous to seek to do so. However, it is important to differentiate between limits to voluntariness that arise from the participants' values and beliefs, and those that limit autonomous decision making being imposed by others.

Ease or difficulty in choosing

All participants described having an almost instant initial reaction to the option of trial participation. This set the cornerstone for their decision making. Only Bob changed his mind from his initial intuitive response to the request. Everyone else progressed to make their decision in line with their first reaction, although with varying degrees of ease or difficulty. For example, Beth reported feeling "prepared" by being given information about clinical trials in general early in her treatment and said that this had helped her a great deal. When she was asked about participation in a particular trial she gave a positive response in principle straight away (without giving formal consent). Later, at home she began to worry whether this had been the right thing to do.

> "No, I still had a lot of fears because, with chemotherapy, it's something outside of nursing. I have sort of nursed the terminally ill and now I'm the sort of reverse, I'm the patient, sort of thing. No, I had my fears." (*Beth*)

The list of side effects and of chemotherapy were her main concerns, although she went on to join the trial anyway. Beth's past experience of nursing terminally ill patients did not appear to help. She felt "overwhelmed" by the necessity to choose and by a decision that could not be avoided. Bob also reports similar feelings.

> "I would have been better off if they'd just sort of told me what I was having. Decisions are always hard to make, especially when they're quite a major decision. I was fazed by it really. You know why, sort of like, why have a trial now, like, at this moment in time? So I've got to make the decision. I'm not going to make the decision till I'm better ... but things like this made me stronger...." (*Bob*)

Both Beth and Bob seem to have felt a form of decision paralysis, caused by their perception that the choice was complex and difficult and simultaneously crucial to their future well-being, and by being put in a position of having to choose at all. (This links back to the section earlier in this chapter on conceptualising choice.) This is important information about the impact of being given the choice, which is not available elsewhere. This is the hidden cost of autonomous decision making and why research governance is important to ensure that being given a choice is not in itself harmful to potential participants.

Adrian was living alone and dismissed the trial quite quickly on seeing the list of side effects, which he thought represented an additional physical burden. Involvement in the trial, he felt, would exacerbate and prolong his 'cancer patient' status and he therefore wanted to avoid the symbolic significance that he attached to participation. As described here, overall, he preferred not to think about it and as a result declined entry without a great deal of deliberation.

> "I read through this. Well I didn't … when you're in this position and you come down to the hospital and there's all this sort of bad news, when you go home you want to think about something else, you know? You don't just want to think about yourself just as a piece of cancer with a human body around it, you know? I didn't find it difficult…." (*Adrian*)

This is an important point about identification with the population group and relates to other chapters in this edited collection where research focuses on identified participants groups, whether the definition is health, experience, or demographically defined. In this case, the fact that group identification would be prolonged was seen as a potential harm to the participants.

Alternatively, Alastair and Bob (who declined one trial and consented to involvement in another) were in a state of indifference between the two treatments on offer. They perceived negligible risk to themselves of participating and therefore reported that the decision to enrol in the trial was relatively simple.

> "And what he said to me was, instead of giving six weeks of radiotherapy, it's seven. I thought, 'Well …' [shrug, suggesting 'fine']. As I said, my trial was so simple there was no need for me to ask the doctor, what would you do? It was just seven weeks instead of six, that's all it was." (*Alastair*)

All those in this group of participants who reported finding the choice a relatively easy one spoke of making up their minds quickly. Unlike the others reporting ease of decision making, Bob still spent a good deal of time thinking through the decision. What seems to have made the second trial easier to decide about was that (a) he was less ill; (b) taking trial nausea tablets entailed less risk; and (c) he had no preference for trial treatment over standard tablets. So, like Alastair, who also perceived risk as minimal and understood that clinical equipoise existed, the decision was made much easier.

Factors that seemed to make the choice easier were having a strong expectation of personal benefit from trial participation, or and equally strong belief that the trial was not in their personal interests or perceiving the risks of participation to be low, or being genuinely indifferent to which treatment was received (personal equipoise). Using the option to withdraw as a form of insurance was one way of mediating the balance between risks and benefits and finally having a strong altruistic commitment made volunteering the self-evidently right thing to do for one person. Factors which made choosing difficult were perceiving the personal stakes involved to be very high, feeling forced into the position of having to make the decision at all, and struggling to achieve an 'objective' evaluation of the risks and benefits of participation from the information provided.

Risk

In the focus groups for this research, there was very little explicit mention of risk as an abstract concept. Rather, risk was conceived by participants as something concrete and was contextualised by their experiences of having cancer. In the main, the conversation focused upon the implications of the risk of participation versus standard or no treatment, rather than on dealing with numerical probabilities or the comparative nature of the trial. In this way, the perceived risks and benefits were 'rounded off' or made into general rather than specific considerations and couched in terms of uncertainty. By definition, having cancer makes one's life more risky. The 'certainties' of life that are generally taken for granted are jeopardised on receiving the diagnosis. In addition, standard treatment involves risk and one's newly precarious physical state means that normal activities entail risks that did not apply previously. Michael's comments suggest that the effect of this is a decreased sensitivity to risk taking. It may also be that this familiarity with bearing risks in relation to one's health, results in a quickly gained competence in juggling the contingent risks. Whether or not this interpretation is correct, it seems reasonable to suggest that weighting the risks and benefits of trial participation take place within the context of this multifaceted overall risk to one's survival.

> "Why bother? If I'm ... why would I want to go through the whole chemo business and lose hair and generally feel terrible? Why do I want to do that? Why bother? But I was happy to take the chance to see. Because they say to you if it's going to affect you, you come off it immediately, don't you? Any chance is better than nothing. Because when you're actually told you've got cancer, though you've got a pretty good idea that you've got it, at least I had, it's still a big slap in the face, so you're still going to take any chance possible aren't you...?" (*Michael*)

As mentioned above, the uncertainties involved in the trial are experienced as part of this larger picture was also apparent when the participants were asked about their first general reactions to being offered the choice. As all the participants had a clear and confident understanding that they could withdraw from the trial if they had second thoughts about participation later (this presumably would include finding side effects too unpleasant), this represents a strategy for managing risk. Michael described this 'opt out' clause explicitly, as did others in the groups. It seems to have been a way of prospectively dealing with the uncertainty inherent in accepting the risks of trial participation. Thus, a higher degree of risk could be taken in the knowledge that they could withdraw from the trial situation to the relative security of standard treatment. This maximised the chance of benefiting from taking the risk in the first place, while leaving one's options open.

Risk information was dealt with in terms of the imaginability[4] of the effect rather than the chance of it happening. One person was particularly sceptical of all risk information and compared it in the clinical trial information to the manipulation of statistics outside medicine (the BSE controversy). The risks of side effects were often discounted in favour of the chance of benefits in the decision making of those who gave consent. Three people who chose to decline the trial did so to avoid the risks described in the information to patients. Declining trial entry and relying on the option to withdraw are two pragmatic ways that participants described of managing contingent risks.

Self-interest

The possibility of personal health gains from trial participation is, by definition, uncertain. Research so far points to a weak 'trial effect' that appears to arise from the imposition of increased monitoring on protocols rather than the effect of new drugs or treatments (Braunholtz et al, 2001). The prospect of improving their health status was the primary concern of all the participants bar one. Statements about the possibility of benefiting their health were usually supported by comments to the effect that at least others would benefit if this did not occur. Helping to contribute to medical knowledge was seen as a worthy and worthwhile aim and yet for most of the participants it was a form of added value rather than the main motivation.

The potential benefits suggested by participants went beyond the physical. Sally astutely noted that the benefit might in part be psychological, and also that the closer monitoring of patients in a trial may be beneficial.

> "That's right, I think psychologically you think, 'If I'm having two drugs, I'm on a trial, that's better for me' [animated selfish voice], like you say you're probably selfish, but … do you feel that, being on the trial, they're keeping a closer look at you or…? I think, probably, it's just selfish again. I think you just go for, you know, if you think it's going to do you good then you take it." (*Sally*)

Sally's use of the word 'selfish' was picked up from Arthur's repeated description of trial participation as 'selfish'. This was initially puzzling. Jeremy had also used the word in a different group to describe non-participation. This was more in line with the professional understanding of trial participation as essentially altruistic, given the uncertain risks and benefits involved for the volunteer and the certain benefit to future patients. It became clear that Arthur's insistence that trial participation was a selfish act was based on his certainty that new treatment was better treatment and his misunderstanding of randomisation. He had decided almost instantly to enrol in the trial because he thought that there was a good chance that it might prolong his life. He even goes so far as to say that he "didn't have to think about it" to the extent that later in the discussion he reported not having read the patient information sheet.

Bob provided a second pragmatic reason for declining trial entry in addition to pleasing his mother. He fully understood that the trial was being run to establish whether marginally shorter treatment was as effective as standard treatment. Although he appreciated the benefits of this healthcare economics exercise generally, he decided against being involved in the experiment to establish the clinical basis for making the economic saving.

Not surprisingly, perhaps, self-interest therefore operates in some cases to prevent patients enrolling in clinical trials. This was the case for Jeremy, Jack and Adrian who all felt that avoiding the possible side effects of the trial and associated inconveniences was in their best interest. In addition, Adrian wanted to protect his image of himself from being defined as a cancer patient any longer than necessary, and felt that trial participation would prolong this.

Altruism

Braunholtz et al (2001), identify two concepts of altruism to explain the attachment of moral value to being involved in a trial: 'strong' and 'weak' forms of altruism. This is a useful distinction to make because, while the majority of participants mentioned altruism as a motivating factor, this was usually a demonstration of the weaker form. It is a consideration or even motivation, but it is not a deterministic factor in the choice. Strongly altruistic choice occurred much less frequently in these participants, and involves an individual consenting to trial participation in the expectation that, as a result, he or she will probably not benefit and may even be worse off. While only Alan described volunteering without any expectation of personal benefit, most of the participants mentioned the possibility of benefiting others by their trial participation but most usually as a secondary outcome of benefiting themselves. For example, Beth said:

> " … and having the nursing background, I think for me it was slightly easier for me to make that decision because, you know the type, once you've done this you want to help as much as you can, so for me it was wanting to help other people too, in the future." (*Beth*)

Those who declined to participate also acknowledged the moral value of volunteering for medical research. Jeremy, who rejected trial entry, said that his first thoughts were "largely yes, you know, I'd like to give something back". Adrian also declined the trial but acknowledged the necessity for altruistic actions in this context but felt that others would be in a better position to volunteer. The weight attached to this as a motivating factor however was related to their individual ideas about the kind of person they were. Some of the participants thought of themselves as essentially altruistic people. Arthur for example (despite the number of times he called himself 'selfish' for jumping at the chance to take part), likened trial participation to carrying an organ donor card and so showed himself to be a person who had previously made a commitment to helping others. Bob had a strong religious faith and placed his trust in God. His "thank God" comment was entirely authentic, on the basis of other comments in the interview in which he disclosed his faith. The first time he was asked to join a trial, his initially positive response (which he later changed) was influenced by a 'moral' sense that he ought to enrol to help other people.

> "But you know, they caught it early, thank God, so there was only one choice really. Although that sort of moral thing about helping someone down the line was so strong that I would have gone for it straight away."
> (*Bob*)

He rejected the first trial to avoid upsetting and worrying his 74-year-old mother, among other reasons. However, he gave informed consent the second time that he was asked to join a trial (without telling his mother!). There were also pragmatic reasons why the second trial was acceptable where the first was not. Protecting those who loved him and being fair to himself had moderated his inclination towards altruistic action in the first trial where the risks to him personally were much higher.

Altruism was described as a reason that one 'ought' to participate; in other words, it was recognised as a moral principle relevant to the situation. For some, it was mediated by pragmatic concerns, specifically with the protection or advancement of self-interest. However, for Alan it was the overriding principle that necessitated his involvement in the trial in spite of his expectations that this would be an unpleasant experience.

Discussion

This research project on patients' decision making about taking part in medical research was inevitably research on the process of research. The discussants, however, seemed to view the process positively as an opportunity to talk about an issue that was important to them with others who had the same or very similar experiences. As a researcher, this involved cultivating relationships to some extent with the participants purely for what I could gain in terms of research data. However, that is too bald a description of the relationships I developed. For example, I learned something about the lives, circumstances and families of these people who bothered to come to these meetings on the basis of a letter asking for their help with the research. As a researcher, it was my intention and my hope that I could repay this by offering general support and advice where I was able (for example, on health services available or sources of information), to analyse the data honestly and thoroughly and to relate it directly to the professional groups best placed to use it to improve the experiences of future patients.

Conclusion

This chapter has looked at the process of patients' decision making when asked to take part in clinical research, in order to identify the ethical problems that arise within the relationship between patients and researcher. The combination of the 'patient role' (which encourages compliance, dependency and deference) and the ethical requirement that patients make an autonomous decision about participation in a project that is not primarily designed to benefit them, presents an extremely difficult scenario. The informed consent interview is difficult to negotiate because of this combination of ethical requirements and communication difficulties, compounded by a shift in traditional roles. If patients can be perturbed by the introduction of clinical uncertainty, so can recruiting doctors who may not be the principal investigator.

In this small qualitative project, the participants reported making initial intuitive decisions, which they supported by selective use of information. The inclination is an understandable search for certainty, which is so much more comfortable than confronting uncertainty when ill. This suggests that the way in which participants are approached by researchers is extremely important. If potential participants are allowed to avoid an understanding that medical research is an experiment with uncertain outcomes, or the implications of randomisation, for example, problems of confusion and resentment are stored up for the future of those persons' involvement. Research in medicine may suffer in general from damage to recruitment figures by negative 'word of mouth' reports (long waits in outpatients are wonderful opportunities to chat).

The data presented in this chapter raise concerns about participant group identification by illness. In this example, cancer patients questioned whether they would want to maintain that identity categorisation beyond treatment. 'Getting one's life back' is the driving motivation away from hospital treatments and bureaucracy, which may include being involved in research. From participants' testimonies, we can observe that a number of the patients considered being defined by their illness as something potentially harmful.

Being given the choice can be problematic for the reasons above, thus highlighting the important role which governance plays in protecting particularly vulnerable people from this negative impact of choice. Paternalism can easily creep in to fill the void, which also has implications for the collection of unbiased data in quantitative studies. The skill of the recruiting researcher is an awareness that these factors need to be balanced and most importantly that the interests of the patient come first. While other chapters in this book may have been critical of the 'gate-keeping' role of RECs, the data presented here suggests that this is or could be important.

Harm is not just about physical harm. Even in cancer RCTs, it is the emotional impact of recruitment that is raised alongside disappointment from raised expectations arising from misunderstandings, such as expecting direct feedback at the end of participation. The symbolic value of participating can also include emotional benefits. For example, positive feelings of being altruistic (weak/strong) as well as feeling special on account of the act of participating in worthwhile or prestigious research.

The relationship between patients and those recruiting patients onto trials is a problematic one. Most individuals do not wish to identify with the defining characteristic of the population. The pressing concern of most is to get well and remain well. As such, although in some circumstances they might benefit from participation, this is not always going to be the case. It is the desire to succeed in this primary aim that leads researchers to conduct new RCTs so that subsequent treatments will improve the survival chances of future patients. It could be argued that this is a more human interpretation of the more abstract concepts addressed in the Declaration of Helsinki. What the data presented in this chapter shows us, however, is the way in which the conflict between individual harm and wider social good impacts on the relationship between participants and researcher.

Notes

[1] Vulnerable groups include children, prisoners, members of the armed forces, people with mental illness, students or those in a subordinate employment position to the researcher (for example, medical students/junior doctors) (COREC, 2002).

[2] This reaction is very like that expressed by Thornton, a breast cancer patient who described feeling betrayed and let down by the clinicians she most relied on at the time (Thornton, 1992).

[3] Paragraph 5 of the World Medical Association (2000) states that, "In medical research on human subjects, considerations related to the well-being of the human subject should take precedence over the interests of science and society".

[4] 'Imaginability' is a function of the cognitive bias of 'availability'. See Kahnemann et al (1982, pp 12-13).

References

Alderson, P. and Goodey, C. (1998) 'Theories in health care and research: theories of consent', *British Medical Journal*, vol 317, pp 1313-15.

Beauchamp, T.L. and Childress, J.F. (1994) *Principles of biomedical ethics* (4th edn), New York, NY: Oxford University Press.

Braunholtz, D.A., Edwards, S.J. and Lilford, R.J. (2001) 'Are randomized clinical trials good for us (in the short term)? Evidence for a "trial effect"', *Journal of Clinical Epidemiology*, vol 54, pp 217-24.

Brody, B.A. (2001) 'A historical introduction to the requirement of obtaining informed consent from research participants', in D. Len and T.S. Jeffrey (eds) *Informed consent in medical research*, London: BMJ Books.

CIOMS (Council for International Organisations in Medical Science) (2002) *International ethical guidelines for biomedical research involving human subjects*, www.cioms.ch/guidelines

COREC (Central Office for Research Ethics Committees) (2002) *Governance arrangements for research ethics committees*, www.corec.org.uk

Donovan, J., Mills, N., Smith, M., Brindle, L., Jacoby, A., Peters, T., Frankel, S., Neal, D. and Hamdy, F. (2002) 'Improving design and conduct of randomised trials by embedding them in qualitative research: ProtecT (prostate testing for cancer and treatment) study', *British Medical Journal*, vol 325, pp 766-70.

Ellis, P.M., Dowsett, S.M., Buttow, P.N. and Tattersall, M.H. (1999) 'Attitudes to randomized clinical trials among out-patients attending a medical oncology clinic', *Health Expectations*, vol 2, pp 33-43.

European Parliament and the Council of the European Union (2001) *European Directive on good clinical practice in clinical trials*, Strasbourg: Council of Europe.

Featherstone, K. and Donovan, J.L. (1998) 'Random allocation or allocational random? Patients' perspectives of participation in a randomised controlled trial', *British Journal of Medicine*, vol 317, pp 1177-80.

Freedman, B. (1987) 'Equipoise and the ethics of clinical research', *New England Journal of Medicine*, 87, 317, 3, pp 141-5.

General Medical Council (2001) *Research: The role and responsibilities of doctors*, London: GMC Publications.

Hewlett, S. (1996) 'Consent to clinical research – adequately voluntary or substantially influenced?', *Journal of Medical Ethics*, vol 22, no 4, pp 232-7.

Kahneman, D., Slovic, P. and Tversky, A. (eds) (1982) *Judgment under uncertainty: Heuristics and biases*, Cambridge, New York, NY and Melbourne: Cambridge University Press.

Kemp, N., Skinner, E., and Toms, J. (1984) 'Randomized clinical trials of cancer treatment – a public opinion survey', *Clinical Oncology*, vol 10, pp 155-61.

Maslin, A. (1994) 'A survey of the opinions on "informed consent" of women currently involved in clinical trials within a breast unit', *European Journal of Cancer Care* (English language edition), vol 3, no 4, pp 153-62.

Searight, H.R. and Miller, C.K. (1996) 'Remembering and interpreting informed consent: a qualitative study of drug trial participants', *Journal of the American Board of Family Practice*, vol 9, no 1, pp 14-22.

Snowdon, C., Garcia, J. and Elbourne, D. (1998) 'Reactions of participants to the results of a randomised controlled trial: exploratory study', *British Medical Journal*, vol 317, pp 21-6.

Sugarman, J., Kass, N.E., Goodman, S.N., Perentesis, P. and Faden, R. (1998) 'What patients say about medical research', *IRB: A Review of Human Subjects Research*, vol 20, no 4, pp 1-7.

Thornton, H. (1992) 'Breast cancer trials – a patient's viewpoint', *The Lancet*, vol 339, pp 44-5.

WMA (World Medical Association) (2000) *Declaration of Helsinki: 52nd World Medical Association General Assembly*, Edinburgh: WMA.

Appendix

The focus group interviews held were structured around five theoretically defined questions:

1. Think back to when the possibility of being involved in a trial was first mentioned to you. (If you have been in more than one, think of the first time to start with.) Where were you, who was there and what were your first reactions?
2. How easy was it for you to ask questions?
3. What did you think would happen to you if you said 'No thanks'?
4. What did you think your doctor thought about the trial?
5. Is there anything else about the way that you were asked to give informed consent for the trial that you would like to add? Have we missed anything?

Individual interview questions

1. I'd like you to think back to when the possibility of being involved in a trial was first mentioned to you. (If you've been in more than one, think of the first time to start with). Where were you, who was there and what were your first reactions?

2. How easy was it for you to ask questions?
3. What sort of questions came to mind?
4. What was the information like that was offered to you?
5. How well did this help you to understand?
6. Was there anything that wasn't mentioned that you think should have been?
7. Who else was important in helping you to make the decision? How did they help?
8. What did you think your doctor thought about the trial?
9. What did you think would happen to you if you said 'no thanks'?
10. How long did you have to make up your mind about whether to go into the trial or not?
11. How easy or otherwise was it to make your decision?
12. How did you feel about signing the form?
13. To what extent were your expectations about the trial met? Did anything happen that was unexpected?

Is there anything else that you'd like to add that we haven't covered?

THREE

Ethical protection in research: including children in the debate

Trudy Goodenough, Emma Williamson, Julie Kent and Richard Ashcroft

Introduction

This chapter considers participants' views of ethical protection in longitudinal epidemiological genetic research. The data presented in the chapter was collected as part of a project called 'Ethical Protection in Epidemiological Genetics (EPEG): Participants' Perspectives'. This was a three-year, qualitative research project designed to consider how adult and child participants in a major longitudinal epidemiological and genetic study of child health (the ALSPAC study; see Chapter Nine of this book) perceive and understand their involvement in that research, with particular reference to the ethical protection of participants[1].

This chapter is particularly concerned with how child participants describe their relationships both to research and researchers, and to what extent and at what point can they be said to have consented to participate in the study. It offers insight into the way in which the 'objects' or 'subjects' of scientific enquiry perceive that role and contextualises that within wider contemporary debates about the role of children within society. Following a brief outline of the EPEG project methodology, this chapter first considers how children perceive their initiation into research within various processes of consent and proxy consent. This includes an examination of what children thought about the content of research, as well as whether they thought they would take part in research if asked now. We look at the choices that children make and their perceptions of the implications of such choices before examining what participation itself meant to this specific group of children.

What does this chapter contribute to an edited collection such as this one? It offers a unique insight into the perceptions of child research participants and focuses on their views of decision-making and ethics. The chapter is deliberately descriptive in terms of the presentation of children's voices in order to ensure that the diversity of 'participants' is represented. This chapter offers the reader an opportunity to consider how child participants of research perceive their own roles in the research process and the relationships that inevitably develop between researcher and researched in long term studies such as that considered.

EPEG study sample

The EPEG study sample is drawn from participants in the Avon Longitudinal Study of Parents and Children (ALSPAC), also known as the Children of the Nineties Study, which is an extensive epidemiological genetic longitudinal study of children born in the Bristol area with an expected date of delivery between 1 April 1991 and 31 December 1992. The specific aim of ALSPAC is

> to determine ways in which biological, environmental, social, psychological and psychosocial factors are associated with the survival and optimal health and development of the foetus, infancy and child, and ways in which the causal relationships might vary with the genetic composition of the mother and/or child. ALSPAC has the long-term aim of following the children into adulthood to answer questions related to prenatal and postnatal factors associated, for example, with schizophrenia, delinquency, reproductive failure on the one hand and realisation of full educational potential, health and happiness on the other. (www.ALSPAC.bris.ac.uk 2002)

The EPEG project interviewed children, mothers, and fathers involved in this longitudinal epidemiological genetic study as well as a control group of parents not involved in such research. Forty interviews were carried out with children (an equal number of 20 boys and 20 girls took part) with an age range of 9-11 years. In the final sample of children interviewed, 23 children were from the inner city, 16 lived in or very close to a small country town, and one child was from a rural village. Interviews took place at school [n=31] or at home [n=9], according to the wishes of the parent and child (Williamson et al, 2003a, 2003b).

Child-centred knowledge

As stated in the project aims, EPEG seeks to discover how children in epidemiological genetic research perceive and understand their involvement, and how these perceptions might affect their participation and expectations of the research itself (Williamson et al, 2003a, 2003b). Our overall objective was to discuss ethical issues relating to health research with the children in a way that did not impose adult-centred approaches to knowledge and understanding. Society is changing: children across the world are increasingly viewed as active participants in society and accorded 'rights' (UN Convention on the Rights of the Child, 1990); hence our effort to no longer view them as simply subjects of research but as active participants and co-researchers.

Reflecting on these considerations, the interview schedule used with the children was initially developed from information gained at five Children's Focus Groups (Goodenough et al, 2003), and then intensively assessed by two Children's Reference Groups (drawn from children who had already attended one of the focus groups). At the reference groups, we gave the children the opportunity to express any thoughts or feelings that they might have, concerning not only the questions, but also our approach to the interview process. The children were also given cards (green = good, red = bad), so that they could express how they felt about the interview questions without needing to articulate their reasons in the first instance. Researchers experienced in working with children were also consulted about the nature and content of the questions, prior to construction of the final interview schedule.

Questions in the interview concentrated on the children's experiences and perceptions of participating in the ALSPAC study. In order to discover how the children perceived ethical issues such as joining ALSPAC, consent to continued participation, and the reasons for their continued involvement in ALSPAC, the target questions were embedded in experiential discussions, with further prompting from the interviewer as the children themselves raised questions or commented on these issues. At the end of each interview, the children were asked to reflect on their experiences of the EPEG interview process. All of these initiatives were intended to ensure that the research process was, in as many ways as possible, both collaborative and inclusive.

Results

We were interested to discuss with the children how they felt about their involvement in ALSPAC, particularly as for most of them recruitment into the study occurred by proxy, with their parents (usually their mother) enrolling them, while they were 'in-utero' or as a baby or young child. Thus, the children did not give their informed consent to participate initially, but at the time of interview aged 9-11 years, it seemed likely that the balance of decision making would be changing (Goodenough et al, 2003). The children reported that in their everyday lives they were used to being offered choices and were gradually making more decisions for themselves, which might also have had an impact upon their involvement in ALPSAC.

Joining

The children were asked about how they joined ALSPAC in order to give an indication of whether they viewed their participation as something they chose to do, or something that was chosen for them, who made that choice and whether there would be any changes in their responses if they were given the chance to join the study now (aged 9-11 years). These questions were developed to discover how children might discuss issues relating to ethical matters such as proxy consent, informed consent, assent/dissent and continued participation.

First, we asked the children how they joined ALSPAC and later in the interview we asked the children to imagine how they would respond if they were invited to join the study now.

Responses to the first question indicated diverse perceptions of 'joining'. Sixteen of the children were not sure, or had forgotten, how they became part of ALSPAC; ten children said they knew how they had joined. When we prompted the children to try and say when they joined the study, nine of the children thought that they joined when they were invited to go to their first Focus Session[2], 13 thought that they had been recruited when they were a baby, and 12 when they were young children.

Examples of the diversity of response can be seen in the following extracts:

CI018

"I didn't even know that I was part of it, until I got sent this, um, like all the information telling you where you are going ... I was like, 'What's this?'" (*ALSPAC child participant, girl, 11 years old*)

CI011

"My mum just said, 'Do you want to take part in this club thing?', and I said yes, and then I went and saw lots of different children and felt a bit scared but my mum got ... when I went there I saw there was lots of activities and stuff so I decided to join." (*ALSPAC child participant, boy, 10 years old*)

CI007

"Um, well, my mum said like, when I was born or something, a lady came round and said 'Would [you] like to be in the "Children of the Nineties?"' Well, she didn't ask me because I wouldn't be able to hear her; she asked my mum and mum said, 'Yes, all right'. Or maybe, yeah I was like, I just came out of hospital. I think someone gave us a letter and then I think I was five [years old] or something and I remember getting my first one, I can't remember, and I was really excited and I read it straight away and I send it straight away." (*ALSPAC child participant, girl, 10 years old*)

Only one child perceived that their consent had been sought prior to participation:

CI041

"Um, well, 'cause she got a letter when I was around three, then it's like if you want you can sign up your child and then she wasn't so sure but, and later when I could, you know, kind of think for myself and stuff, then I got one when I was seven then I said that I wanted to, and now I've done Focus @ 8 and Focus @ 9." (*ALSPAC child participant, boy, 10 years old*)

For some children, their perception was that the ALSPAC study was able to enrol them without any obvious parental involvement at all.

CI025

"I think I was born in the 1990s and I think, um, Professor Jean Golding registered my name down when I was born." (*ALSPAC child participant, boy, 9 years old*)

It is testimony to the strategies used by the ALSPAC study to engage participants, both children and parents, that this child, along with several others whom we interviewed, could name the founder and lead researcher of this project, Professor Jean Golding.

We asked the children how they felt about not knowing that they were part of the study until they were six or seven years old. As can be seen from the following quotations, the children we spoke to did not appear to question their parents' decisions to enrol them into the study, and one or two commented how pleased they were that their parents had made that choice.

CI053
"Well, um, my mum I think, when I was born, um, a couple of days after she got this letter or … I think someone at the hospital asked her if, um, she would like me to be part of, um, um, a scientifical-like research place called Children of the Nineties and she agreed and, um, I didn't know until I was about seven, but that's basically how I joined I think."

Interviewer
"And what did you think when you were told about it? Can you remember what you thought?"

CI053
"Well, I didn't know exactly what it was then but it sounded good.... I liked the bit about the, um, scientifical research on children and stuff." (*ALSPAC child participant, boy, 10 years old*)

For some children, their involvement in ALSPAC has become part of their 'growing up' story.

CI031
"I think it was because they knew I was born in Avon, and I was born in 1992, so they, I can remember when I was about five, my mum told me how I was invited and they told me, and she told me that she was sent, they talked to her and asked if I could join and my mum said yes because she thought that I would like it so that's what I did.... 'Cause at the time, that's the sort of thing that I would do, I liked having exciting things even when I was a baby." (*ALSPAC child participant, girl, 9 years old*)

Due to the nature of the ALSPAC study, the children have, from the earliest age, been providers of the data resources for analysis rather than active participants shaping the research process. In this process, the adults have been the knowledge holders, permission granters and the rule setters (Grue and Walsh, 1998), with parents often interpreting the meaning of ALSPAC for and to their children. Thus, it is unlikely that the children would perceive participation as their choice, but as a decision made for them by parents or the research team. It appears from our discussions with the children at nine to eleven years of age, that they perceive little influence on whether they participate in ALSPAC or withdraw.

Would you join now?

As stated earlier in this chapter, for the majority of the children, their initial recruitment in ALSPAC was by way of proxy enrolment, with the expectation that their participation would continue well into childhood. In order to discover more about the children's perceptions of their involvement and their commitment to the ALSPAC research, we sought to discover whether or not, if given the choice now, the children would still opt to participate. To do this, we asked the children to say how they would respond if they were asked to join ALSPAC at their current age. Thirty-two of the 40 children said they would definitely join ALSPAC if invited now, and three were quite certain that they would not (interestingly, however, these three were not planning to leave).

The children's responses offered insight not only into how the children made decisions but also how involvement in ALSPAC interacted with the rest of their life experiences. The reasons for saying 'yes' to joining, although diverse, appeared to fall into two main categories: direct benefit to self derived from taking part (fun, something to do, exciting, good, like it, meet new people) and the benefits of the research for others (helps other children, good research).

CI014

I'd like to be part of it and see other children and make new friends."
(*ALSPAC child participant, boy, 10 years old*)

CI011

"I would check, say, what it was like and what do you do there, and then I would listen to what they say. And then, if they say good things about it, I would go and tell my Mum and then she'll sign up for it. If they say it's boring or its rubbish, I wouldn't bother."

Interviewer

"What are the good things?"

CI011

"Like the, if they like, if they're kind to you if they give you like some energetic things and things that are not boring." (*ALSPAC child participant, boy, 10 years old*)

CI012

"Um, don't really know how I'd decide.... It's good, it's helpful and by me doing it if I get ill or something it could help me...." (*ALSPAC child participant, boy, 11 years old*)

CI022

"Because I know that they are doing it for a good purpose and I would be helping with some good research." (*ALSPAC child participant, boy, 9 years old*)

For the children who said 'no', the response seemed to reflect what was happening in their lives at the time of the interview:

CI044

"At the moment, probably not.... Now I am joining I really enjoy it but if they said you'd have to got to all these focuses, but it would be really, really fun, you'd do all these activities, seeing as the amount of other stuff I'm doing at the moment, I'd probably say no because it would be too much, just like something else to add to the collection and it would be too much." (*ALSPAC child participant, boy, 10 years old*)

CI018

"Possibly not, because I think when you get older you tend not to do what they do, and stuff.... Possibly because the things you do, I think, are possibly maybe a bit younger, I don't know." (*ALSPAC child participant, girl, 11 years old*)

As part of the discussion, we asked the children to describe *how* they would decide.

Twenty-eight of the 40 children outlined the process as one of gathering information and then weighing up costs and benefits, to themselves and others, of participating. Although several children drew on their current experience of ALSPAC to answer the question, the children were able to imagine 'not belonging' and described actions such as talking to parents, friends, and staff at ALSPAC, and perhaps having a trial period to see if they liked the study enough to continue. Almost all of the children perceived that the final choice to participate would be theirs. The children were reflective in their answers, and could clearly weigh up costs and benefits in making their choice.

CI024

"Um, I think I'd find out some more information first, ask them to send some leaflets, and then, if I agree with everything, I think I'd join, yeah."

Interviewer

"What would you like to see in the information that you'd received?"

CI024

"Um, telling me about what would happen to the research and make sure it didn't get wasted, them doing all these tests on you and then not bothering looking at them and things." (*ALSPAC child participant, girl, 10 years old*)

CI031

"I wouldn't want to join if I had been hurt, I'd have probably have one go at it and see what it's like and if I don't enjoy it then I would probably leave." (*ALSPAC child participant, girl, 9 years old*)

CI035

"Like, what sort of stuff they did. Like, do you have to fill in forms and stuff? And do they, like, treat you not like you're younger so you're less important, not like that. Like, if they said that children are just as important as adults, which they do, then I think I'd definitely want to join." (*ALSPAC child participant, girl, 10 years old*)

These extracts reflect other research – for example, Alderson (1995), Alldred and Edwards (1999) – which suggests that children are capable of making carefully thought out decisions about choices they are offered. The children were able to describe the importance of information gathering as a vital part of this process.

Choices in taking part

While the children may not have consented to their initial participation in the ALSPAC study, as they have grown older they are being asked to assent to many different types of activity. These activities include completing questionnaires (which often ask for extensive information about all aspects of their lives, from perceptions of skills and abilities, self awareness to information about their environment at school and at home), to providing physical measurements and giving biological samples, including blood samples for genetic analysis. Whereas parents or guardians are required to give formal consent for their children to participate in the ALSPAC study without the children's assent for their own active involvement, assessments and data gathering could not occur. Twenty-five children in EPEG recounted that their participation in the ALSPAC study began when they were babies or young children. At this stage, parents would have been viewed as having the authority to give consent on behalf of their child. As the children become older, they are viewed in the law regarding medical treatment as 'competent minors' (Alderson, 1995, p 75). This raises questions about how children in research are perceived, how children in research view themselves, and those whom children perceive as making decisions. In relation to EPEG, we are interested in how these perceptions influence the nature of their membership of the ALSPAC study.

We asked the children about how choices are made about which parts of the ALSPAC study they are involved in, and what they would do or have done if there is an activity or question that they do not want to complete or answer. The discussions that followed raised questions about the nature of the activity, and how the children constructed the meaning of the activity to themselves and/or others, as well as who determined whether the child decided to agree with what was being requested.

Several children described incidences when, although they felt unhappy or embarrassed to complete an activity/assessment, they did not feel able to refuse participation. Some of these children felt that they were powerless to change what was happening to them, while for others it was not difficult to decide whether or not to participate.

Interviewer
"So, would you feel you could say 'no' if you didn't feel like doing something?"

CI007
"I'd just be too shy, really, so I'd say, 'Yeah, OK'." (*ALSPAC child participant, girl, 10 years old*)

Interviewer
"Would you be able to say, 'I don't want to do that?'"

CI038
"I'm not sure. Um, I wouldn't want to cause problems." (*ALSPAC child participant, girl, 11 years old*)

CI049
"Um, if there was something like I really didn't want to do like talk about my, my life, that's quite private or stuff like that, I wouldn't want to talk about it."

Interviewer
"And would you say 'no'?"

CI049
"I'd say 'no', but I would still feel a bit embarrassed." (*ALSPAC child participant, girl, 9 years old*)

Participation in the Focus Sessions is preceded by invitations to attend, along with information sheets and questionnaires with facts about the activities/ assessments in the session being sent out to the children and their parents. Most of the children reported reading the information with their parents, and 22 of the 40 children said that they alone decided which activities they would do at the Focus Sessions:

CI051
"That would be totally my choice. My mum and dad wouldn't interfere, they'd let me do what I want and the Children of the Nineties people would as well." (*ALSPAC child participant, girl, 10 years old*)

CI035

"Well, when I get there [Focus Session], they give me a sheet with what I'm going to do. And then they show me, they tell me all what they're going to do and then they ask me if I'm OK with all of that and will I do it? And then if I say 'yes' or 'no' and mum doesn't get to decide." (*ALSPAC child participant, girl, 10 years old*)

One child said that he was now being asked more formally for his consent to take part in a particular activity and that he thought this was good as this process gave him more autonomy:

CI056

"... and before I had to go on that machine thing, they came round with a leaflet and I had to sign it and tick a box that I was happy to and it was legal for them to do that ... I think it's like a really good idea because then, like, if I don't want to do it, then you don't tick it and sign it, and if I do then I can just sign it." (*ALSPAC child participant, boy, 10 years old*)

Four children said their parents made the decisions at the Focus Sessions; ten children said the decisions were shared between themselves and their parents.

CIO37

"If I had said 'no' she would have said, 'Yeah, you've got to have it done', or something... [And then] I would have just had it done..." [This child felt that when she became over 16 years old, then the decision would be hers.] (*ALSPAC child participant, girl, 9 years old*)

Where it was reported that parents had made the decisions, children often commented that the decision-making process would gradually change, with the children having more control as they got older. Children in the 'joint decision makers' group reported similar views.

What does participation mean?

When the children talked about having the choice to participate in the ALSPAC study now, their discussions often touched on how they perceived the relevance or meaning of ALSPAC. In order to investigate in more depth what participation in ALSPAC might mean to the children, we asked them to consider two questions. The first was a general question about their perception of the overall purpose of ALSPAC; the second asked what being part of ALSPAC meant to them.

The first question, asking about the purpose of ALSPAC, came at the end of the interview when the children had spent some time talking about their ALSPAC experience. Part of this discussion drew out the children's thoughts on the purpose of particular questions or activities that they had described.

There was a wide range of responses to this question. Some children, while able to provide detailed thoughts and ideas on the purpose of particular activities, did not feel able to articulate an overview or a summary of the ALSPAC study aims. On the other hand, others could provide a more comprehensive account of their beliefs about ALSPAC's purpose. Six children said they did not know what the purpose of ALSPAC was. Where children did express an opinion, most of their responses indicated that the aim of ALSPAC was to find out about children's health and development (this is a message repeated in a variety of media sent or available to both children and parents). Some thought that the research would be of benefit to children in ALSPAC now or later on. However, more responses indicated that ALSPAC was conducting research that would be of benefit to other children in the future. The ideas that the children expressed often echoed discussions that they reported with family members, or friends who were also part of ALSPAC. When children said they did not know what ALSPAC was for, some wanted to know more, and others were not particularly interested to find out more.

CI051

"Making a better future … for children, for adults for everyone, making the next generation better and less illness...." (*ALSPAC child participant, girl, 10 years old*)

CI056

"Yeah, um, just to see how, um, people are and I think it's just like are you doing the right things or are people not doing the right things or are there too many people being bullied or are there too many people eating too much junk food or are there anybody who hasn't got, like, if there were lots of people who had no friends, then they might be able to do something about that." (*ALSPAC child participant, boy, 10 years old*)

CI044

"I think it's basically to, they study what the information they get off children and then use that to help other children who aren't as well off … I think they see what part of their body actually fights off these diseases 'cause they are healthy and then they use that sort of thing to try and recreate something like it. It may not make any sense but they then try to create something like what's in a person's body that's healthy to fight off [in] other people that aren't so well." (*ALSPAC child participant, boy, 10 years old*)

CI043

"I know it's a project but I don't know what it's like about." (*ALSPAC child participant, boy, 10 years old*)

CI031

"Um, I don't know at all." (*ALSPAC child participant, girl, 9 years old*)

CI029

"Um, finding out about you and things." (*ALSPAC child participant, girl, 10 years old*)

CI008

"Discovering about what children like and what they don't like, basically, and find out about different children's abilities and some not abilities, some disabled, some special." (*ALSPAC child participant, boy, 9 years old*)

The second question asked the children to explain what being part of ALSPAC meant to them. The opinions that the children expressed varied from reporting benefits for themselves only, to more altruistic explanations where they described feeling good as a result of being part of something that would help others. The recurring theme in the children's descriptions of the significance of the ALSPAC study to them, with 33 observations, was of seeing themselves as 'special or different' and included in something that was only available to a limited number of other children. Eight children's explanations combined both perceptions of 'being special' with benefits to others.

CI034

"I'm glad I'm part of it. One, because it's fun, and the other one it would help, it would help me and other children." (*ALSPAC child participant, boy, 10 years old*)

CI046

"Special ... because they want to find, they want to find a lot more about you and I think it's a good idea ... because they'll know what you think and how you view things ... because they can help kids that have problems, so then that go to ALSPAC." (*ALSPAC child participant, girl, 11 years old*)

CI051

"Um, well, I feel glad that they're gonna try and use my information to make everything better, but apart from that I don't really know, I haven't really thought about it." (*ALSPAC child participant, girl, 10 years old*)

Twenty of the 40 children commented that being part of ALSPAC made them feel special/different or included in something, that other children could not be part of.

CI004

"I feel great and really, it feels good to be part of something that, um, I would, I would only be able to that loads of other people wouldn't be able to do and well I feel good 'cause it's really, I find it really exciting and I like it loads." (*ALSPAC child participant, boy, 9 years old*)

CI007

"It feels as though I belong, I belong to something quite very special that will go on for a long time. I feel, I feel, I feel sort of as though more included of the whole of the world because I'm included in quite a big thing, history really.... It feels as though when you've got those things it feels as though it's very precious...." (*ALSPAC child participant, girl, 10 years old*)

The children's descriptions of being part of ALSPAC indicate that, overall, they perceived the experience as positive. Not all the children could put into words the overall aim or purpose of ALSPAC, but most could articulate what being part of such a study meant to them. The descriptions that the children gave also appeared to reflect how the ALSPAC study was portrayed within the family.

CI054

"Um, sometimes, you know, like, my mum says, 'Maybe you should write a letter and say how grateful you are to be in this really big helpful scientific thing'...." (*ALSPAC child participant, girl, 10 years old*)

Lessons for the future

The children's expectation to be given more choice and control over their involvement in the future has implications for the future provision of information to the children and their families for informed consent decisions, including, for example, what information children and parents should be given and when, as well as when children are able to make their own participation decisions independently of their parents. It is worthy of note that, although the children already believe that they can say 'no' to any activity, the reality of their experience is that dissenting is difficult, especially in the context of the Focus Sessions which involve face-to-face encounters between researchers and participants. Such conflict suggests that children perceive the adults around them as more powerful in this context. This has implications for consent decision made on behalf of the children and how they may interpret such decisions as they get older. It also emphasises the importance of creating an accepting, non-pressurising environment in which children can have a real choice about participation in research generally (Alderson, 1995; Morrow and Richards, 1996) and recognises the basic human needs and rights of the child in any research context (WMA, 1964, 2000; UN Convention of the Rights of the Child, 1990). Despite the good intentions behind such moves, often children's life worlds remain silenced and ignored. If the trend towards asking children to take part in research for the benefit of other children increases, then it is imperative that every opportunity for children to participate actively in such research be taken.

Reflecting on our epistemological position, that wherever possible children should be involved in the research process, in the final part of the interview we asked the children to say what they thought about the EPEG interview. The purpose of this was to provide the children with the opportunity to comment on their experience of EPEG and, if they wanted to, to add to the research process by suggesting changes to the interview process and the interview itself. The children responded to the brief evaluation by commenting on the interview process, the nature of the questions and the purpose of the EPEG interview.

CI006

"Well, I think it's quite fun, you interviewing and stuff and I'd quite like to do it again." (*ALSPAC child participant, boy, 10 years old*)

CI013

"Um. I found it interesting 'cause I have never done an interview ever before. It's my first ever one.... [Which questions were best?] Probably what sort of, what they did at ALSPAC, what activities and what's my favourite one...." (*ALSPAC child participant, boy, 10 years old*)

This extract demonstrates how the data collected in these interviews confirms the responses of the reference group children, namely that children preferred the questions based on experience and rather than those testing knowledge.

CI040

"I reckon they were really good. I'd probably prefer if you did me all the time, like every year you come back and asked, have some questions again and see, then after about six years say compare ... see the difference ... 'cause I maybe say that blood taken is really annoying at the moment then I'd say three years later or two years later that I don't mind any more." (*ALSPAC child participant, girl, 10 years old*)

This extract raises questions about different types of knowledge collection and the importance of consultation with children. This child acknowledges, very eloquently, that their priorities, opinions and concerns may change, illustrating that some children are in a position to discuss their views about their own development in a reasoned fashion.

Other responses from children about their experience of answering EPEG questions raised important issues in how children perceive adult's questions:

CI031

"Some of them were a bit worrying and I didn't know what to say, so I just said I don't know, and lots of them were just fine and I could answer them easily."

Interviewer

"Why did the questions worry you?"

CI031

"Because I didn't know the answer."

Interviewer

"And when I said it doesn't matter whether you know?"

CI031

"Oh, when you told me that I just thought, 'Oh good!', and said 'I don't know'." (*ALSPAC child participant, girl, 9 years old*)

This extract emphasises the importance of listening to children at all times during the interview process, providing further explanations and renegotiating consent as necessary. Consent to participate does not always represent consent for the whole process, particularly when the activity is completely new to the children involved. In order for the consent given to be valid throughout the process, it is imperative that children understand, and act upon, their right to withdraw from the research at any point. There is a danger that, when the negotiated consent is given by proxy, this right to withdraw might not be fully understood by the child participant. This right should be reinforced with the children at all times.

Conclusion

This chapter has considered how children perceive their participation in a specific genetic epidemiological study in relation to processes of (proxy) consent, participation, engagement, choice, and decision making. It thus contributes to our understanding of child participants' perceptions of research participation. The children raised a number of issues, which we attempted to address in the epistemological framework of the EPEG project from the outset. Most importantly, by asking children questions which were centred around their own experiences and willingness to answer, we were able to ascertain that children do indeed have concerns about the types of questions and activities they are asked to take part in within a research context. Alongside these concerns, this particular group of children feel 'special' on account of their participation in a prestigious research study, and believe that by taking part they are contributing to some kind of greater good, whether helping other children or helping a more abstract notion of science. Absent from the views offered by children, despite being asked, was an understanding about how, specifically, the information and samples they have given are used. This raises wider ethical questions about informed consent within research (an issue addressed in Chapter Two of this book, for example).

Since the focus here has been on children's views, this chapter has not examined the corresponding views of ALSPAC parents. Interestingly the parents we interviewed were clear that they would never 'force' children to take part in research which they perceived as not directly beneficial to them. The parents' position is congruent with current research guidance and law. However, the majority of adult respondents believed that they could 'persuade' their children to take part in an activity if they felt their child's reasons for not wanting to take part were unjustified.

In addition, longitudinal research, by its design, raises questions about the ongoing nature of consent which emerge as particularly important in longitudinal research involving children. The children who took part in this project recognised that their views, as well as the relationships they had with adults, were changing, resulting perhaps in substantial shifts in such views and relationships over the lifetime of a longitudinal piece of research. It is important, therefore, that researchers involved in longitudinal research continue to listen to children and amend their consent and participation procedures accordingly.

Such consultation would include:

- enlisting the views of children recruited to research prior to their birth as early as possible;
- including children's views in the process and content of research;
- allowing children to make their own risk/benefit evaluations which will include evaluation of how their data has been used and the conduct of researchers;
- ensure that children do not underestimate the amount of choice that their parents give them when consenting for them to take part in research;
- and explaining that consent is an on-going process.

As active participants, children should also be given the ability to contribute to the development of research tools. Done properly and in a child-friendly environment, this not only includes children in this process, but also addresses issues about public engagement in citizenship activities. Research, after all, is a social endeavour and one which in the majority of cases is advocated in order to benefit society as a whole. Children as a group should not be excluded therefore from these wider ethical debates, particularly if they are to be given the opportunity to participate within research for the benefit of others.

Acknowledgements

We would like to thank all of the children (and parents) who participated within the EPEG Project. In addition, we are grateful to members of the EPEG advisory group, the Wellcome Trust who funded this project (Grant number 059812), and members of the ALSPAC staff team, especially its director, Professor Jean Golding, for their cooperation and assistance.

Notes

[1] This chapter focuses on the research conducted with children. For further details of interviews and focus groups conducted with parents see Williamson et al (2002, 2003a, 2003b).

[2] Focus Sessions refer to regular, in depth, hands-on assessment of children at an ALSPAC centre, such as physical measures: weight, height, body mass, cognitive testing, psycho-social measures and taking of biological samples, for example, blood.

References

Alderson, P. (1995) *Listening to children: Children, ethics and social research*, Essex: Barnardo's.

Alldred, P. and Edwards, R. (1999) 'Children and young people's views of social research', *Childhood*, vol 6, no 2, pp 261-81.

Goodenough, T., Williamson, E., Kent, J. and Ashcroft, R. (2003) 'What did you think about that? Researching children's perceptions of participation in a longitudinal genetic epidemiological study', *Children and Society*, issue 17, pp 113-25.

Grue, M.E. and Walsh, D.J. (1998) *Studying children in context: Theories, methods and ethics*, Berkeley, CA: Sage Publications.

Morrow, V. and Richards, M. (1996) 'The ethics of social research with children: an overview', *Children and Society*, vol 10, pp 90-105.

UN Convention on the Rights of the Child (1990) *The convention on the rights of the child. (Official text) Know your rights! Translation for young people*, London: Committee for UNICEF.

Williamson, E., Goodenough, T., Kent, J. and Ashcroft, R. (2002) 'Ethical protection in epidemiological genetic research (EPEG project): participants' perspectives. Preliminary findings', Paper presented at European Association for the Study of Science and Technology conference (EASST), York, August.

Williamson, E., Goodenough, T., Kent, J. and Ashcroft, R. (2003a) 'How research participants perceive and construct "risk" in relation to genetic and non-genetic data collection', Paper presented at the First Interdisciplinary Conference on Communication, Medicine and Ethics, Cardiff University, 26-28 June.

Williamson, E., Goodenough, T., Kent, J. and Ashcroft, R. (2003b) 'Genetic epidemiological research: participants' perspectives on "drawing the line"', Paper presented at the Who Twists the Helix? Conference, 16-19 March.

WMA (World Medical Association) (1964: Helsinki) (2000: Edinburgh) *Ethical principles for medical research involving human subjects*, Helsinki: WMA.

FOUR

'An equal relationship'?: people with learning difficulties getting involved in research

Beth Tarleton, Val Williams, Neil Palmer and Stacey Gramlich

Introduction

During the 20th century, there has been no shortage of research into medical and cognitive aspects of learning difficulty. During this period, the medical profession has had an enormous influence on the construction of knowledge about 'learning difficulty', known in previous eras by terms that are now considered to be abusive and derogatory, like 'subnormality' or 'mental handicap' (Rioux and Bach, 1994). Researchers were concerned in the main to find out what 'learning difficulty' actually was, and what negative impacts it had on individuals. As Walmsley (2001) points out,

> [until the late 1960s] people with learning difficulties were tested, counted, observed, analysed, described and frequently pathologised, but never asked for their views. (Walmsley, 2001, p 188)

It has only been relatively recently that researchers have paused to consider what people with learning difficulties themselves have to say about their lives, and to consider their views to be a focus for research (Goodley, 1996).

This chapter aims to re-examine the relationship between researchers and those who are researched, by taking an insider look at examples of inclusive research that have been carried out with and by people with learning difficulties. This is still a controversial area, with dilemmas that are rehearsed often within the academic literature. For many, as Walmsley (1997) pointed out, it seems a contradiction in terms to speak of researchers with learning difficulties, since research by its nature implies a high level of cognitive ability. Critics also question the authenticity of inclusive research in which non-disabled supporters are involved; the work carried out by the supporter or advisor is extremely important to many authors:

> If people with learning difficulties need non-disabled allies in the research process in order to convey their experiences in a way which is acceptable to the research community and its gatekeepers, how can the integrity of their accounts be maintained? (Chappell, 2000, p 41)

There have been many debates in academic arenas about the distinctions between *emancipatory research* (Oliver, 1992; Zarb, 1992), which is research initiated and controlled by disabled people and their organisations, and *participatory research* (Chappell, 2000), where disabled people are involved in others' research projects. Emancipatory research, which is often seen as the 'gold standard', sprang from the concerns of disabled people themselves, and is a central part of the disabled people's campaign to take collective control of their own lives and issues. People with learning difficulties, however, are seldom fully in control of every aspect of research that concerns their lives. Most research projects in the field of Learning Difficulty have been started by non-disabled researchers, who have involved people with learning difficulties in their work: as co-presenters (McClimens, 1999), as co-researchers (Mitchell, 1997; Minkes et al, 1995), or as consultants (Rodgers, 1999). The issue of power, and how this is played out within projects, is therefore another frequent theme in the debate about inclusive research with people with learning difficulties.

Involving people with learning difficulties in research is still a developing field, and it is vital now that people with learning difficulties are included within its theoretical development. That is what we hope to do in this chapter, which contains perspectives from disabled as well as non-disabled researchers.

Since the Norah Fry Research Centre supported all the projects mentioned in this chapter, we start with a few words of explanation about the centre. We then present a range of examples, from different perspectives. Val Williams and Beth Tarleton are both non-disabled researchers who have sought to support people with learning difficulties to carry out research, and to have their views heard; Neil Palmer and Stacey Gramlich are both members of groups run by people with learning difficulties, and have done research in their own right. In the concluding section, we return to the controversial questions of skills, support and power, in the light of the accounts given in the chapter from these different viewpoints.

The Norah Fry Research Centre

From its beginning in 1988, the Norah Fry Research Centre at the University of Bristol has been committed to a programme of research that aims to make a positive difference to the lives of people with learning difficulties, and to their families. This is achieved in two ways. First, research can have a practical value through influencing policy through a top-down approach to change. We ensure our research findings are fed into relevant policy forums. Many of our projects evaluate particular policies and their impact on people with learning difficulties. Second, our research aims to adopt a bottom-up approach through partnership with people with learning difficulties (Ward and Simons, 1998). Not only is it assumed that people with learning difficulties will have valid and important things to say about their own lives, but also that they will have valuable advice to give on the conduct of research which concerns them (Minkes et al, 1995; Rodgers, 1999; Williams, 1999). As Ward and Simons (1998) point out, involvement in research can happen at many different levels. The projects described in this chapter are only individual examples, among a growing number of very different models. As Mitchell (1997) observes:

> It is important not to raise up one particular level of involvement as a pinnacle. For many people full involvement in a research project may be liberating; for others it may be daunting, for others it may just be plain tedious. (Mitchell, 1997, p 8)

In this chapter, we describe projects where people with learning difficulties were consulted about the research before going on to the insider perspective, with the experiences and views of people with learning difficulties who have done research in their own right.

In order to refer to such a wide range of involvement, we will follow Walmsley (2001), who coined the phrase 'inclusive research'. The questions that concern us are to do with the 'why' and the 'how' of inclusive research, as it was played out within several different research projects. By exploring these questions, we hope to contribute to a clearer understanding of the perspectives of those who were involved in the research, and the issues that faced them.

Examples of research involvement

One of the main ways that people with learning difficulties are involved in research is through advisory or consultative groups. Therefore, we start this section with an example of such involvement, from the perspective of the researcher, Beth Tarleton. Following this, Neil Palmer and Stacey Gramlich will each present their views about projects in which they did their own research. In both these projects, Val Williams acted as research supporter, and she will conclude the examples with a few comments about her experience of that role.

Beth Tarleton: Involvement in advisory or consultancy groups

The first research project I was involved in with people with learning difficulties was a national survey of short break (respite) services undertaken in 1998 (Prewett, 1999). This national survey included a qualitative component in which service-users were asked their opinions of the services they received. This aspect of the research was undertaken by convincing the gate keepers, service providers and parents that the child or adult who had short breaks would be able to give their opinion using the method of communication most appropriate for them. Seventeen children and 21 adults who used services were supported in coming to focus group meetings by appropriate independent supporters and by the use of pictures and symbols and photographs of all of the individuals involved in their short breaks. The service-users had been provided with a throwaway camera and a record sheet (often completed by parents and carers) so that, as a facilitator, I knew who the individuals were and could use their names appropriately.

In addition, the project benefited from a research advisory group (project steering group). One task undertaken by this group was ensuring the focus group interviews with children and adults who used services were appropriately focused to enable the children and adults to contribute.

A very able adult who received short breaks enthusiastically contributed to the advisory meetings, which also included parents, service providers and researchers. She was an expert participant in meetings and contributed freely drawing on her own long-term experience of very positive short breaks with a carer whom she dearly loved. She was involved in the research because of her recognised enthusiasm for promoting short break services and ensuring their appropriateness. As she was very able to get her message across in a mixed meeting, she was a seemingly obvious choice for a research advisory group. She supported our aims and was able to guide us regarding the issues that were relevant for the children and young people we wanted to communicate with. In this context, she could not, if she had wanted to, easily challenge the notion of the provision of 'respite' care. The concept of 'respite' care is frequently cited as inappropriate because of its artificiality and difference from 'normal' patterns of behaviour, in talks and presentations by self-advocacy groups on the issue. Therefore, it can be said that we had the power to set the agenda.

In order for this service-user to be able to contribute appropriately, the agenda of the meeting had to be accessible and all the advisory group participants needed to be aware of the jargon they were using and the speed at which they were talking. Accessibility is a key issue for people with learning difficulties who are increasingly taking part in consultation exercises and joint planning with local authorities, and there are published guidelines for accessibility (Simons, 1998). Nevertheless, as the meetings for this research focused not only on the consultation with service-users but had to discuss the details of questionnaire design and distribution, much of the meetings were no doubt boring and inaccessible. The question should be asked as to whether this method of involvement was appropriate. Was it respectful to include her in the main advisory group as an equal, and then to bore her, or would it have been better for her to have a separate session? The problem with this solution is that it would have split the reference group and created a less inclusive approach.

In a more recent project about the provision of short breaks for children and teenagers with autistic spectrum disorders (ASD) (Tarleton and Macaulay, 2002), one of the fundamental research questions regarded the overall appropriateness of short break services for children who are stereotypically regarded as needing routine and disliking change. It was vital, therefore, that we investigated the issue of short breaks from the point of view of individuals with ASD. As we believed that it would be very difficult to elicit the views of children with ASD about short breaks if they had not had them, we decided to work with adults with ASD who could draw on their own experiences of different environments.

We consulted with adults in two ways. First, I spoke to consultants with ASD who had experience in expressing their views. We met at a time and location of their choice and with the clear understanding that the discussion was for the purpose of research and we wanted their opinions on the provision of short breaks for children with ASD. While a seemingly easy option, these consultants, who were both well-known speakers, did have some anxiety about the meeting, as it was a new social situation. Therefore, time was taken to ensure they were happy to be involved in a discussion and to become comfortable in my presence.

The second strategy was to invite local young adults with Asperger Syndrome to consult on the issue of short breaks for children with ASD. These young adults were very able academically and verbally, and knew me well from my on-going involvement with their pub group. I had met them on a monthly basis for nearly a year and they were happy to come to a meeting to talk about short breaks. We had a conference evening in a city hotel which was planned in detail, with the date, start and finish times and location confirmed in writing and the evening itself planned out with an agenda which included the timing of the food break. The concept of short breaks was explained using a video and a sheet describing the different types of services.

The young adults provided a unique perspective on their own lives and the benefits and issues they foresaw regarding short breaks for children with autism. Their views have been recognised as a first step in consulting with people with ASD about the services they received and are fundamental to the recommendations from the research. However, while their freely expressed contributions were extremely valid and form a baseline for the research, the overall power was not theirs: they were not involved in the conceptualisation nor in the development of the research proposal. They were thanked for their expert contribution, as were the adults and children in the focus groups above, with a present of gift vouchers.

While the inclusion of people who use services as advisors is a seemingly obvious approach to ensure research is relevant and useful from their point of view, it is very time consuming to ensure that they can make a valid contribution. Taking this approach within traditionally funded and time-limited research is not easy. When the research proposal has already been written and approved by a funding body without this element, it is difficult to seriously involve people with learning difficulties. This inclusive process takes time, detailed thought and appropriate funding for the practical support required which includes provision of supporters, accessible information, and appropriate venues and transport arrangements.

Can people with learning difficulties really achieve any control of the research when taking the role of advisor or consultant? We need, first, to question our aims. Is it just advice and guidance that is being sought, implying that researchers could choose to ignore the advice or guidance given? Is there a real commitment to ensuring that expert advice from people with learning difficulties is central to the research process?

Within consultation exercises, there are certain practical steps that the researcher can take in order to ensure that power is more evenly shared. For instance, the following questions can be addressed in setting up the exercise:

- Who is invited to contribute and how are they chosen?
- Do they have expertise in the area or are they representatives of self-advocacy groups (organisations run by disabled people)?
- How many individuals are invited?
- Are the service-users expected to be involved in the research advisory groups or a series of specialist meetings just for them?
- How will they be supported to contribute?
- Is the agenda/venue accessible?
- Can they bring supporters?
- Is a pre-meeting needed to support the formation of their views?
- Are the people with learning difficulties able to check the information they provide?
- Will there be an accessible output?
- Are they rewarded for their contribution?

In the final analysis, it must be acknowledged that the involvement of people with learning difficulties as consultants to research is never going to result in full engagement with the research questions and issues. Such a process takes time and energy, and will require the research to be set up in a different way. Stacey Gramlich now describes his experience of a project in which people with learning difficulties took lead roles.

Stacey Gramlich: Journey to independence

From 1999 to 2002, I was part of a team of three researchers, who worked for Swindon People First on a project about direct payments[1]. Swindon People First is an organisation run by people with learning difficulties, and all the researchers were people with learning difficulties. The Community Fund funded our project, and it was called Journey to Independence. It was about the support that people with learning difficulties want, so that we can use direct payments and have control over our lives. In our report (Gramlich et al, 2002) we talk about how the project got started:

> Back in 1999, our committee at Swindon People First got together. They had put in for some money to run a direct payments support scheme, because they thought that direct payments was such a good idea. But they also wanted to learn from it, and be able to tell others about it. So, they talked

with Ken Simons at the Norah Fry Research Centre, and decided to go for a research project. In the summer of 1999, they heard they had got the money from the National Lottery (now the Community Fund) for that research project. Great news!

That was where we came in. The project was planned to include a post for a self-advocate researcher, and so this was advertised. We were the people who applied and got the job, as a job-share, and we started our job in November 1999. (Gramlich et al, 2002, p 109)

When we first started doing research, we were all new to it, so we had to learn. That is why we had a researcher and a supporter to help us. We had to learn about two things – about the topic we were researching which was direct payments and how to do research.

Researchers often try to include people with learning difficulties, but the real power lies with the non-disabled people. People do not always believe that research can be done by people with learning difficulties, but we have found our way of doing it, and it has worked for us. The important things for us were that we had paid jobs and we had lots of time to talk about our research, and make sure we all understood. We had a People First supporter, as well as a research supporter from Norah Fry Research Centre. We were involved in all the planning of the research (making phone calls, writing letters, chairing the research meetings and we had our own ideas about how to do the work).

It was hard work, but we did it by teamwork. Our research project was in partnership with the Norah Fry Research Centre. We were like one big team, all working to the same goals, but in different ways. We all had equally important goals, and we could not have done it without each other. We would not have been able to get where we are so quickly.

The best way of learning about research is to get out there and do it. We went all over the country, looking at different examples of direct payments schemes, and we interviewed many people. In the end, we did 88 interviews on our visits, with a whole lot of different people – people with learning difficulties, their families and parents, social workers, commissioners and direct payments officers. We also talked with other self-advocacy groups. This was an awful lot to do! We taped all our interviews and brought them back to Swindon People First.

The Community Fund gave us money for our research because they think it is important that the voices of people with learning difficulties get heard. For many years, non-disabled people have controlled most of the system for people with learning difficulties. They look on us as something inferior, and they can restrict us. This is what we wrote about doing research:

We want to do our own research because it's first-hand, and then we don't have to learn from second-hand research. It's first-hand because it's our own. Other research is clouded by the fact that it's done by professionals, it's from their point of view, and they're effectively only guessing how we feel. Also, other research is very hard for us to understand. (Snelham et al, 2002, p 5)

Are we 'people with learning difficulties'? I think it is wrong to label people, but in this research we had to think about why it was us doing the research. We all need support, and that was important for this project. That is why the research was special for us. Having a learning difficulty is not something to be ashamed about. I am proud of who I am. If I resented it, then I would be a wreck.

People have often asked us how we did the research. What sort of problems did we face? In fact, we had to face the same kind of problems that any researcher faces. Here is an example of one of them.

In our research, we wanted to interview parents of people with learning difficulties about their views on direct payments. We thought they did not know much about direct payments, and that they may be part of the barrier. However, we decided that we had to get consent from the people with learning difficulties, because disabled people often get talked about behind their backs. They should be able to say yes or no; if we went over their heads and asked their parents, that would not be self-advocacy. Instead, that would be taking power away from the people with learning difficulties.

We had three choices. We could go straight to the parents; we could go and talk with parents' groups to explain the research first; or we could make a consent form, so that the son or daughter could understand and give consent.

We decided that we would stick to our plan, and go through the person with learning difficulties first, and get their permission. The problem was, we found it was very hard to get the people with learning difficulties to understand why we wanted to speak with their parents, and so very few gave permission. We talked about this problem a lot, in our advisory group and in our own meetings. In the end, in the second year of our project, we agreed that we would do some interviews in carers' groups.

We were quite right – when parents get together, they do talk about their sons and daughters behind their backs. On the whole, however, it was useful to hear what they said. Most parents we met really wanted their child to get independence, but many had never heard of direct payments. This was important for us to know.

Our research supporter did not do the work for us. She had the contacts, and we did the research. It would not have been the same if she had done it for us. When we do research, it is different. It proves to others that we can do research. It is important, because it is our point of view: we can now be the artists of our own lives, and not the exhibits.

Neil Palmer: Finding Out project

I do research, because it makes me feel so happy to see my name as an author. My mum might say to me, 'What are you doing, and where has this come from?'. People see me as a person who works outside, doing research projects and doing my own thing.

A few years ago, a group of us in Bristol decided to get together in our own research group. We were all people who had been labelled as 'people with learning difficulties', and we called ourselves the Bristol Self-Advocacy Research Group. We already knew Val Williams, and she helped us as a volunteer to get things going. We did a project called Finding Out which was mainly about discrimination issues. Different people in the group had different subjects, and we had to decide how each person wanted to do it.

Research is the main way that you are going to have a chance to express your opinion on things. One of the things I feel very strongly about is disability and discrimination. I have written things about that, and spoken at conferences. If a researcher goes to a conference, and they see the book, they can see the sort of thing that I have done. It is really down to the skills the person has.

When we did our Finding Out project, we got some money from the National Lottery Charities Board, just a small grant. But it was enough for us to get to the places we wanted to visit, and to pay ourselves a small fee. We visited lots of self-advocacy groups, and we got information from them, about discrimination and what they were up against, and also labelling. We had a whole list of questions, and it helped us to get the information we needed, so that we could get the answers back. In the minutes of one of our first meetings, this is how one of our members talked about what we aimed to do:

> To find out – 'Are other people hitting their heads against a brick wall like we are?'. (Research Group, minutes, 17 January 1997)

There were just four people in our group when we set out to do this research, and we wrote all our own questions. We could decide exactly how to do this project for ourselves. As a research group, we were working on our own, with support from Val. She was not there to tell us what to do, but we told her what to do. The four of us were running the thing ourselves, and we had to tell her what we wanted to do. For instance, we wanted to ask questions about transport, and we told her what we wanted.

We wrote up our project in a chapter for a book (Swain and French, 1999), and we have also had articles published (Palmer and Turner, 1999; Williams, 1999). But we also wanted to write something for other self-advocates, so we put in for some more money from the Lottery, and we got a grant to make an easy-English book about the research. This is called Finding Out, and we have sold it to many people. Research is a two-way thing, because when people read our book, then they talk about it with us. Everyone can take part in research.

Now we sometimes have links with Norah Fry Research Centre, and as I see it, I represent other people with learning difficulties. People at Norah Fry need to be connected to other people outside, who have problems. When I come up to Norah Fry, it always gives me a very good feeling of communication –and making things more established. People who are doing research should be connected to people who have a learning difficulty.

Why can't we all work together? It is simple. We do our research for ourselves, because it is about how we think and see and understand. We should have an equal relationship with researchers. We are all human beings, and working to a common goal of equality.

Val Williams: Reflections from a research supporter

The three accounts in this chapter are about quite different research projects, and yet there are certain common themes that appear to be important for all of them. I was the research supporter in both of the projects described by Neil and by Stacey. In this final part of the chapter, I will try to draw out some of the main themes, and in so doing, I will attempt to give a flavour of the support role, including some of the dilemmas I faced. I will also address some of the common criticisms and doubts about inclusive research that were raised in the opening part of this chapter.

Skills for research

When people with learning difficulties (or, to a lesser extent, any impairment) get involved in research, academics are often sceptical (Walmsley, 1997; Aspis, 2001). Research is associated with advanced cognitive skills. Surely, people with learning difficulties, by definition, cannot have those skills? That is how the argument goes.

Both Stacey and Neil write about the skills involved in actually conducting a research project. Doing research involves learning, as well as sheer perseverance. Neil in particular, writes about his sense of achievement on seeing his name in print. Although all researchers and authors may share this sentiment, being a published author is an unexpected achievement for someone who has a learning difficulty. Beth's account of consultation with service-users equally draws on their skills. One of the consultants was picked out in particular as having expert skills and experience, and so was a natural choice as an advisor to the first project about short breaks.

From my own perspective as a research supporter, it seems important to consider carefully the question of skills and learning in the context of *why* people with learning difficulties are getting involved in research. The question of learning, and teaching, research skills was an issue that occupied me greatly, during both the projects described by Neil and by Stacey. At the start of the Finding Out project, in January 1997, I had no one except group members to dictate my role. I was engaged in the project in a voluntary capacity, having previously been supporting People First members with their European work, and 'research' was not a familiar activity for any of us. At the outset, I think it was fair to say that none of us were fully aware of the roles that we would be playing in this new venture.

By contrast, when the Journey to Independence project was set up in Swindon People First, we had full funding for salaried posts for the researchers with learning difficulties, myself and others in the team. Setting up well-supported inclusive research is inevitably costly. My role was quite specifically to support the disabled researchers, and to enable them to learn the necessary skills to play their own important part at the centre of a large-scale research project. We were all accountable to the Community Fund and to the wider community to do the research tasks for which we were funded. Therefore, the process we followed, and the issues and dilemmas we faced, were somewhat different to those in the Bristol project.

In both projects, the conclusion I came to was that inclusive research depends on the researchers' identity as people with learning difficulties. When Stacey and Neil get involved in research, they are doing so precisely *because* they have a learning difficulty. If they did not, then they would not be there. Learning the skills for research, therefore, is not about overcoming in some way their cognitive limitations. As Walmsley (1997) pointed out, that would be an extreme manifestation of normalisation tendencies. On the contrary, one of the skills people with learning difficulties bring to research is their understanding of how it feels to face cognitive limitations. Thus it is vital that we do not conceive of inclusive research as an academy to produce people with learning difficulties with advanced skills of reading, writing and memory. Researchers with learning difficulties should have an understanding of who they are and why they are doing the research. They must be able to listen to others and have empathy with their experiences and views and the confidence to think how things can change and to communicate this to others.

Researchers with learning difficulties will turn to supporters for help with many of the technical tasks of research. This does not mean that the researchers do not have control over the process; on the contrary, it will give them more control and power to represent others who face the same barriers.

Support

Conscious that the outside world sometimes doubts their own ability to manage as researchers, both Neil and Stacey are anxious to make it clear that the supporter is simply there as a back up, and does not take over. From the supporter's point of view, the subtle skill required to actually achieve this stance is also worth considering. However, as with the question of researchers' skills, I will argue that the question of supporter's skills is not just about the technical tricks of 'doing support'. The question also has to be considered in the light of the ethical issues central to this chapter, which are issues of identity and power.

Different research supporters will undoubtedly operate in very different ways, and the assistance required by different people with learning difficulties will also vary from individual to individual. However, the central feature of good support, from the point of view of self-advocates, is that the supporter does not dominate. The ideal would be for the disabled person to truly control his or her supporter, asking for the help that he/she needs to accomplish a particular task. That is the goal towards which one is constantly working. In my experience, however, the difficulty arises in attempting to achieve this stance while also ensuring that the research gets done.

In each of the projects described earlier in this chapter, the researchers with learning difficulties needed guidance at the beginning to understand their role. They all approached this learning enthusiastically. However, even when understanding was achieved, they still needed guidance to know how to plan their working day, and encouragement to carry through all the tasks, such as interviewing, presentations and analysis. As research supporter, I was employed in order to support the teams to do these things, but I was also responsible for ensuring that the research proceeded according to plan. On occasions, these two aims could conflict. For instance, in research interviews I was there to support the researchers with learning difficulties. However, what should I do during an interview if the interviewers ignored a topic, which clearly needed to be followed up? Should I intervene or not? If the research supporter's role is at least partly driven by a commitment to the research, then there has to be a constant shifting between the roles of guide, teacher, personal assistant and research manager.

These dilemmas about support within research are matched by dilemmas in supporting people with learning difficulties to achieve independence throughout their lives. In the research on direct payments, the whole team discussed these very ideas about independence, as a key part of their research analysis. As Morris (1993) points out, independence does not mean isolation and lone achievement. Our lives are in reality all interdependent. Disabled people's demand for independence does not imply that they want to be entirely left on their own; it is because those who care for them often take over their lives and their decisions. The Swindon People First research team fully grasped this concept in relation to direct payments:

> Everybody can make choices, but who has control over their whole life? Like everyone, we all need other people. Because we want things, sometimes we want help for those things, and that does depend on other people. (Gramlich et al, 2002, p 8)

Instead of independence, then, researchers with learning difficulties need to have autonomy and control in their own research. Stacey does in fact touch on this when he talks about teamwork. Every member of the team has his or her own role, and the supporter is just one part of that team.

Power

The dilemmas inherent in the support role are very much to do with power struggles. Neil and Stacey both appreciate that taking on the researcher role can give them power and control to have a voice in their own affairs, and by implication, in the affairs of those whom they represent. Stacey, in particular, is very clear about the value and purpose of people with the label of 'learning difficulty' representing themselves. It is easy to agree with this statement, but much harder to achieve it in reality. My own experience as a supporter was that the struggle was often about desperately trying to hand over power. It would have been far easier for all the team if the supporter could simply tell them what to do!

In research consultation exercises there is also an issue of power, although the expectations here may be quite different. The researcher is going to have the final say over decision making in the project, and the consultants are there simply to give advice. Their power will depend on the degree to which their views are really central to that decision making. In her part of the chapter, Beth gave some practical pointers towards setting up consultation exercises to ensure a more equitable balance of power.

In the projects Neil and Stacey described, there were also practical questions to be considered. For instance, in the Swindon project, we found that power was more evenly distributed when a researcher with learning difficulties took on the role of chairing team meetings. We also took pains to ensure they made their own agenda, and felt in control of the meetings.

The concept of power can signify different things. On the one hand, it can mean something akin to feeling good about yourself, or having a powerful persona. There is no doubt that doing research can produce this feeling, as Neil commented after the Finding Out project:

> It is definitely a challenge to me, more of an upgrading challenge. (Quoted in Williams, 2002, p 230)

On a continuum from the personal to the collective, Neil's comment is definitely towards the personal end.

Many would argue that inclusive research should challenge traditional power bases on a much broader front. When a group of people share and develop their own knowledge, they achieve a collective form of power. This is what can happen when research is both conceived and carried out by organisations of people with learning difficulties. However, it can also happen when people achieve a sense of representing other people who are in the same position as themselves.

Final thoughts

In the act of becoming researchers, people with learning difficulties are enabled to have a voice. People whose voices are often submerged (Foucault, 1980) are now working out their own opinions about their worlds and their experiences. It is very important, therefore, that this new type of research does not simply encourage people with learning difficulties to blindly copy the position and discourses of academic researchers. A true sense of power will emerge only when people with learning difficulties are proud of their own distinctive identities.

If inclusive research of this nature is to develop and continue, however, it will need more than a shift in thinking. At present, the power of academic researchers is backed up by streams of funding to which they have privileged access. Generally, it is far harder for disabled people, let alone people with learning difficulties, to successfully bid for research funding in their own right (Ward, 1997), although there are recent examples of progressive thinking among some funding bodies. Shifting this balance in favour of disabled people implies a shift in the power of the traditional, academic system.

The various models and examples we have described in this chapter are all aiming to enhance the possibility of people with learning difficulties developing their own knowledge base. The challenge for all of us, disabled and non-disabled researchers, is to find ways to share the debates about inclusive research. We will also need to question our own power base, and the way in which research is commissioned. As Neil put it so eloquently in his part of this chapter,

> We should have an equal relationship with researchers. We are all human beings and working to a common goal of equality.

Note

[1] 'Direct payments' (DoH, 1996 Community Care [Direct Payments] Act) is a scheme whereby disabled people can opt to get the cash, instead of a community care service. They generally use the money to employ a personal assistant. The scheme has been slow to include people with learning difficulties as direct payments users.

References

Aspis, S. (2001) 'How valid is your research project?', *Community Living*, vol 15, no 4, pp 17-18.

Chappell, A. (2000) 'Emergence of participatory methodology in learning difficulty research: understanding the context', *British Journal of Learning Disabilities*, vol 28, pp 38-43.

Foucault, M. (1980) *Power/Knowledge: Selected interviews and other writings, 1972-1977*, London: Harvester Press.

Goodley, D. (1996) 'Tales of hidden lives: a critical examination of life history research with people who have learning difficulties', *Disability and Society*, vol 11, no 3, pp 333-48.

Gramlich, S., McBride, G., Snelham, N. and Myers, B. (with Williams, V. and Simons, K.) (2002) *Journey to independence: What self advocates tell us about direct payments*, Kidderminster: BILD.

McClimens, A. (1999) 'Participatory research with people who have a learning difficulty: journeys without a map', *Journal of Learning Disabilities for Nursing, Health and Social Care*, vol 3, no 4, pp 219-28.

Minkes, J., Townsley, R., Weston, C. and Williams, C. (1995) 'Having a voice: involving people with learning difficulties in research', *British Journal of Learning Disabilities*, vol 23, pp 94-7.

Mitchell, P. (1997) 'The impact of self advocacy on families', *Disability and Society*, vol 12, no 1, pp 43-56.

Morris, J. (1993) *Independent lives*, London: Macmillan.

Oliver, M. (1992) 'Changing the social relations of research production?', *Disability, Handicap and Society*, vol 7, no 2, pp 101-14.

Palmer, N. and Turner, F. (1998) 'Self advocacy: doing our own research', *Royal College of Speech and Language Therapy Bulletin*, August, pp 12-13.

Prewett, B. (1999) *Short-term break, long-term benefit*, Sheffield: Joint Unit for Social Science Research.

Rioux, M. and Bach, M. (1994) *Disability is not measles: New research paradigms in disability*, North York: Roeher Institute.

Rodgers, J. (1999) 'Trying to get it right: undertaking research involving people with learning difficulties', *Disability and Society*, vol 14, pp 421-34.

Simons, K. (1998) *A place at the table*, Kidderminster: BILD.

Snelham, N., McBride, G. and Gramlich, S. with Myers, B. (Swindon People First) and Williams, V. and Simons, K. (Norah Fry Research Centre) (2002) *Journey to independence: Doing research as self-advocates*, Consumers in NHS Support Unit Newsletter, Summer, pp 5-6.

Swain, J. and French, S. (eds) (1999) *Therapy and learning difficulties: Advocacy, participation and partnership*, Oxford: Butterworth-Heinemann.

Tarleton, B. and Macaulay, F. (2002) *Better for the break? Short break services for children and teenagers with autistic spectrum disorders and their families*, Bristol: Shared Care Network.

Walmsley, J. (1997) 'Including people with learning difficulties: theory and practice', in L. Barton and M. Oliver (eds) *Disability studies: Past, present and future,* Leeds: Disability Press, pp 62-77.

Walmsley, J. (2001) 'Normalisation, emancipatory research and inclusive research in Learning Disability', *Disability and Society*, vol 16, no 2, pp 187-205.

Ward, L. (1997) 'Funding for change: translating emancipatory disability research from theory to practice', in C. Barnes and G. Mercer (eds) *Doing disability research*, Leeds: The Disability Press, pp 32-48.

Ward, L. and Simons, K. (1998) 'Practising partnership: involving people with learning difficulties in research', *British Journal of Learning Disabilities*, vol 26, pp 128-31.

Williams, V. (1999) 'Researching together', *British Journal of Learning Disabilities*, vol 27, pp 48-51.

Williams, V. (2002) 'Being researchers with the label of learning difficulty: an analysis of talk in a project carried out by a self-advocacy research group', Unpublished PhD thesis, School of Health and Social Welfare, Open University.

Zarb, G. (1992) 'On the road to Damascus: first steps towards changing the social relations of research production', *Disability, Handicap and Society*, vol 7, pp 125-38.

Part Two:
The review and governance process

FIVE

Research with psychiatric patients: knowing their own minds?

Sarah Nelson

"I couldn't cope at home; the house didn't feel safe any longer. The walls I felt were closing in. I saw eyes everywhere, they were just black eyes to begin with, but when I confronted my abuser I realised they were his eyes. I went back to the same [psychiatric] ward, back and forward ... they would change my tablets, or up my tablets, then send me out. It helped in the sense that it gave me time out, but it wasn't dealing with the problem."

"One night I had an urge to talk. I said to the night nurse, 'Could I wait until it quietens down a bit and talk to you?' She said, 'I don't have time', told me to take my sleeping tablets ... but the charge nurse was brilliant. He said, 'Talk to me if you need to…. He admitted 75% of people coming through the doors had been abused; and they didn't know how to deal with it."

Introduction

What is ethical behaviour when it comes to consulting vulnerable, mentally distressed people, like the woman quoted above, about their experiences of psychiatric care? This question became a source of dispute with a Research Ethics Committee (REC) in my own Scottish study of women with mental health problems, who had survived childhood sexual abuse (Nelson, 2001). Issues about research participants' freedom of choice, the independence of social researchers and gaps in understanding between the worlds of social and medical research have relevance that goes beyond this particular study.

This chapter highlights my experiences as a researcher within the Beyond Trauma project, in order to examine the ethical issues that arise within the ethical governance process in more detail. By considering a specific example, this chapter reflects on the governance process from the social researchers, professionals' and participants' perspectives. This chapter also considers the impact that REC decisions have on research, knowledge and services.

The qualitative Beyond Trauma research project had the practical aim of improving mental health services for female survivors of childhood sexual abuse.

It explored their experiences of services, and their views on how these might be improved. It also consulted mental health professionals and voluntary sector agencies working with survivors for their perspectives on the issue. Six months into the study, the local REC suspended its approval of the project, putting the survival of the project at risk.

The dispute that followed illustrated how there can be genuine disagreements about research ethics in mental health. It is the assertion of this chapter that this range of views needs to find greater expression, particularly from service-users themselves, both in major funding bodies and in these 'gate keeping' local RECs. The local RECs are meant, after all, to be independent of professional influences, and to "protect the dignity, rights, safety and wellbeing of all actual or potential research participants" (Scottish Executive DoH, 2002)

As our research progressed, it became clear that, ironically, the fears which mental health professionals on the REC had about researchers like myself interviewing these women paralleled the fears of many professionals in the study about raising, or responding to, abuse issues with the women as patients. The reasons which were given for not opening 'the can of worms' were similar in both cases: it might do more harm than good since:

• the women would be too upset, damaged, destabilised and self-harming;
• the women might be unreliable or untruthful;
• staff working with them were not suitably trained or qualified;
• I, as a social researcher, was not suitably trained or qualified.

In contrast, every survivor who was interviewed stated that they would have valued the opportunity to identify and talk about the issue. Some had spent decades of frustration under mental health care, without their legacy of abuse being addressed or even recognised. Thus, the silencing which sexual abuse survivors with mental health problems have experienced as children may be replicated several times over: by having the issue ignored or minimised in the mental health system; by the scarcity of research studies which consult them directly about their needs; and by attempts to restrict their participation in research when studies do take place. Patients diagnosed as psychotic, in particular, are usually excluded from research studies (Read, 1997).

Background to the Beyond Trauma Project

The impetus for this particular piece of research came from a growing realisation through years of working with female survivors of childhood sexual abuse that most had experienced both mental distress and contact with psychiatric services at some point in their lives. Often the contact with these services that they described seemed to be unhappy and unsatisfactory, although some had met very helpful staff. As a result, a qualitative research study was designed in order to capture a range of their experiences, and their own views on the shape of services they wanted to see, and the kinds of support they had found most helpful.

The influence of childhood sexual trauma sat uneasily with dominant medical models of mental illness and had long proved controversial. In addition, campaigns by accused adults, such as the False Memory Societies, placed new pressures on mental health professionals (psychiatrists, psychologists and psychiatric nurses) doing therapeutic work with sexual abuse survivors (Andrews, 2001). Was it relevant to question whether these factors made an impact on professionals' work? How did they think services could be improved? What were the main areas of agreement and disagreement between professionals and service-users?

The planned research, in a Scottish city, was a collaboration between a mental health charity and a university department of sociology. We hoped that a qualitative study would prove a basis for wider-ranging research, and for useful policy initiatives in care and support for adult survivors.

Our study drew on four sources of data:

- semi-structured interviews with the survivors;
- semi-structured interviews with mental health staff;
- a voluntary-sector questionnaire;
- a 'consultation day' attended by participants, where mental health staff and service-users alike considered the preliminary findings and discussed what the priorities for the recommendations should be.

One result of that exercise was that survivors of sexual abuse insisted on including public education, awareness raising, and work to combat social stigma as part of the recommendations to improve the treatment of people who had been sexually abused in childhood.

Some of the ethics committee problems that we experienced were foreshadowed in our difficulties with funding the project, and we had several 'knockbacks' from major funders. Peer reviews of the application revealed anxiety that the women might be unreliable because they might not be telling the truth that they had been sexually abused. It was unusual to find the basic life experiences of prospective interviewees being challenged, and a sharp reminder of the heated political debates (such as 'false memory syndrome') surrounding child sexual abuse (CSA).

Potential funders who rejected our application, along with several advisers who were medical specialists, also argued that the sample of women would not be representative. However, this concern was inconsistent: no one raised as a problem that the psychiatrists, psychologists or social workers we interviewed might be unrepresentative too. In particular, critics argued, the women in the sample would be more dissatisfied than others with mental health services. That seemed to reflect anxieties about health service-users who voiced their opinions, and also about the militancy of people who joined voluntary sector support agencies. In fact there was no discernible relationship between the women's source of recruitment as interviewees and their level of discontent irrespective of whether they volunteered to take part after publicity in the media, through the psychiatric hospital, through mental health charities, or through other survivors.

Eventually, the research proposal gained National Lottery funding, unusual for such a project, but much appreciated.

The dispute

Approval from an NHS REC is normally required for any research proposal involving NHS patients, particularly vulnerable patients. The local subcommittee for psychiatry and clinical psychology confirmed written approval for the project and even waived its usual rule that patients' GPs or consultants must be informed of their participation. This decision was made since survivors might not want to reveal they had been abused to a third party. This subcommittee consisted mainly of psychiatrists and psychologists.

It could be argued that we did not need to take this route. Indeed, we would not have needed ethical approval to approach interviewees who were clients of voluntary sector organisations, or indeed those who are not clients of specific organisations. However, we also wished to be free to approach outpatients of psychiatric services and interview staff inside a major psychiatric hospital. Since the client group was potentially vulnerable, it was especially important to be seen to have thought through as carefully as possible any ethical issues that might have arisen. It was also felt that professional mental health staff would only take the project seriously if such approval had been sought and given. In any case, we did not foresee the difficulties that arose.

Six months after the project began, a consultant psychiatrist on our project's advisory group wrote to the mental health charity that he was concerned whether I, as principal investigator, "had any supervised clinical experience or clinical training of a kind which might be appropriate to someone who is to hold intensive interviews with people who have been severely sexually abused as children".

This consultant had previously been very supportive of the project, had been involved from an early stage of planning, and had never previously raised any such concerns. The subcommittee immediately suspended the project from ethical approval. Their letter of suspension stated that this was happening "after a consultant psychiatrist expressed serious concerns about the ethical propriety of your study". The rules of operation seemed autocratic since the mental health charity was never shown a copy of the psychiatrist's letter, and approval was suspended before the researchers had any chance to respond to the claims. The committee was dominated by mental health professionals; there were no service-users, and the substantial mental health voluntary sector in the city was not represented among the statutory 'lay members', who did not have specialist knowledge of this field.

Ethical approval was not reinstated for nearly six months. The widely circulated suspension letter seriously undermined the project's credibility, so all interviews had to be stopped during the suspension. The months of delay to the work meant that the mental health charity had to look for extra funding in order to complete the project.

The committee accepted one of the psychiatrist's claims – that we were not gaining written consent from interview 'subjects' – as untrue. We designed detailed information brochures and consent forms that we had elaborated further on their advice. This proved a helpful aspect of having contact with an ethics committee. We also arranged that every woman involved in the project had a support person or group to talk with afterwards if the interview proved upsetting.

However, we fundamentally disagreed that the project needed 'clinical supervision' in interpreting interviews or choosing interviewees. We believed this would compromise our independence as social researchers, and the women's independence as service-users, who had every right to comment freely on their care. In addition, the interviewees had not consented to, or been asked to consent to, submission to any clinical process. Methodologically, this objection to the research implied that people with mental health problems might be less reliable, and that only doctors and psychiatrists had the skill to interpret their claims within a clinical context.

The concern ethics committee members had – namely, that I lacked the training and qualifications to interview these vulnerable women – was not about my training in interview techniques, nor my training in qualitative research methods. Rather, it was about my ability clinically to interpret the claims of the mentally ill. This implies that even when asking about patients' experience of services, there are specialist skills which only clinical staff possess. This position poses a direct challenge to social science researchers and other researchers without medical training. This was social research about services, in a medical context, and not medical research carried out upon a group of people. It was fundamental to our position that psychiatric patients were just as capable of commenting upon services as anyone else. We did, however, agree to put in place clinical support and advice for the researcher, should she need it at any time (if, for instance, she was concerned about the mental stability of an interviewee).

In some ways, this might be seen as a 'professional territory' dispute, and certainly for some members I appeared to be encroaching on their professional territory. But it was not simply this. I was not a rival attempting to offer different treatments to their patients, nor suggesting that they did not need treatment at all. I was trying to explore patients' views on services, and was in a sense simply a conduit for those views and experiences. The committee had difficulty accepting the legitimacy of the views of particular users of medical services, as did the professionals.

The need to consider the ways in which service-users evaluated services had been considered particularly important just because therapeutic interventions with survivors of abuse had tended to ignore, and sometimes to silence, their experience of sexual abuse trauma. It was because of the failure of mental health professionals adequately to address the issue that external research was particularly necessary.

The charity, researchers and academic advisers presented their case personally to the ethics subcommittee. It proved extremely difficult to explain to many members that the foci of the research were the services, not the women themselves, and this difficulty continued in the correspondence afterwards. If that is a widespread problem, it may impact on many contemporary consultations with service-users about both mental and physical health services.

Psychiatrists, in particular, worried that women would be seriously "de-stabilised" and would self-harm if I asked them to talk about their abuse, with professionals being left to pick up the pieces. Almost identical concerns about self-harm were expressed later during the research itself. For instance, a psychiatrist thought it "inappropriate" to explore a possible sexual abuse history with young psychiatric in-patients in his specialist unit. This also raised worrying child protection issues, especially since the unit worked closely with the patients' families. Suppose, for example, that some of those family members were implicated in the sexual abuse of their young patients?

Following the ethics subcommittee meeting at which we presented our case personally, we were later told that ethical approval would be reinstated if, among other conditions (and reversing an earlier decision), women's GPs or consultants were told that they were taking part. If the women did not agree, they should be "excluded from the study population" (sic).

We put our ethical objections, that women had the right to keep their sexual history private and to take part if they wished, and a long correspondence took place. Eventually the charity reluctantly agreed to the conditions, in order to save the project. We at least won an assurance that doctors would not be told the content of interviews, and that women would have the right to read anything doctors wrote about them. The new chair of the subcommittee, who wanted to be as helpful to us as possible, asked us to let her know if any problems developed with the ruling.

As it happened, most women in our sample had been involved with mental health services for a long time and did not mind their consultant or GP knowing, because their abuse history was already recorded somewhere. This reduced the dilemma we faced, but in another research project, where survivors were less mentally distressed or had more diverse histories, this condition might be offensive and exclude people from taking part simply because they could not agree to it. I also found it awkward and disagreeable as a researcher that I had to ask women to agree to this condition before interview. It created unease at the early stage of trying to build trust. It was hard even to imagine how the subcommittee could fail to understand why people might be offended or embarrassed at a professional knowing their abuse history, if they were not ready to reveal it. The condition came across as an assertion of medical power.

Evidence challenges professional fears

Were the subcommittee's fears – that the women might be upset or destabilised by talking about abuse – realised? The experience of our research suggested they were not. Nor were the fears of many practitioners. In our study, 22 women who had been sexually abused in childhood gave in-depth, semi-structured interviews. Of these, it emerged that ten had experienced psychotic episodes at some time; all had faced severe mental distress, and for most, bouts of being mentally unwell were recurrent features of their lives. Thus we had not simply selected 'the worried well'. Further, we asked each person if they could outline basic details of their abuse history. Therefore, the cohort consisted of upset people speaking of upsetting subjects, and some who had faced extremely traumatic early lives.

Apart from one extremely distressed and damaged teenager, where it was impossible to say whether or not the interview had assisted her in any way, every woman interviewed stated that she found value in being able to put her views across. Three of the women spoke publicly at our final conference and all said they experienced this as very empowering. Every woman interviewed was also able to describe rationally and coherently how her abuse had affected her, and the issues with which they needed help, advice or support. This ranged from therapy for violent or intrusive thoughts to support for grief and bereavement issues, legal advice, and practical help for their partners and children. They told traumatic life stories with dignity and often with sadness and regret as well as with pride in their survival, but without collapsing or descending into destructive self-harm.

They described clearly their own experiences of assessment and treatment, and when a sub-sample of their remembered treatment histories was checked (with their permission) against their medical records, accuracy of recall was high. When the survivors were asked to describe the kinds of staff they found most helpful, there was so much consensus that we were able to draw up a 'pen portrait' of helpful attributes which applied across sectors, disciplines or job status, from consultant psychiatrists to volunteer counsellors. Responses from across Britain after the report was published, and invitations to speak about the project, showed that these findings were of particular interest to professionals working with survivors.

The women did not see qualifications as important, although basic human qualities of warmth and empathy were highly valued. So were:

- informed awareness of sexual abuse trauma;
- courage to 'stay with' clients during (sometimes traumatic) disclosures;
- willingness to face their own issues in relation to abuse;
- non-hierachical approaches, such as a willingness to consult respectfully with the women;
- efforts to reach joint decisions about support and therapy.

The research interviews thus challenged assumptions that psychiatric patients are unable to give coherent accounts of their experiences and needs, unable to know their own minds, or inherently unreliable, especially if they have suffered psychotic episodes. They also challenged fundamentally the assumption that survivors of sexual abuse would be more distressed if they addressed issues relating to their trauma than if they left things as they were. The women were already in pain and distress, and years of silence had exacted their own toll.

Every woman who was interviewed told researchers they would have welcomed help to deal with problems arising from the abuse. This suggests that there is particular value in consulting directly the views of service-users rather than assuming knowledge of what they wanted, or what was best for them. The issue of 'opening the can of worms' in fact emerged as the sharpest point of difference between survivors and a majority of staff interviewees. This strengthens the argument of researchers and clinicians like Dr John Read, who believe that, due to the frequency of a CSA history in psychiatric patients, even in those diagnosed with schizophrenia, questions about CSA should routinely be asked at assessment (Read and Fraser, 1998a, 1998b).

Research perspectives on psychiatric patients

It is useful to consider the description by Pilgrim and Rogers (1993) of three ways in which the psychiatric patient's voice has typically been portrayed or conceptualised: as *patient*, as *consumer* and as *survivor* (meaning here survivor of the psychiatric system, rather than survivor of child abuse). First, clinical research on users as patients has tended to exclude their views, or to see them as passive objects of study. Clinicians and researchers question the validity of users' views. They would still tend to agree with the outlook of Jones (1962), despite the changes in official rhetoric, since he wrote:

> It would have been a basic precaution to check the objective value of (patients') statements with the medical records or the responsible psychiatrist. (p 343)

According to this perspective, patients' lack of insight is seen as part of their mental condition, and their ability to make informed decisions about treatment is compromised by their impaired mental status. This perspective was evident in responses from some of the psychiatrists, psychiatric nurses and psychologists we interviewed for the study, as well as among some peer reviewers for funders, and among sections of the ethics committee.

When psychiatric patients are also known to have suffered childhood sexual abuse, their witness risks being seen as even less reliable. While the 'recovered memory' debate has seen sceptics focussing on allegations that therapists implant the memories in such vulnerable clients, the two psychiatrists quoted below refer rather to the possibility that fantasising sexual abuse may be part of a patient's illness:

> You have to remember the context. We have patients on the ward who
> have delusions about their family, who say people are trying to kill them....
> If someone was in the ward having an acute episode of a first psychosis or
> something ... forgive me, one wouldn't automatically necessarily take
> everything at face value. Because [some] people are saying.... Martians are
> beaming rays down at them.... (Nelson, 2001, p 48)

> Sometimes people are extremely unwell with schizophrenic illnesses and
> when they are unwell, they say they have been sexually abused. But if you
> sit down and talk to them about it at some length, the accounts are very
> bizarre ... and sometimes when they get better it is clear there never was
> sexual abuse and that person will deny it vehemently. It is part and parcel of
> their illness, in other words.... (Nelson, 2001, p 48)

In such situations, the significant contributory reason for the patient's trauma
is denied. If people are not permitted to be the people they believe themselves
to be, and are not given credibility for their own life experiences, their views
will have no value and they will not be consulted for their own expertise.
These people are also in a double bind. Being a victim of sexual abuse has led
to them being regarded as inherently unreliable and untrustworthy, therefore
incapable of giving evidence, or of knowing their own minds – which could
be seen as further abuse.

Pilgrim and Rogers (1993) describe how a second view, of the patient as
consumer, is linked to the introduction of general management principles into
the NHS since the 1980s, and the redefinition of welfare services as commodities
that can be freely chosen by patients as consumers. This approach is certainly
perceived as a more positive one, which should encourage respect for individuals.

However, before governments, health service managers or research designers
embrace it too eagerly, they need to address how problematic, even perhaps
inappropriate, it is for psychiatric patients. Most have little choice or buying
power, and, if compulsorily detained, they have none. It has also been argued
that the actual consumers of mental health services are relatives, the police, and
the state as a whole. Outside the hospital, the consumer of mental health
services remains more likely to encounter employment discrimination, stigma
and other disadvantages rather than benefits, while inside the hospital,
stigmatising conditions and diagnoses, graphically described by interviewees
in the Beyond Trauma project, may be underplayed by those who optimistically
embrace the consumer approach. The anti-stigma campaign embraced by,
among others, the Royal College of Psychiatrists ought to address not just the
attitudes of the general public, but also the attitudes of the psychiatric professions
themselves (Nelson, 2003).

Third, writings on service-users as survivors of the psychiatric system have
focussed on analyses of the structural position of users as a social group, or
phenomenological understanding of their position and identity. These have
often taken the form of personal accounts of life in psychiatric wards or other

settings (Goffman, 1961; Barham and Hayward, 1991; Rogers et al, 1993), which have given many valuable insights. Issues of rights, freedom of expression, human dignity, discrimination and advocacy have been prominent.

The mental health survivors movement has issued a powerful challenge to traditional views and practice, although its influence remains limited. That is because it still remains stigmatised and relatively marginalised as a pressure group; because support structures and resources have been patchy across the country; and because the movement itself has been far from united on specific issues, for example, when considering acceptance or rejection of medical paradigms of mental illness, and on whether users should seek to reform the system, or create alternative care outside it.

One problem has been that the perspective of 'user as survivor of the psychiatric system' has, like the 'anti-psychiatry movement' (Szasz, 1972; Breggin, 1993), been viewed as inherently political, biased and suspect by those who feel defensive – and protective – of conventional mental health services. It is important to stress that studies like our own did not set out with some political point to make, and made no prior assumptions about what the research would find. Women who described the squalid, frightening and shaming conditions in acute psychiatric wards, or the double-bind situation of being assessed as too upset and unstable for the counselling they sought, were not demanding to be treated as any special political category. They were simply asking to be given the same dignity and respect as other human beings. Part of ensuring that this basic respect is given to psychiatric patients as a whole is surely to regard their perspectives without prejudice and with an open mind. It is also to value the expertise that comes from personal experience.

Signs of encouraging change

Our published study has contributed some impetus to change in the mental health treatment of sexual abuse survivors. The Scottish Executive Minister for Health has formally asked all health boards and local authorities to consider its findings, while a Scottish Executive working group on the care of adult survivors of sexual abuse was set up in 2003 and is expected to make wide-ranging recommendations. In Scotland, there have also been changes in the guidance issued to ethics committees, which may encourage in future a more sympathetic appraisal both of qualitative research, and of research that consults vulnerable or stigmatised service-users.

Representation of the views and values of users and social (not just medical) researchers has become particularly important, given the significant and growing emphasis in national and local policy on 'user involvement' and 'user consultation' in health service provision, and on assessment of consumer satisfaction with health services. Understanding of qualitative methods, which explore processes, values and relationships, is also essential. Ethics committees now confront far wider issues, research topics and methodologies than the 'randomised controlled drugs trial proposals which have understandably played such a major part in their work. There are changes in the revised 'Governance arrangements for NHS research committees in Scotland' (Scottish Executive DoH, 2002), which, if implemented by local RECs, would represent encouraging movement and a more inclusive policy. For example, the term 'subjects' has been replaced with 'participants' throughout. This change in itself conveys a sense of shift in the relationship towards greater respect and away from seeing people as passive recipients of the research gaze, or even as somewhat dehumanised.

Membership numbers have been extended up to a maximum of 18, and the guidance states that the committee should ensure that it includes "expertise in qualitative and other research methods applicable to health and community care research". At least one third of the committee should be lay members independent of the NHS. The committee is also urged to make community considerations, for instance the extent to which the research contributes to capacity building (for example, enhancement of local healthcare and the ability to respond to public health needs). New policy also urges committees to take into account principles of justice, where the benefits and burdens of research are distributed equally among all groups and classes in society.

Conclusions

Recent policy initiatives are welcome and long overdue. They go some way to redressing the research governance balance, which, as this chapter has illustrated, can be damaging to specific types of research. However, the concern to avoid recruiting members in a 'representative' capacity remains problematic. Fears that numerous groups would want to be represented if the principle was conceded are understandable. Nonetheless, there are major, broad interests which ought to have a place at the table and service-users undoubtedly fall into this category, even if those recruited would not (and could not) claim to be representing all users. At the moment, Dr X and Ms Y may not be officially representing psychiatrists or psychologists, but their perspectives as psychiatrists and psychologists still strongly influence the committees, and it would be disingenuous to pretend otherwise. Likewise, voluntary-sector organisations, which make a major contribution to physical or mental health services in the area, need a voice. They are surely capable of arranging among themselves a rotating system of membership if all cannot gain a seat at the table. To fill lay places instead with people with minimal knowledge or experience of mental health issues makes little sense unless there is a conscious attempt to preserve the status quo.

On a more fundamental level, there remains the inequality of relationship between medical professionals and others. Venturing into medical areas for the first time after experience of working with (and doing research with) many professions, I found a disconcerting gulf between the worlds of social and medical research. This gulf was fuelled by arrogance, a hierarchical approach and a narrow vision of acceptable research paradigms, of which my own experience with the ethics committee was only one example. Even the fact that medical researchers have, from tradition, routinely referred to human beings as 'subjects', with the underlying attitudes that this suggests, was a shock and remains so.

I believe it is important that the medical professions as a whole open themselves (as many individual members have done) to other research paradigms and values, and that they reach out in a spirit of equality, fellowship, and collaboration to the inquiring minds, expertise and experience of other disciplines and (most urgently) of their own service-users. It will also be important that, in the increasing tendency to emulate scientific and medical criteria in the drive towards 'evidence-based practice' and 'systematic review', the social sciences do not sacrifice their breadth of vision in their understanding of human behaviour, their creative flexibility, or their humanitarian values.

References

Andrews, B. (2001) 'Recovered memories in therapy: clinicians' beliefs and practices', in G. Davies and T. Dalgleish (ed) *Recovered memories: Seeking the middle ground*, Chichester: John Wiley & Sons.

Barham, P. and Hayward, R. (1991) *From the mental patient to the person*, London: Routledge.

Breggin, P. (1993) *Toxic psychiatry*, London: Fontana.

Goffman, E. (1961) *Asylums*, Harmondsworth: Penguin.

Jones, K. (1962) 'Review', *Sociological Review*, vol 8, pp 343-4.

Nelson, S. (2001) *Beyond trauma: Mental health care needs of women who survived childhood sexual abuse*, Edinburgh: Edinburgh Association for Mental Health.

Nelson, S. (2003) 'Diatribe', *Mental Health Today*, February.

Pilgrim, D. and Rogers, A. (1993) *A sociology of mental health and illness*, Buckingham: Open University Press.

Read, J. (1997) 'Child abuse and psychosis: a literature review and implications for professional practice', *Professional Psychology: Research & Practice*, vol 28, pp 448-56.

Read, J. and Fraser, A. (1998a) 'Abuse histories of psychiatric inpatients: to ask or not to ask?', *Psychiatric Services*, vol 49, pp 355-9.

Read, J. and Fraser, A. (1998b) 'Staff response to abuse histories of psychiatric inpatients', *Australian & New Zealand Journal of Psychiatry*, vol 32, pp 206-13.

Rogers, A., Pilgrim, D. and Lacey, R. (1993) *Experiencing psychiatry: Users' views of services*, London: Macmillan.

Scottish Executive DoH (Department of Health) (2002) *Governance arrangements for NHS research ethics committees in Scotland*, available from Department of Health, St Andrews House, Regent Road, Edinburgh, WEH1 3DG.

Szasz, T. (1972) *The myth of mental illness*, St Albans: Paladin.

SIX

Researching end of life in old age:
ethical challenges

Ailsa Cameron, Liz Lloyd, Naomi Kent and Pat Anderson

Debates about the most appropriate way to research the relationship between old age and death highlight many of the ethical dilemmas facing all researchers, and social researchers specifically. In this chapter, we review the ethical issues that arose when developing the methodology for a one-year pilot study exploring the lives of 100 people over the age of 80. These ethical dilemmas included whether older people with dementia can or should consent to research participation; whether it was appropriate to obtain proxy consent from carers; how the ethical issues which arose were addressed through a Research Ethics Committee (REC); and how we, as researchers, dealt with ethical issues as they arose within the research interaction.

Introduction

The relationship between old age and death is poorly understood (Harper, 2000). Despite increasing concern about the care of older people, recent health and social care policies on ageing make few references to death and dying. The emphasis is on maintaining and restoring the independence of older people (DoH, 1998; Royal Commission on Long Term Care, 1999). This results in an inadequate policy framework for developing services for older people who are increasingly dependent on others and for whom rehabilitation services are no longer appropriate (Lloyd, 2000). The *National Service Framework for Older People* (DoH, 2001) marks a new development in government health policy in acknowledging the need for better end-of-life care in old age and for rehabilitation and support as health declines. However, increased awareness does not necessarily translate into improved practice. Evidence suggests strongly that the responses of health and social services to older people's needs are patchy and inconsistent (Henwood, 2001).

The research project discussed in this chapter aimed to explore these issues in depth from the perspective of older people themselves. By listening to older people's accounts of their lives, we hoped to better understand their involvement in key decisions made about their lives by health and social care professionals. The project was funded as a pilot study to test and refine our prospective longitudinal approach prior to undertaking a larger study. While older people were the focus of this project, they were also actively involved in the project advisory group helping us to plan and fine tune the research methodology.

Ethical considerations

Inclusion

The involvement of patients and 'the public' in the planning and provision of services is a powerful theme that has informed all aspects of public policy of the present Labour government. In relation to health and social care services, the National Service Framework (NSF) for older people points out that, while older people are the main users of these services, their needs are not always adequately addressed. The NSF calls for better representation and involvement for older people in local decision making, in particular the need to seek out "views about how services can be improved" (DoH, 2001, p 21). Standard 2 calls for professionals to treat older people as individuals and ensure that "older people and their carers should receive person-centred care and services which respect them as individuals and which are arranged around their needs" (DoH, 2001, p 21). While such policy statements can be interpreted as being aimed narrowly at older people's involvement in planning the services they directly receive, they also provide powerful supporting arguments for researching older people's views in a more general manner. It is this spirit of inclusion and empowerment that forms the backdrop of this study. However, this raises some problems.

Sensitivity of subject

From the outset, we were acutely aware of the ethical challenges of this study. A major concern was to ensure that our approach would be inclusive of all older people whatever their circumstance, that it was not threatening or distressing to participants and that our approach would enable older people to express their own perspectives of events in their lives. At the same time, we were concerned that our approach to the inclusion of people with dementia would pose problems both in terms of the ethical considerations of gaining consent and also the reliability of the responses. At the heart of our approach was a tension between our objective of ensuring that our sample was inclusive of the total population and at the same time developing an approach that was sensitive to the needs of older people with dementia.

Since we anticipated that some potential participants might have difficulties in giving consent through the period of the research, we chose to take advice from members of a local research ethics committee (LREC). Additional advice was sought from a national voluntary organisation about how best to communicate with people with dementia, how to make arrangements for participants to give consent in different ways and how to ask questions. For example, we realised that people with dementia may be better able at some times than others to give consent, depending on their state of health on any particular day. With an over-riding interest in ensuring that people with dementia should not be excluded from the study, we also decided that, in some circumstances, a family carer or other close friend or relative might give consent by proxy. While this decision might pose concerns about the authenticity of data collected from a 'proxy', we decided that data collected from a third party would help our understanding. However, we decided that this data would be analysed separately. This decision was invaluable in enabling us to clarify our approach to the LREC.

Developing the methodology

Since the relationship between old age and death is so complex, it is hardly surprising that this is a methodologically challenging sphere of enquiry in which a variety of approaches have been used. In some of the key studies in this field, researchers have used the recollections of bereaved relatives as a way of examining the deaths of older people (Seale and Cartwright, 1994; Addington-Hall and McCarthy, 1995). However, limitations to this approach have been noted. Higginson et al (1994), for example, suggest that, while relatives' retrospective assessments of service provision are valid, their assessments of pain, symptoms and anxiety are not. They also suggest that family members' views change over the period of bereavement.

To counter this view, we decided to undertake a prospective longitudinal study. We decided that, over a longer period, we would be able to explore the ways in which participants' lives changed and how their families and friends (as well as professionals) responded to their changing circumstances. We believed that the factors that influence older people's ability to gain access to sources of support and help when they need it can be better appreciated through exploring the processes they go through over a longer term. It is important to emphasise that the experiences of all participants, whether or not they may be considered as dying during the period of the research, are equally important. The focus was on establishing trends and patterns in the ways older people's lives change so that these can be better understood and prepared for.

Researching significant life events

We wished to explore prospectively events in the lives of participants that may be significant in terms of the circumstances of their eventual deaths. The focus on significant life events was a development of the concept of 'critical junctures' in the process of dying (Glaser and Strauss, 1968). Events such as bereavement, hospital admission or moving house are associated with an increased risk of death, but the nature of this association is often hard to establish (Harwood and Ebrahim, 1992; Ebrahim et al, 1995). While recognising that the significance of such events may be understood only in retrospect, our prospective approach enabled us to examine these as they occurred and, most importantly, to capture older people's own views of these rather than rely on the recollections of professionals or bereaved relatives.

Since we were interested in gathering data from older people's perspectives, it was necessary to develop appropriate qualitative instruments. One of the advantages of a longitudinal approach is that it provided opportunities for data gathering over a period of time. So, for example, on some days, participants may feel more inclined to engage with the researcher than on others. We also believed that a retrospective understanding of the significance of different events needs a long-term view. For example, the death of a pet might set off a number of adverse reactions on appetite, mental health, social and emotional life. A qualitative approach to interviewing older people has a good chance of allowing such information to emerge, particularly over a longer time frame.

The local research ethics committee

In compliance with the NHS Research Governance Framework, we applied to the relevant LREC for ethical approval. We were initially advised that committee members were concerned about the inclusion of people with dementia in the sample. Their concern centred on the issue of consent to participate. Their view was that, unless a person was able to give consent, they should be ruled out of the study. Our view was that, because dementia affects approximately 20% of people aged 80+ (DoH, 2001), we should include them. Otherwise, only a partial view of the lives of this age group would be gained. In order to begin fieldwork without delay, we negotiated a provisional agreement to invite only people that were able to give consent to join the study. Subsequently, the LREC decided we could proceed as originally intended with a 'close relative' or 'close friend' giving consent where an older person was unable to do this.

Concerns were also raised about the content of our questionnaire. Some committee members considered that asking for information about income, housing tenure, and so on, was not relevant to our study and was too intrusive. We argued the relevance of these factors for health and well-being and pointed to the large number of studies where such information was gathered. Approval was subsequently granted five months after our initial submission.

Ongoing consent

The issue of obtaining ongoing consent from participants is always an important consideration in longitudinal research. Researchers should not assume that participants remain happy to be involved in a project over a long period particularly when, as in this case, the research touches on potentially sensitive issues. It was also important to secure ongoing consent with this specific research population because for some participants there may be an increase in mental impairment during the course of the study.

In terms of an individual's ability to consent, the research team developed an 'informal rule' that if the older person remembered the interviewer when they spoke to them and remembered the research, then we were happy that they were able to consent. Indeed, in reality the majority of participants remembered exactly who we were and were expecting us to contact them. We recognised that it was essential to ensure that participants were still willing to be involved at each stage of the project and took action where necessary. For example, if at any stage during the study the researchers had concerns about an individual's ability to consent, a home visit was arranged at a time when someone else was present.

Sampling, recruitment and response rates

Clearly, it would be both unethical and impractical to attempt to identify potential participants who are likely to die but who are not 'terminally ill' in the accepted sense. While our intention was to be as inclusive as possible, and achieve a sample of all those older people aged 80+, we wanted to ensure that the potential risks to participants were minimised. With that in mind, participants for the study were selected from the patient list of two GP practices in Bristol and, although no formal exclusion criteria for the study were set, GPs were asked to examine the list to determine whether they felt anyone had grounds for exclusion. For example, two people were excluded on the grounds that they had a terminal diagnosis.

In accordance with the LREC requirements, recruitment for participation with the study was based on an 'opting-in' model. The selected older people were approached with a letter of introduction from the GP practice, explaining the aims of the research and what they could expect from participating in the study, a Patient Information Sheet and a reply form. A reminder letter was sent to those who had not responded within two weeks, although the reminder letter had only a limited impact. The final sample for the study was 96 individuals, which was comprised of 55% older people under the age of 85 years and 45% aged 85+ (the average age was 85 years).

Attrition

During the fieldwork period, the aim was to achieve the baseline interview and four follow-up interviews, covering a total period of between eight and nine months for each participant. Over the year, only two participants decided to leave the study. One left due to health problems necessitating hospitalisation, then a nursing home placement, and their spouse did not wish to continue with the study. The second participant who left did so due to domestic circumstances, which made telephone follow-up interviews difficult to conduct.

Overall, six of the participants died during the fieldwork period. A protocol was developed for responding to these deaths, which addressed issues such as sending condolences, the appropriateness, timing and sensitivity of any follow-up interviews with the next of kin and putting in place the necessary administrative arrangements for access to GP and hospital records, and interviewing health and social care professionals. However, the experience of following up these deaths led us to the conclusion that decisions surrounding follow-ups with next of kin need to be taken on a case-by-case basis. For example, the daughter of a 102-year-old woman living in a nursing home was interviewed and spoke calmly about the prospect of her mothers' death:

> "I know she can't go on for ever. I won't grieve for her when she does die. She's had a good life and she says she'd like to go in her sleep now."

Shortly afterwards, the project team was informed that the woman had fallen and was in traction in hospital. She died 11 days later in the hospital. Due to the distressing period of hospitalisation, the nursing home staff advised the team not to contact the daughter until after the funeral. Although we would ideally have wanted to gain prospective information from the daughter about the period leading up to death, we were led to believe that this was not appropriate in this case. While the researchers were guided by this advice, it does illustrate the tensions that exist between wanting to learn as much as possible about the circumstances of the death and the need to be sensitive to the emotions of the next of kin. This example also illustrates the role within research of intermediaries or 'gate keepers', in this case the nursing home staff.

Approach to data gathering

Baseline interviews and follow-up contact

Detailed face-to-face interviews were conducted with older people when they first entered the study. These interviews were conducted in older people's own homes at a time and day to suit them and took an average of 75 minutes. The interview schedule included a lot of open questions to enable older people to put forward their own perspectives and talk about issues that they felt to be important. However, it also included the use of some standard validated measures, such as the GHQ12 (or General Health Questionnaire, a standardised measure of psychiatric morbidity). Information gathered during the interview included demographic information; family and support networks; health status; use of health services and social services; activities of daily living and instrumental activities of daily living; types of help and support received; significant events in the past year; quality of life issues and plans, worries or fears for the future. After the baseline interview, each participant was followed-up every two months with a short telephone interview. In instances where a significant life event had occurred, such as a fall, hospitalisation, a new diagnosis (such as Parkinson's), close bereavement or house-move a longer face-to-face interview was conducted.

Contact with professionals

A key aim of the research was to examine health and social care professionals' responses to older people's needs and their decision-making processes in relation to significant events. An initial procedure was set up in the two participating GP practices whereby GPs and district nurses would alert the research team when an event that they felt was significant occurred. It became apparent that the procedure was not working effectively for a variety of reasons, including different administrative systems between the GP practices, recording locum visits and telephone calls, differing interpretations about what constitutes a 'significant event', and workload pressures. In the majority of instances, the researchers were alerted to significant or non-routine events through the follow-up interviews with participants (although at times this was later than we would have wished).

Gaining information from different sources was a useful strategy for identifying different perspectives on a range of events. However, it also raised an ethical issue: all participants gave consent for the research team to have access to medical and social services records. At times, the information that came to our attention via the records contradicted the accounts of the participants. For example, in one case, medication for depression had been increased. In another, a participant consulted the GP and was prescribed medication for a newly-emerged health problem. In both these cases, the participants had said that there were no changes to their health.

The protocol we developed was to ensure that participants were reminded regularly that they had given permission for us to look at their records and to give them the opportunity to share information with us, but not to raise the matter of what we had discovered in their records. We took the view that this would be inappropriate, because participants may feel coerced into giving an explanation.

The importance of qualitative interviews

The interviews carried out over the year demonstrate the importance of qualitative interviews in terms of illuminating a story; this was particularly evident with regards participants' use of hospital outpatient services. During the fieldwork period, 13% of the sample of older people had an inpatient stay in hospital and 5% visited accident and emergency. In the vast majority of these instances, older people themselves spontaneously mentioned these during the follow-up telephone calls. However, nearly half (44%) had visited hospital as an outpatient during the study. In many cases, older people did not spontaneously mention outpatient visits to the hospital when we asked about things that had happened in their lives in the intervening period between interviews. Older people often had to be prompted before providing information on these visits; they were not always thought to be significant. It appears that, for some older people, their worries and concerns about their health were more important than the visit to hospital for tests and they spoke more about their feelings than the events that had taken place.

Reflections on the methodology

Participants' reactions to the baseline interview

One of the aims of the pilot was to identify any adverse effects on participants from taking part in the project. The older people generally appeared willing and interested in answering the majority of questions at the baseline interview. There were no particular areas of the interview where significant proportions of older people were either unwilling or unable to provide responses. The vast majority of older people were willing to be interviewed and many expressed their enjoyment either at the end of the interview or at the follow-up telephone calls. One participant commented:

> "It's been good to talk to you. You probably think I'm being silly, but you've listened to it all. I'm not sure what you're getting out of this, or if I've been any help, but I've enjoyed our chats."

The final part of the baseline interview was a validated cognitive impairment assessment (6CIT[1]). Despite some initial concerns within the research team, that conducting the test might undermine the rapport developed between the interviewer and older person, our concerns were not generally borne out. The majority of older people were happy to take part in this exercise and it did not effect their continued involvement in the project. Indeed, as interviewing progressed, the research team felt it necessary to tell participants that this was not a speed exercise and they could take as long as necessary to answer the questions.

Even for those older people who were unable to complete all of the tasks in the cognitive impairment exercise, the interviewers did not detect any negative consequences, although a few older people did exhibit a defensive response, such as "I have never been any good with names", when they were unable to remember the details of the exercise.

There were only three instances where the interview process appeared to have had a negative effect. In one case, an 88-year-old man was unable to answer many of the questions at the baseline interview due to memory problems and exhibited some anxiety while carrying out the mental impairment assessment. It was determined at subsequent contact with his spouse that the participant had increasing memory problems and was worried that the purpose of the interview was to assess his ability to live independently. At a later date, we learnt that the man had been taken into hospital with viral pneumonia and that his wife was trying to find a long-term care home for him. His wife subsequently decided to withdraw from the study because she was finding caring for her husband stressful. In the second instance, the participant was happy with the interview process, but their spouse questioned the purpose of the research to the extent of becoming verbally abusive which made further contact difficult. These two cases reinforce the importance of clear information for participants and their relatives, which is presented in a way that is useful and accessible to them as a reference throughout the research, not only at the point of recruitment. In the third case, the participant herself talked about the effect of the baseline interview at subsequent interviews:

> "I wanted to tell you that following the interview I was quite depressed. I am over it now and I talked to my doctor about it. I think the questions made me think about things more than I usually would."

The GPs involved in the research did not report any increased anxiety or consultations with GPs as a result of participation in the study. However, at follow-up interviews, a small minority of respondents have reported that the initial interview led them to either thinking about issues that they normally try not to think about, or considering issues in greater depth than previously; for example, about what they would do if they were ill and unable to get out of bed. Whether the research process has a negative impact on participants is a concern that all researchers must address. However, it is probably more obvious for those working in sensitive topic areas or in longitudinal studies, particularly when, as in this case, a deliberate attempt is made to ask participants to reflect on the process of involvement. The interviewers working on this study were encouraged to reflect on the content and style of the interviews and alter these if they were perceived by participants to be too intrusive. In the end, no substantive changes were made. It was also important for the interviews to emphasise the on-going nature of the consent process so that participants understood that they could refuse to take any further part in the project.

Changes in nature of follow-up over time

Over the year that this research project lasted, the relationship between the researchers and many of the participants developed. The telephone calls were received positively and many older people were expecting to hear from the research team. As the fieldwork continued, many older people began to talk about wider issues, other than just health problems that many assumed we were primarily interested in. It was possible to overcome participants' original assumptions about the types of events we wanted to hear about as time progressed.

For a significant minority of participants, the developing relationship resulted in older people revealing more personal details during subsequent interviews. For example, a 95-year-old widow who had been living abroad but was "enticed" back to Britain by a relative following a diagnosis of cancer and a subsequent colostomy described how she regretted the move and had never really settled. She had lived in a total of five residential homes since moving back. All contact was by necessity face-to-face, as this participant had poor hearing. At the third follow-up visit, when asked about going out socially, she spoke for the first time of the distress and discomfort of being incontinent, saying "I get so wet it's very uncomfortable. I have asked the GP if there is anything I can use that will help but he didn't suggest anything 'modern', only what I already use". At the fourth and final interview she talked about the difficulty she has managing her personal care with a colostomy.

> "The other problem is my colostomy. They told me once I had moved in that this was only a residential home and that if we required nursing care we should have to go! So I have to be very careful to keep my condition in check and be very careful with what I eat. I have had to clean the carpet with a toilet brush and hot soapy water before now. [Could you not have asked the staff?] *I* had to do it – the staff wouldn't."

This interview extract was insightful and graphically demonstrates the lengths to which an older person would go in order to preserve their independence. Potentially, there could have been some tension between balancing the confidentiality of the participant against a duty of care if we felt she was at risk. However, in this instance, our respect for the participants wish to remain autonomous outweighed any sense that she was 'at risk'.

At the final follow-up interview, participants were asked about how their experiences of taking part in the research and their responses were very positive. One older person described the process as "A most agreeable inquisitor", while another said, "It's been nice to let off steam. I wouldn't talk to my GP or family this way". While it is impossible for us, in retrospect, to know why they found the experience positive, it may be that our participants welcomed the opportunity to discuss their health and well-being in this on-going manner.

Including supporters for participants

Partly as a result of our experience of gaining ethical approval, we have decided that in future research we should include as part of the sample at least one other person in each participant's family or social network. Participants will be invited to nominate a relative or friend who can be contacted for information in the event of changes in the participant's circumstances and these contacts will be required to provide formal consent to take part. This will not only help to alleviate anxieties about the position of frail or confused older people in the research; rather, it will also reduce the difference in our approach to those with dementia by including nominees of *all* potential participants as part of the general research process and will improve ongoing contact with those who become frail during data gathering.

Such ongoing participation is valuable to the process as illustrated in the following case example. An 82-year-old man (Mr M), who had been diagnosed with Parkinson's, was originally interviewed with his wife present throughout.

During the interview, he became tired and was happy for his wife to help answer some of the questions. At the first follow-up telephone contact, his wife reported that her husband had been admitted to hospital and was unable to come home as he was confused and having balance problems. Since his wife had been present in the initial interview and knew about the research, the researchers asked if she was happy to continue her involvement in the study. Since then all follow-up contact has been with Mrs M, and we asked her to sign a consent form, which she duly did. In this way we have been able to keep abreast of developments. We know that Mr M had a six-week stay in hospital; then, after six weeks at home, went into a nursing home (for ten days) so that his wife could have respite care as she found it hard to cope with his confusion and "wilfulness". She then fell and broke her arm and the only place that could be found for Mr M was a nursing home across the city, where he remained till the end of the study. This next of kin contact has been invaluable in providing a clearer picture of these events of the past eight months, but it does raise wider questions about the nature of consent – and proxy consent in particular. In this study, proxy consent raised methodological and epistemological issues due to the way in which the autonomy of the participants, and role of carer proxy consent-givers, was also the subject of the research. The example given earlier illustrates how, pragmatically and ethically, it is important to include secondary participants. Rather than take a very narrow view of autonomy as relating to the individual, it has been important in this study to consider the autonomy of the participants as part of a wider social network where dependence is more important than individualism. For example, the relationship that a participant has with their support networks or carers can have a major impact on their ability to assert independence. As such, the autonomy perspective we have taken in relation to proxy consent-giving is consistent with the lived experiences of the participants.

Conclusions

This pilot study has proved invaluable in demonstrating how issues about end of life in old age can be researched in a sensitive and inclusive manner. The ethical challenges in researching vulnerable groups, such as older people, are not to be underestimated, in particular, the ethical issues around including subgroups such as older people with dementia. From the outset, it was our contention that this group has particular needs relating to health and social care and that these could be understood both objectively through the use of standard measures but also subjectively through interviews. Not to include older people with dementia and their carers would effectively have excluded their voices, a position that the research team regarded as inappropriate and unethical.

The opportunity to reflect on the appropriateness of methods used in this pilot has helped us refine our approach before commencing a larger longitudinal study. In particular, the study has confirmed the importance of a longitudinal approach to this area of research, allowing the researchers to build up a rapport with individual participants and their carers. This approach appears to be acceptable to older people: it offers them the opportunity to discuss any concerns they have about the research with the research team while our approach to on-going consent means that they are free to withdraw from the study at any time. The on-going nature of our work also helped ensure that researchers avoid the traps which occur because of expectations, in this case that the older people sometimes presumed that we were only interested in a very narrow definition of health and well-being. Over time, participants became familiar with our broader notion of health and the data suggests that they felt comfortable discussing their experiences. Our decision to include carers or nominated representatives in the formal consenting process has also helped us gather richer and more detailed information than might otherwise have been the case.

Acknowledgements

Funding for the study was received from the Nuffield Foundation on the basis that this would be a pilot study to test and refine our prospective, longitudinal mixed methodological approach prior to undertaking a larger study.

Note

[1] The 6 Item Cognitive Impairment Test (6CIT) is a screening tool developed to assess cognition and memory loss. It was originally developed as a cognitive test suitable for primary care usage and was chosen for use in this study due to its brief and non-intrusive nature.

References

Addington-Hall, J.M. and McCarthy, M. (1995) 'Regional study of care for the dying: methods and sample characteristics', *Palliative Medicine*, vol 9, pp 27-35.

Addington-Hall, J.M., Fakhoury, W. and McCarthy, M. (1998) 'Specialist palliative care in non-malignant disease', *Palliative Medicine*, vol 9, pp 295-305.

DoH (Department of Health) (1998) *Modernising social services: Promoting independence, improving protection, raising standards*, Cm 4169, London: The Stationery Office.

DoH (2001) *The National Service Framework for Older People*, London: DoH.

Ebrahim, S., Wanamethee, G., Walker, M. and Shaper, A.G. (1995) 'Marital status, change in marital status and mortality in middle-aged British men', *American Journal of Epidemiology*, vol 142, pp 834-42.

Glaser, B. and Strauss, A. (1968) *Time for dying*, Chicago, IL: Aldine.

Harper, S. (2000) 'Ageing 2000: questions for the 21st century', *Ageing and Society*, vol 20, no 1, pp 111-22.

Harwood, R.H. and Ebrahim, S. (1992) 'Is relocation harmful to institutionalised elderly people?', *Age and Ageing*, vol 21, pp 61-6.

Henwood, M. (2001) *Future imperfect? Report of the King's Fund Care and Support Inquiry*, London: King's Fund.

Higginson, I., Priest, P. and McCarthy, M. (1994) 'Are bereaved family members a valid proxy for a patient's assessment of dying?', *Social Science and Medicine*, vol 38, no 4, pp 553-7.

Lloyd, L. (2000) 'Dying in old age: promoting wellbeing at the end of life', *Mortality*, vol 5, no 2, pp 171-88.

Royal Commission on Long Term Care (1999) *With respect to old age: Long term care: rights and responsibilities*, London: The Stationery Office.

Seale, C. and Cartwright, A. (1994) *The year before death*, Avebury: Aldershot.

Part Three:
Researchers' relationships
with participants

SEVEN

Interviewing: the unspoken compact

Jean Rafferty

Introduction

My ethical approach developed before I knew about the National Union of Journalists' (NUJ) Code of Conduct, before I ever understood the pitfalls of the industry I was working in. I can speak only for myself. As a freelance journalist, I have written for many different publications, from the *Sunday Times Magazine* to the *Sunday People* newspaper. If any of them had a house policy on matters of research, I did not know about it.

Investigative journalism

I consider bearing witness to be one of the most important functions of investigative journalism, not just about the public events of politics and society, the wrongs that need righting, but about the personal things, the human things that touch us all. What does it feel like to have a terminal illness, or to lose a child? What leads a person to torture another or to commit suicide? These experiences of the darker side of being human are often airbrushed out of newspapers, whose editors are driven by the twin imperatives, first, of hanging on to circulation, and second, of hanging on to their jobs.

Investigative journalism holds an uneasy position in the world of newspapers. On the one hand, it embodies the virtues that most people associate with the romantic image of the journalist as crusader. One thinks of Hollywood films such as *All the President's Men*, which dealt with the Watergate affair and which featured Robert Redford as one of the most good-looking men ever to grace a newsroom. This type of journalism is seen as high-minded, driven by idealism, and the journalists are seen as incorruptible. It can expose wrongdoing even at the highest levels of society, uncovering truths that vested interests would prefer suppressed. It is the reason that society tolerates many of the excesses of less serious journalism.

On the other hand, it has become seriously devalued in newspaper circles, because it takes too long, devours too many of a publication's resources and leads to risky legal cases. Apart from an elite few journalists, who are given huge resources on the basis of their reputation, those who practise it are given less money, less prestige and less interest from editors, despite the fact that the best investigative journalism can add thousands to a paper's circulation, as Watergate enhanced the circulation and reputation of the *Washington Post*.

Truth, knowledge, and communication

Investigative journalism differs from academic and medical research in its immediate consumption by the public. Unless the public reads it, it is worthless, whereas academic research can be lodged in libraries or circulated through the medium of lectures. Academic work often only reaches the public through the mediation of the journalist. The groundbreaking linguistic work of Deborah Tannen, for example, was a modest success compared to the worldwide best-seller, John Gray's *Men are from Mars, Women are from Venus*, which covered much the same ground but presented it in a populist way.

Where academics focus on a limited part of a wider field, attempting to reveal verifiable evidence of a piece of information or insight, journalism's first task is to *communicate* that knowledge or insight. Journalists break down the information they gather in a different way from that of academics, which is both deductive and reductive. The traditional view of academic research (although this has begun to change) is that it deduces common patterns from research and presents them in terms of facts and statistics. Working to this pattern, academic researchers reduce the material they have gathered to a narrow conclusion, based on what they consider to be the facts they have 'proved'. They discard what they consider to be soft or unproved information, such as anecdotal evidence from witnesses who claim to have experienced something first hand, although in fact anecdotal evidence is the basis not only for much of journalism but for much of what is presented in our courts.

Investigative journalists too are under an obligation to 'prove' their case by using reliable material, but they use the material they have gathered primarily to present a narrative. Rather than reducing their material to come to a conclusion, they often come to a conclusion about a wider situation by extrapolating from limited material, an expansionist rather than reductive technique. Where an academic will interview 300 prostitutes in Glasgow to prove that over 90% are addicted to heroin, a journalist will interview one and use her experiences to convey the reality of what that means and feels like. In journalism, the one stands in for the many.

For that reason, journalists often use academic statistics to lend credence to their stories, as academics use case studies to lend credence and life to their statistics. Each relies on core material gathered by the other's method as back-up evidence for the validity of their own method. In fact, nowadays academics use ethnography and qualitative methods, and their operations have more in common with journalism than either journalists or academics might be comfortable admitting. There are, perhaps, fewer differences between us now than before.

The public

The journalist's way of presenting material obviously has a much more immediate and emotional effect on the public. The story is the most powerful and ancient tool we have for disseminating information and is one of the reasons the mass media reach people in a way that academic research does not. Journalism is a collective form, shared by the whole of society. The products of journalism are accessible to society as a whole, and indeed are driven by society. Not only do newspapers consult their readers about what they want to read through focus groups and other market research, they also use input from the public at every stage of the process. Many articles come from readers' tip-offs, and most would not be possible without interviews with members of the public, who provide human interest and authenticity to an article. Journalists often actively seek the public's opinion, adding people's comments to the end of contentious articles or recording the results of vox pops in the street. Academic and medical research may ultimately benefit the whole of society, but is initially shared by an elite. It may never reach the wider public, whereas journalism exists only for that purpose.

Interviewing informants

There are a number of issues which for me affect the relationship between journalist and interviewee: power; the political environment of the newspapers in which journalists have to operate; the nature of the story and interviewee; and the role and motivation of the journalist.

Power and the process of journalism

The interview is not naturally an equal transaction. Journalists have more chance of controlling the process because they are trained to do so, whereas the interviewee may never have previously spoken to a journalist. The more ruthless might all too easily exploit the public for their stories, simply seeing them as pawns in the larger purpose of writing about an issue. On the surface it looks an exploitative process. Journalists pump people for information, drain them emotionally, and then discard them. Indeed, most journalists cover so many different stories that it would be difficult to satisfy the needs of every interviewee. It is easy to forget the courtesies – telling people when the piece will appear, checking that you have reported things accurately and so on.

The way to avoid exploitation lies, I believe, in what Martin Bell calls the "journalism of attachment", a recognition that no writer or broadcaster can be truly objective; rather, we are all bound up in thought systems that we may not even be aware of. Martin Bell was referring specifically to the writing or broadcasting of material, but I believe the journalism of attachment extends to the interview too.

It is a common technique of journalists to empathise with interviewees, to make them feel safe, that they are not being judged. I have even cried with people as they told me about their lives. It is hard not to, when a woman tells you about her husband's head being crushed with a boulder by Afghani mujahideen, or a mother mourns her dead child. It would be cynical in the extreme to embark on that kind of intimate human exchange in a spirit of exploitation, although no doubt there are some journalists who are capable of it. Just as Arthur Miller says, there is a promise made in every bed (*The Crucible*), there is a promise made in every interview: that the journalist will be aware of the impact of their words on the person to whom they have just spoken. Many people share deeply upsetting experiences with journalists because they want their story to have a wider audience or they want an issue discussed. They depend on the journalist to disseminate the story on their behalf, just as the journalist depends on the interviewee for raw material.

This mutual dependence leads to an implicit contract between interviewer and interviewee. In return for telling the journalist intimate details of their life, the journalist pledges to bear witness to them in as truthful a manner as possible. A deal is made, whether financial or otherwise, between two people who both have something to offer.

'Getting' the story

The public image of the journalist is as manipulator and exploiter, extracting personal details from people for the sake of a big splash in the newspaper or a front-page headline.

There are plenty of bloodsuckers working in the press; they exploit people at their most vulnerable in order to get a story, hang about in the bushes outside their houses and pester them to talk; they refuse to take no for an answer. This kind of coercion may be part of the compact celebrities make with the press, in order to gain positive publicity. However, unless there is a huge public interest concern, it is not acceptable with private members of the public. Public concern about such intrusion in the past has exerted such pressure on the press that more and more journalists are suspending competitive practices and agreeing to pooling arrangements at times of disasters. The stereotype of the exploitative journalist fails to recognise that sometimes a person actually wants to break out of their privacy and talk. When that happens, the journalist has to engage with them at a deep human level.

The journalist is often the recipient of confidences that the person has never told anyone before, things that would take months of teasing out with a social worker or counsellor or those other professionals who also deal with extremes of human emotion. The compact between journalist and interviewee differs from these in that the newspaper industry is deadline-driven and the journalist usually has to extract information in a very restricted time.

The counsellor's aims are therapeutic: the information is expected to emerge at a time when the interviewee is emotionally ready. The interviewee's emotional readiness is taken for granted by the journalist, whose aim is not therapeutic.

There is an implicit understanding that the transaction is not about therapy, but about communication to a wider audience, about bringing situations or issues to public attention. Trust has to be established very quickly for the process of disclosure to be short-circuited in this way. This makes the journalist–interviewee relationship a pressure cooker. The telling of the story is telescoped, even if the interview takes as long as 24 hours. This has occasionally happened to me, usually where child sexual abuse was concerned. What was being said in one day would normally have emerged piecemeal over a long period of time.

There is a tacit understanding that the person telling the story must try to present reality as they see it in its totality and not prevaricate or protect themselves, as they might be tempted to do in a more therapeutic setting. Ironically, that in itself can be therapeutic for interviewees, enabling them to see the patterns in their story, sometimes for the first time, even though this is not the primary purpose of the interview. There is often a sense of striving for wholeness, a scrupulousness that informs in-depth interviews. I believe it springs from the joint commitment of both journalist and interviewee to bear witness to a particular truth. It is not just the two of them present in the room, as is the case with psychiatrists and counsellors; rather, the outside world is there in the room too, as an understood element of the process. The journalist's job is to communicate the story and, for that, the interviewee must move from shared contemplation of a private world to sharing that world with the public.

This is particularly true of 'death knock' interviews, when someone has just died. Younger journalists are often afraid to do this for fear of intruding into private feelings, but if the person agrees, it is a privilege. If they do not, the journalist should simply accept that and leave, although I see no ethical problem with sending a follow-up letter requesting an interview at a later date. Those who *are* prepared to talk to the press at the most difficult time of their life want the world to know that the person they have just lost was worth mourning. They want the world to know who that person was. Somehow they feel that if it is in the newspapers or on the television, it proves that they are right to grieve as they do.

I was once sent out by *Sunday Today* newspaper to investigate the murder of two elderly sisters in Manchester. Susie and Florrie Egerton had been brutally battered to death in their own home. The police were releasing no details other than that Susie was 92 years of age, Florrie was 81, and the attack was bloody. There were a number of journalists in the street looking for people to talk to, but eventually they went away and I was on my own when the sisters' niece, Barbara Watson, arrived at the little terraced house. Susie and Florrie had paid her way through teacher training college, so when they became too frail to cope entirely on their own, she popped in every day to visit them.

What surprised me was that, rather than being angry at my presence, Barbara was eager to talk. She loved her aunts and wanted to tell me – and through me, other people – what they were like. Susie was clever and adventurous and had often worked away from home; Florrie was timid and quiet; in later life she became rather forgetful after a serious illness. They were both independent and kind, adhering still to the more community-minded values of a previous age. It was extremely moving to hear how well these old ladies had lived, who had died so terribly. I felt that Barbara Watson had given me a gift in telling me about them and I in turn had a responsibility to tell others.

People and stories

As was mentioned earlier, the driving force of journalism is communication. Whether it is a fact, an opinion or even just a funny story, journalism requires it to be delivered to a wider audience. In fact I believe that the primary duty of the journalist is to the story and that wider audience, not to the person interviewed or even to the editor. It is taken for granted that interviewees understand this.

This approach is not usually a problem when journalist and interviewee share the same view of the nature of the story. For example, in 2002 I interviewed an extremely religious woman, Bernadette Roberts, about bereavement for *The Observer Magazine*. Her son Matthew had died in a motorbike accident. At first we talked about the material things, the way she wanted his dressing gown because it contained his smell; the beer mats and bar paraphernalia he had rigged up in his room for fun. But gradually Bernadette began to talk about her spiritual experiences of bereavement. Knowing I was not a believer in God or the afterlife, she still needed to convey the visions she had seen of her son, the dream farewell where he had said goodbye to her after his death. Although we both believed different things, together we came to a joint and respectful understanding of her grief. It was equally important to us both that the article reflect the whole of her story and not just the parts that the public – or the writer – would consider comfortable.

In such a situation, where there are no public interest considerations, the journalist should avoid causing further hurt to the interviewee, who is already sharing a painful experience. In other situations, the relationship between journalist and interviewee is less benign. Interviewees are not always satisfied with a journalist's approach to a story – inevitably, given that journalism is a process of selection governed by the writer's own beliefs and feelings. Sometimes the public interest is in conflict with what the interviewee is trying to convey. For example, one would not necessarily accept a Mafia member's version of events. I am not suggesting a two-tier system where one treats 'good' people one way and 'bad' people in another – that, in fact, would work against the journalist's interests. Only by treating murderers and thugs with common decency and respect is one likely to gain their trust – and therefore their story.

It would, however, be disingenuous to pretend that the journalist is always totally honest in investigative situations. I believe it would be morally acceptable – and indeed politic – to say that one accepted the Mafia member's version of events, even if one did not. Such a lie is the sort that permeates our social life anyway. In this case, the public interest value of the story outweighs the personal hurt to the Mafia member.

I once worked undercover in an old people's home, where the experience of being on the premises for eight hours at a time was far more revealing than any inspection visit could be. I had no compunction about deceiving fellow members of staff. Their behaviour towards the old people in their care was so unkind and humiliating that I felt it should be exposed. The newspaper, *The People*, was asking the one thing that did give me pause for thought: to take pictures. Many of the residents were suffering from dementia; they were confused and sad, unable to remember exactly where they were. Since I believed it was very important to get the story of the old people's treatment out to a wider public, I agreed to take the pictures. It was an upsetting experience, pointing the camera at an uncomprehending and fearful old lady, but I believed that the story was too important to let her distress, which I assumed would be temporary, stand in the way.

For me, however, the difficulty in the situation was emotional rather than ethical. My justification lies in the NUJ Code of Conduct:

> [the] journalist shall obtain information, photographs and illustrations only by straightforward means. The use of other means can be justified only by over-riding considerations of the public interest.

Exposing the abuses that go on in old people's homes is clearly covered by such considerations.

For many people, however, the problem in this is that the journalist defines the public interest. This suspicion is a luxury, born of living in a Western democracy. In many countries, the public interest is defined by dictatorial government and there is no opportunity for the media to expose the truth. Obviously some journalists in this country abuse their ability to speak out freely, quoting public interest arguments when really they are talking about public curiosity. This is the price we have to pay if we are to have a free press, able to discuss government policy and actions without fear of reprisals. Post-Hutton, that freedom has taken a battering, with the resignation of Greg Dyke in particular. The sight of BBC staff actually standing up and supporting a director-general bore witness not only to the high personal regard in which Dyke was held, but to their concern for the future of editorial independence.

In practical terms, subterfuge is an essential part of undercover work, and is usually necessary for the writer to establish the truth of the story. This is the case not only in journalism but also in some academic research, particularly in the field of armed conflict and researching insurgent movements. Adopting conventional methods just does not achieve the same results. A couple of years ago, I did an undercover investigation into a homeless hostel in Glasgow. The hostel was a disgrace and was closed down some time afterwards. Simply phoning up and asking the council would just have produced a string of excuses, as I found out when I phoned them up *after* having done my research.

Even the tabloids, with their love of exposing public figures, rarely take on undercover work unless they are sure the resulting article will expose something that should be exposed. One may not appreciate their public spiritedness in exposing the contents of the bins of the famous, but their reporting on criminal activity and fraud is far more proactive and powerful than that of the broadsheets. The main problem with the use of subterfuge, it seems to me, is not its morality but the practicality of carrying it out. Sustaining a role – that is, remembering the details of a fabricated life – is not easy.

Personally, I would find it difficult to do as Martin Bashir did, and behave sycophantically and dishonestly with Michael Jackson over a period of months in the making of the Granada documentary 'Living with Michael Jackson', although it was clearly the only way to get Jackson to trust the reporter enough to let him film. One may sympathise as a person with the sense of betrayal felt by Jackson, but as a journalist I feel that the deception was justified. The story was in the public interest not only because of Jackson's popularity and therefore influence over young people, but also for his continued contact with young children at his home, Neverland. Martin Bashir's responsibility was to communicate the story, not to spare Michael Jackson's feelings.

The irony is that, despite his hostile agenda, Bashir's film actually did a great deal for Jackson's credibility, because it let us see the human being underneath the image. Over 50% of the UK audience watching that night thought that Jackson's relationships with children were innocent. Now that the singer has been charged with child sexual abuse, we have more chance of assessing, not necessarily whether he is guilty, but why he behaves the way he does. Telling the story, even in a negative way, opened up new information for the public.

The realpolitik of journalism

Machinations which would not be out of place in a Medici court go on all the time: journalists jostle for power and promote the work of their friends, while the management of many papers deliberately set colleagues against each other. It is not unknown for two people to be appointed to the same post to see which of them comes out on top. The competitiveness is not just internal but external too, with different publications constantly striving to beat each other to the same material. *The Observer*'s famous celebrity interviewer, Lynn Barber, recalled chatting for 20 minutes to Andrew Billen, an interviewer for a rival paper, before he told her that the person they had both come to see had said to send her straight up. He was a friend but had managed to decimate her interview time with the celebrity interviewee.

The competitive ethos that permeates the industry can lead the journalist to ignore the human needs of the interviewee and concentrate on satisfying the editor. There is constant pressure on the journalist to get the story, any story, as is attested by the death of Sky News reporter James Forlong. Forlong committed suicide in October 2003 after he was exposed as having passed off library film as live. Although an award-winning journalist with many fine years as a foreign correspondent behind him, he was sacked from his job and found himself unable to find another. During the Iraqi conflict, he had secured an invitation to board nuclear submarine HMS Splendid, but because of security regulations was restricted in what he could report. He reported as if from the Persian Gulf, failing to mention that shots of missiles being launched from the submarine included library footage and were actually taken during an exercise. He lost his job, but the ridicule he received from rival journalists seems to have been even more painful for him. One even compared him to Damien Day, the fraudulent character from newspaper comedy, *Drop the Dead Donkey*. His sister-in-law, Christine Toomey, herself a fine writer, was excoriating in her condemnation of the media, which can, she said, "Be the most brutal of industries and never more so than when one of its own is wounded". It was, after all, a BBC television crew which exposed the error, not the Royal Navy.

On top of the brutal competitiveness of the industry, the writer also has to deal with the particular political ethos driving each publication. My failure to understand that led to the most difficult time in my life as a writer, a period when I was under contract to *Night and Day*, then an investigative magazine attached to the *Mail on Sunday*. (It is now a celebrity magazine.) The *Mail on Sunday* is an extremely right-wing publication, a champion for the values of both Middle England and the business community. However, the magazine's editor, Jocelyn Targett, had come from *The Guardian* and swore that we were independent, that we would not be bound by the politics of Associated Newspapers. My own beliefs are the opposite of the *Mail*'s, so I was naive enough to be relieved by this. I did not understand that however honourable the intentions of the editor, it is very difficult for any single person to work against the culture of a newspaper.

The first test came over Rwanda. Jocelyn Targett sent me to Zaire in 1994, when a million Rwandan refugees were camped on the volcanic lava of Goma after weeks of genocide in their own country. The trip came about because the *Mail on Sunday* newspaper had been offered a seat on a charity plane going there. Their editor had refused it, on the grounds that that sort of thing would not interest their readers. I spent nine days there, talking to Hutus, aid workers, Tutsis, doctors, and Interahamwe soldiers and, with Jocelyn Targett's encouragement, produced a lengthy piece that ran to 7,000 words. He was then told not to run the story by the group's editor-in-chief, David English, who had not read it but felt that *Mail* readers were not interested in "that sort of thing". The article eventually ran in severely truncated form, as one of ten articles in the end-of-year round-up (with a further chunk lopped off at the last minute when another advert came in).

Power and the editor

People outside the industry often fail to appreciate how little power the writer of a piece actually has. Interviewees believe that you write the headlines and you say how much space the story gets in the newspaper. These tasks are, of course, the province of other people and the journalist can be let down by them just as much as an interviewee can be let down by the journalist. If as a writer your views are not in tune with those of your newspaper, you struggle to have your work published, no matter what its quality. If it is not published, you have broken your part of the unspoken contract. The interviewee has given you the information and it is now your job to communicate that to the wider world, so there is a deep sense of failure for the journalist when that does not happen.

The reasons are usually to do with the newspaper's belief system. I was commissioned in 1996 to write an investigative piece for *Night and Day* about a satanic ritual abuse (SRA) case in Ayrshire. The *Mail on Sunday* had received press awards in the past for saying SRA did not exist and that the social workers who brought it to the public's attention were swayed by highly questionable American research. Knowing that, I checked that I would be free to write what I wanted. The commissioning editor said that whatever I discovered would be published. It was – about a year later in *The Guardian Weekend Magazine*.

SRA is a notoriously difficult thing to prove, and many newspapers have publicly and vociferously come to the conclusion that it does not exist. Short of being in the room with a child when it happened, I could not prove it existed either. But I could use interviews with experts and the children's own evidence in court to suggest that it did. It turned out to be terribly important to bear witness to its existence. Years later, I met a survivor of this form of abuse who told me that she had read the *Guardian Weekend* article and been deeply affected by its publication. She had passed it on to other people in her survivors' group. It was crucial to all of them to have their experience recognised and named, not, as had happened to many of them, dismissed as the product of their over-heated imaginations.

The current climate of opinion in newspapers, particularly the conservative ones, makes it almost impossible to discuss SRA from the point of view of its victims. You could write about wronged parents or obsessive social workers, but it would be very difficult to find an outlet for a discussion of the people who practise it or who claim to have suffered it. In this, newspapers are only reflecting current thinking in society. Not one of the cases of alleged multiple abusers has succeeded in court. As soon as one does, the silence on this subject will end, but for the moment it is rare to find an editor willing even to contemplate the idea that it might actually happen. Two years ago I was offered an interview with a survivor of SRA, a rare opportunity as most of them have been traumatised by the press's collective disbelief. I proposed it as a feature to *G2*, *The Guardian*'s daily features tabloid. "It's an important subject but not our style", said the commissioning editor. "It's not my bag", said *The Observer*, as if it was anyone's 'bag'. The young woman at *The Telegraph* said it sounded really interesting and she would get back to me. She did. "We couldn't possibly run something like that", she said.

What I have learned from this is that I will not interview a survivor of SRA without being sure I have a publication prepared to run the story. The process is too distressing for them; it throws their hard-won control of their own lives into jeopardy again. The public do not always realise that the journalist's part of the compact, communicating their story, will not necessarily be fulfilled straight away but perhaps at some unidentified point in the future or perhaps never. Journalists like myself, who work mainly for supplements rather than daily papers, sometimes have to wait for months before their work is published. However, all newspapers are run on such whimsical lines that the date, the layout, the context can change in an instant. With stories about SRA, the date sometimes never comes.

A further feature of journalism is the current cult of celebrity, which is deliberately inculcated by editors and the media industry in general. It fills up space in a sanitised, non-contentious way and pleases advertisers, who may not want their products displayed alongside such topics as grisly abortion wards in Albania or suicide in Cornton Vale, Scotland's women's prison (both subjects I have written about). In both cases, the publication that originally commissioned them refused to print them. They later appeared in others.

Copy approval

Some interviewees seek to protect themselves from the arbitrary nature of the way the press works by demanding copy approval. Like most of my profession, I find this an unacceptable attempt to control my opinions. To me, the interviewee's part of the process is over with the interview and it is then up to the journalist to fulfil his or her side of the bargain. The parallel between journalism and research here is with the independence of researchers, or academic freedom. I do, however, often show the interviewee the article in advance, although this is a practice editors dislike. If the person objects to something powerful in the piece, the editor then may feel obliged to cut out material that they would prefer to have in.

In one case, however, I did allow someone copy approval, believing that the person concerned would not object if I wrote the piece fairly, believing too that I *would* write the piece fairly. In 1991, Margaret Watson's 15-year-old daughter Diane was murdered in a Glasgow playground by 14-year-old fellow pupil Barbara Glover. Mrs Watson had been displeased with previous coverage, so when I went to her house, she was receptive to being interviewed. Her condition was that I should show her the piece before it went into the paper. If she disapproved, it would not go ahead.

During the course of my research, I was directed to interview various people by her. After a while, I felt I needed to speak to Barbara Glover's family too, so that the piece was not just from the Watson family perspective. At first Mr and Mrs Glover refused, but a follow-up letter convinced them that their daughter's point of view would be lost if they did not speak out. The resulting article had background information about both Diane Watson and the girl who killed her.

Mrs Watson read it unnervingly slowly, while I wondered what I would tell the editor of the *Sunday People* if she refused her approval. Luckily she found the piece fair and it went ahead the next day, but I have never given copy approval since. Mrs Watson would not have spoken to me at all if I had not agreed to it and I am afraid that my desire to write the story was so strong that it overrode the basic principle: journalists should not surrender their responsibility to tell the story as they see fit. In practice, of course, journalists make such compromises all the time. Specialist sports writers, for example, sometimes hold back from criticism of the sportsmen whose lives they follow. It would be simply too uncomfortable for them to be in constant contact with people they had condemned. That is why news writers are sent in when a big sporting scandal breaks; newspapers do not want to jeopardise their specialists' relationships with the players.

What I have also found is that many interviewees regret things they have said and later wish to sanitise the piece. It is not easy to predict what they will try to erase from the record. Sometimes they realise publication of some detail will hurt another person, but sometimes their request is simply vanity – they are afraid they will look bad. Occasionally they will even try to say after the fact that what they have just said is off the record. I find this unreasonable and use my own judgement about including such material when it comes to write the article. (Of course, if they have specified that beforehand, the journalist must abide by it, although it is common practice to use the material without attributing it to that person.) I do discuss these issues with people but, although I might feel sorry for them personally, my overriding responsibility is to produce work that is as powerful as I can make it. I would always make factual changes and would be open to suggestions, but I would not willingly dilute my own work.

Moral responsibility and sensitivity

Having said that, I do feel that as journalists we also have a duty not to be cavalier with people's lives. We have power and should not abuse it. Margaret Watson has battled constantly with the press since her daughter died and even blames two journalists for the suicide of her son, Alan, who killed himself in 1992, clutching copies of their articles in his hand. Recently, on the appointment of one of them to a Glasgow newspaper, she sent a vitriolic e-mail of protest to various media organisations.

Few would agree with Mrs Watson that the articles alone caused the death of her son. The torment of the survivor, living with the sadness of losing his sister and unable to assuage his parents' pain, is far more likely the cause. However, one of the journalists, in the course of protesting Barbara Glover's indeterminate sentence, actually attacked the character of the victim Diane Watson, implying she was snooty and the product of a 'white socks' background. Such comment is currently protected by the legal position that you cannot libel the dead, but even the most fervent supporter of press freedom would surely find such remarks appallingly insensitive to the bereaved Watsons.

As well as this emotional responsibility, we have a further responsibility to protect those who help us. This is a moral imperative, contained in both the NUJ Code of Conduct and that of the Press Complaints Commission. Our law does not, alas, back it up. In 1984, Peter Preston, the editor of *The Guardian*, published a story on the arrival of Cruise missiles at Greenham Common. The source was a young civil servant, Sarah Tisdall. When Preston refused to reveal her identity, *The Guardian* was threatened with sequestration. A braver editor might have stood out against the Appeal Court, which would surely have shocked the British public had it carried out its threat effectively to close down a major national newspaper. However, Preston handed over the relevant documents and Sarah Tisdall was sentenced to six months in prison.

More recent governments have been equally dismissive of the journalist's responsibility to protect sources, as the suicide of Dr David Kelly in 2003 demonstrates. Leaking his name through allowing journalists to guess his identity by a process of elimination was surely one of the most cynical acts by any government and seems to have led directly to his death. Early in 2004, Paul Mahon, a postgraduate student of journalism, allowed himself to be pressured by government into revealing confidential sources to the Bloody Sunday Inquiry. They were not even Paul Mahon's sources to reveal. Lena Ferguson, now the BBC's head of political programming in Northern Ireland, and her colleague Alex Thomson had made the recordings, of interviews with five soldiers, for Channel 4 News. Both have refused to release the identities of the soldiers and have been threatened with contempt of court by the tribunal chairman Lord Saville. If convicted, they could face a jail sentence.

Ferguson had insisted on confidentiality to Mahon and had no recollection of even allowing him to tape the recordings. She and Thomson are resolute about their duty to protect sources and are bitter about what Thomson calls "an appalling and grotesque breach of trust". The breach of trust is not just between journalist and soldiers, but between fellow journalists. That is the norm, given the competitive nature of the profession, but the consequences here are potentially dangerous – even life threatening – to the soldiers, and life changing to the journalists. It is a shocking betrayal of journalistic ethics by Paul Mahon, who as a student has not even begun properly to practise his chosen profession.

Protecting sources is a practical necessity, in that otherwise much information would not come into the public domain. Without a guarantee of personal safety, few would come forward to talk about drug dealers, pimps or terrorists, to choose just a few topics from recent newspaper campaigns. More importantly, it is a moral duty. The compact to provide safety and anonymity in return for information is usually spoken, not unspoken as so many journalistic transactions are. Reneging on it is doubly wrong, a betrayal on both human and journalistic grounds.

Payment

The complex balancing of human and journalistic considerations is further complicated when you introduce money into the equation. I have always felt it tainted my compact with the interviewee. It introduced all sorts of questions, such as whether or not the information was worth the price paid, whether interviewees were telling as much as they knew, and whether the truth was being distorted for the sake of cash. My way of dealing with it was to divorce myself entirely from the exchange. To me, that was a compact between editors and the subject, and not the province of the journalist.

This may be because as a freelance I have no vested interest in value for the newspaper. I may be loyal to a particular editor, but my only real concern is my story. (Freelances are not really team players – staff journalists may think differently.) There seems no doubt that, in general, the payment of fees for interviews has seriously damaged media credibility. Press intervention in the Damilola Taylor trial, where the *Daily Mail* offered a young girl £50,000 for her story, caused the witness's evidence to be thrown out after the judge said the money was "an inducement" to her. In the Gary Glitter trial, and in that of Amy Gehring, the teacher accused of sexually abusing her pupils, newspapers offered payments of up to £10,000 to teenagers for their stories. The Press Complaints Commission's new ruling outlawing these payments is to be welcomed – such payments devalue the press, but they also devalue the price we put on the truth.

Interviewing Claire W, a member of the family at the heart of the Orkney ritual abuse case, proved for me that the basic currency of the compact between journalist and interviewee is not financial, but emotional. Claire was living on a very low income and demanded that the *Sunday Mirror* pay for her story. She may also have felt so cheated by her childhood, so devalued as a person, that the money was material proof that she was not worthless. Eventually the newspaper agreed a fee of £750.

Claire cancelled our first meeting; then, when we finally sat down in her living room she was just too anxious to speak freely – we talked for four hours with no breach in her defences. Nerves exhausted at meeting such resistance, I invited her out for dinner, thinking that we would resume talking the next day. But at 10pm, in the taxi back from the restaurant, she suddenly asked if I would like to come back to her house for a drink. That was the beginning of the real interview – and of a relationship that three years later has become a friendship.

I do not know what made her trust me, but in her issuing the invitation and in my accepting it, a transaction was made between us that was quite separate from the financial issue. Claire W's story was so shocking that much of the detail was kept out of the paper. Not by my choice (I believe the more we know about everything the better, particularly in an issue such as child abuse), but editors tend not to want to upset their readers – and advertisers – with too detailed a rendition of reality.

Aftercare and professional boundaries

Our conversation left me sad and angry and also full of admiration for Claire's courage, not just in surviving such a start to her life but also in confronting it all over again through her conversation with me. Although she said she had not actually been involved in Satanism, the early part of her life was filled with degradation, physical pain and mental torture. The material dredged up in interviews such as this emerges from deep trauma, and the people involved are often needy emotionally. Receiving Claire's confidences was a delicate matter, as was explicitly recognised by the social worker who was with us for the initial part of the interview. "Don't worry about her afterwards", she assured me, "You'll be gone by tomorrow but I'll be here to pick up the pieces".

The proffered safety net was much appreciated. The journalist–interviewee relationship is not therapeutic and the interviewee can be left with unmanageable feelings when the journalist walks away. But as a freelance journalist, I make the choice to stay in contact with the person if they require it. (Staffers have less control of their time.) It seems to me that the person who gives you the gift of such dangerous intimacies deserves your engagement with them as a person and not just as a slab of material you will use for your story. Child sex abuse, parental betrayal, murder, and death are all combustible materials, which, once released into the air, require careful handling lest they spill over and destroy lives. The journalist's responsibility in such cases is multi-layered, but one of the essential elements seems to me to be to respond as a human being and not just as a professional. This can have repercussions in your own life. If the material you are investigating is disturbing, as child abuse and torture are, it can lead to depression or at the very least a skewed view of the world for a while.

It can also leach into your own time. Since the article on her story was published, Claire and I have discussed her last job, her current job, the rest of her family, her debts, and the boyfriend who turned out to be violent and possibly a stalker. It is an expensive business, as Claire only has a mobile phone; and sometimes it can be hard to be dragged away from what you are doing, but I do not refuse to listen. I think it is a privilege to be invited into a person's life in this way.

This aftercare aspect of interviewing is rarely discussed in the media. We are supposed to be professionals who set boundaries, like doctors with their consulting hours or the counsellors who cannot listen to suicidal patients after 6.30pm. Sometimes, when it really is inconvenient to talk, we put on our answering machines too, but the journalist's method is not ordered like theirs – it is opportunistic. If the only way to get the story is the 24-hour interview, then that is what we do. The corollary of that is that if someone wants to call us out of hours then we should try to be available.

There is obviously a limit to that: after working on a number of stories, the journalist may well have acquired a number of different people who still want to talk over their problems. However, there are no easy answers to the question of where you draw the line. How could there be? Journalists are people too, with different tolerance levels for intrusion into their private lives. The initial compact is for a single interview and a single story. Anything further should be at the discretion of the individual. I think it would be perfectly acceptable morally to sever contact once a story is over; it is just that on a human level it simply feels ungenerous.

It is certainly easy to forget as a journalist that your interviewees are human beings too. Once you have their words on the paper in front of you it is as if what they say has become your property, there to do with what you will, at least until the sub-editors get their hands on it. But I hope that by opening oneself up to a more human and balanced relationship with the people you talk to, the journalism itself becomes deeper and more human too.

EIGHT

Using participative action research with war-affected populations: lessons from research in Northern Ireland and South Africa

Marie Smyth

Ethics of sleep

I

I'd say she's been trained
in archaeology
to know to dig
intersecting trenches
to know to look
for changes in soil colour
denoting the passage of time
different ages.

Eventually they found the marker string
then a shoe, then the corner
of a blue striped sweater.
Gradually they uncover
a tangle of bodies
arms, elbows, legs
heads pathetically nestling
among fingers, faces.

I don't want to think
about their last fall
about the few who survived
the bullets
only to smother, drown
in this pit
among moans
and warm blood.

Now browned
blackened by death
in earth
they lie like dates
or figs
melding to one another.
Two hundred
men's bodies.

She says it's easier for her
if she doesn't meet relatives.
They seal driver's licences
wedding rings, neck-chains into bags
scrub and measure bones.
On clipboards they calculate height and age
note hair colour – to prove what praying families
know but don't want to hear.

II

Our new computer is so fast
we can scroll up pages in a flash.
Still
it takes time to scroll past
three and a half thousand
names and addresses
ages, causes, locations and dates
of death.

Listening: story after story
Reading: obituaries, searching
in tangles of words, in messes of grief
among decomposing anger,
breathing the stink of fear
searching for missing addresses, ages
details, data, to us – searing punctuations
full stops in other lives.

At night, such archaeologists as we are
we lie awake
beside our sleeping husbands and wives
alone
thinking about what we are doing
thinking about what has been done
wondering would it really be better
if we could sleep?

(Written by the author in Belfast, 1 July 1997, after watching *The grave*, a television programme on the exhumation of a mass grave in Bosnia, and thinking about our work researching the impact of the Northern Ireland conflict in the Cost of the Troubles Study, Northern Ireland.)

Introduction

This chapter describes the experience of conducting research, largely in Northern Ireland but also in South Africa, on issues of segregation, political violence and its human consequences. The chapter describes my experience of being researched as a resident of Northern Ireland, and how that influenced the choice of research paradigm for my own work. The implementation of that paradigm – participative action research – in the selected research projects is provided, and in conclusion, the implications of the paradigm and the context of the research are enumerated and explored.

Becoming a researcher

I trained as a researcher in Northern Ireland in the 1970s, during the early stages of what is referred to as the Troubles, when the violence was at its height. Over 30 years of conflict in Northern Ireland, censorship (including self-censorship), the culture of silence on the one hand, and resistance to that censorship and silence on the other divided the academic and research worlds. Certain topics were considered too controversial, and researchers and journalists who addressed them risked marginalisation. As an undergraduate, I had seen one of my lecturers driven out of Northern Ireland as a result of his research on policing. I had been active in the women's movement and in trade union and leftwing politics, had my share of experiences of the Troubles, and had written journalistically on some taboo areas. However, I did not become involved in research on a full-time basis until after my move back to Northern Ireland from the US in 1991.

I had had an ambition to live as an adult in a society that was not at war, so I moved to the US, where I taught college and worked as a clinician in various mental health settings in Massachusetts. My ambition was not to be realised, since during my time there, George Bush Senior declared war on Iraq. Suddenly, everyone was preoccupied with war, troop deployment and bombing raids. I was taken aback at my own anger at people who espoused support for war, without, in my view, any real appreciation of its consequences. Equally, I was frustrated by the assumption of my professional colleagues in mental health that large sections of the population of Northern Ireland (perhaps including me?) suffered from Post Traumatic Stress Disorder. In spite of the plethora of research on Northern Ireland, I knew of no comprehensive research evidence on these questions.

Whyte (1990, p viii) commented after the first 20 years of the Northern Ireland conflict, it is quite possible that, in proportion to its size, Northern Ireland is the most heavily researched area on earth.

As a resident of Northern Ireland, I have considerable experience of being on the receiving end of the attention of researchers sufficiently frequently to render me 'interviewed out' on certain topics. While some of this experience was enjoyable and useful, much of it was frustrating. Rarely did I receive transcripts or drafts in spite of being promised, and only once did I receive a copy of the final text. I had experience of being misinterpreted, misquoted. On a number of occasions, misunderstandings (sometimes based on cultural differences) led the researcher to ludicrous conclusions, which I had seen only when they were already in print. As a research 'subject', I had developed doubts about the value of much of this research (see Whyte, 1983; Smyth and Darby, 2001). Nor was it clear what its contribution to positive social change might be, in a context in which the need for change was urgent as people continued to lose their lives.

I returned to Northern Ireland in 1991. That year, 101 people were killed as a result of the political situation (Fay et al, 1999, p 137). In the light of my American mental health colleagues' comments, I conducted a small study on the long-term effects of Bloody Sunday on the families of those bereaved on that day, and was shocked to learn that I was the first researcher to ask them how they felt about their experiences. I met with them as a group, to feed back my findings, and drafted a constitution for them to form what became the Bloody Sunday Trust.

I lived in Derry Londonderry, taught on the University of Ulster campus, Magee College. As an extra-curricular activity, I began to participate in dialogue across the sectarian divide, which had to be kept secret, due to the dangerous and divided nature of the circumstances. Prominent Loyalists and Republicans met in the city and explored issues together, one of which was the movement of Protestants out of the city, and the consequent change in the city's politico-religious composition. This was to provide me with my first full-time research project, Templegrove Action Research Ltd (TAR) from 1994 to 1996, interrogating the census data, and conducting field surveys in two enclave areas. At the initiation of this study, the first ceasefires of the peace process were declared, and the sense of possibility of change was intensified. Parties to the negotiations talked of ceasefires, release of prisoners, opening up the city centres, unblocking roads, removal of army installations, disarming the police, and many other things that had been unthinkable.

As a result of my earlier research on the Bloody Sunday families, I was aware of the neglect of those who had been bereaved or injured, and began to believe that they should have a voice in the emerging peace process. Yet there were few opportunities for such people to meet, let alone develop a voice. They lived in a deeply divided Northern Ireland and had every reason to be mistrustful of one another, in the light of their many tragic experiences. Nonetheless, in the wake of ceasefires of 1994 onwards, I brought together a group of people from all sections of the population in Northern Ireland who had direct experience of being bereaved or injured in the Troubles. I was concerned that they had no voice, no lobbying power in a fast-moving peace process. Furthermore, the growing political determination to have violence permanently ended seemed to be based on the implicit recognition of the damage done by the violence of the Troubles; yet there was no reliable collated evidence of this damage. Nor had the needs of those who had been bereaved, injured or otherwise affected been examined, needs that might have to be met should peace break out. Indeed, at that time, there was not even an accurate figure for the deaths due to the conflict.

Together with this group of people, I formed the Cost of the Troubles Study Ltd (COTTS). This study compiled a database of all deaths due to the political conflict in Northern Ireland, conducted (with the research officer, Marie-Therese Fay) a large number of in-depth interviews with people about the impact of that conflict on their lives. A survey of the population examining the impact of the conflict on health, well-being, mobility and other aspects of life was also conducted. The study data was also used to produce two exhibitions, one 90-minute film and several books, articles and reports. Subsequently, I conducted a study on the impact of the Troubles on young people, including a survey of young people's political attitudes that was initiated by a group of young people calling themselves the Joint Society for a Common Cause. More recently, I have conducted research on the militarisation of young people in the Middle East and South Africa, which involved interviewing young combatants and former combatants. In the South African case, I interviewed former combatants, who were identified through contacts in a number of organisations. I travelled to townships to interview them about their experiences of armed combat. These data are being analysed at the time of writing.

Objectivity

Some researchers (for example, Knox, 2001) lay great store by achieving objectivity, while others (for example, Feldman, 1991; Nordstrom and Robben, 1996) are more involved in reflexive subjectivity, which arguably offers a different route to objectivity. In a divided society, impartiality or objectivity is not a stance that anyone in Northern Ireland can easily claim. Even foreign researchers and journalists tend very quickly to identify more with one side or the other (see Smyth, 2004: forthcoming). Outsiders bring their own identities and previous experience to bear, and in researching political conflict, this often leads to the researcher identifying with one or other faction. Such identification can blind the researcher to evidence and can hobble the analysis. In the Derry Londonderry study on segregation, researching life in two enclave communities led me to formally explore working as an explicit part of the research with a co-researcher from the other side of the sectarian divide to me. How ever this is done, whether by working deliberately with the 'other' community, or by making explicit the religio-political identification of the research team and discussing the implications of those identifications for the analysis, I remain convinced that it is essential to the conduct of proper research in Northern Ireland, and perhaps in other divided societies. None of us are above the situation, none are capable of objectivity; but co-researching with a researcher from the 'other' side can improve the quality of the research. This is an ethical issue, in that it bears on the researcher's capacity to observe and interpret certain cohorts without distortion, and the rights of that cohort to relatively undistorted representation. It is also a methodological issue, in that the preferred solution is to ensure the diversity of the research team, and to make the identity of the researcher and his or her relationship to the subject area an explicit part of analysis. This requires a degree of open communication among researchers, and this may run counter to the cultures of silence that often prevail in divided societies.

Methodological orientation

This chapter will describe some of the research experience that ensued and the ethical lessons that might be drawn from this experience. However, it is notoriously difficult to focus exclusively on ethical aspects to the exclusion of methodological considerations. Indeed, the solutions to ethical challenges are often methodological alterations or innovations; hence, the two are sometimes inextricably intertwined. My orthodox education in qualitative and quantitative research provided basic knowledge and training in research methods and approaches. However, my training in research did not equip me to consider the rights of the respondent, nor did it demand that I consider the appropriation of information and the subsequent marginalisation of the respondent from the process of analysis as problematic. Thus, the design and orientation of my research from the 1994s onward owes much to approaches described by Reason and Rowan (1981) (new paradigm research), Roberts (1981) (feminist research), Van Manen (1990) (human science research), and, later, Reason (1994) (human inquiry). All of these approaches are concerned with balancing the power relationship between the researcher and those studied, with improving the accountability of the researcher to those researched, and to ensuring positive benefit to more than the researcher's career. Reason (1994, p 10) summarises these aims thus:

> I use the term human inquiry to encompass all those forms of search which aim to move beyond the narrow, positivistic and materialist world-view which has come to characterize the latter portion of the twentieth century. While holding on to the scientific ideals of critical self-reflexive inquiry and openness to public scrutiny, the practices of human inquiry engage deeply and sensitively with experience, are participative, and aim to integrate action with reflection.

In the context of researching Northern Ireland, I shared some of Reason's other vision:

> I have been much persuaded ... that the purpose of human inquiry is not so much the search for truth but to heal, and above all to heal the alienation, the split that characterizes modern experience.

However, my belief was that robust scientifically collected data that could withstand scrutiny from an inclusive research team and that had been collected and analysed according to reflexive principles could make a positive contribution to understanding and thence to dialogue on topics of division. In particular, quantitative data, censuses and their statistical analyses can provide challenges to political stances, and counteract rumours that often fuel conflict in divided communities. The discipline adopted was to 'find the facts, and face them', however much they contradicted one's own loyalties or orientation. This discipline relied on the diversity of the research team and its advisors, since the constant challenge may not be easily produced in homogenous research teams.

Level of involvement of those studied

Someone once commented that poverty in an age of affluence is being unable to write and having others write about you. Some of my motivation to become a researcher was to write about my own community and society, and the problems it faces in a way that is useful. I wished to move out of the passive position of being the 'researched' into one with more control, more power – that of the researcher. I have worked on research topics that have arisen out of my membership of the local community as much as out of my academic interests. Topics have been selected by identifying issues that concern me, that appear to be neglected, and which could stand some illumination. After I began working as a researcher, others approached me with topics, such as the group of young people who asked for help in researching their own age group's political attitudes across Northern Ireland. From the outset, the relationship between researcher (me) and those researched is affected by whose idea it is to conduct the research. All of the projects described have met with enthusiastic participation by participants and board members, and this has assisted with the issue of 'ownership' of the research itself, The New Paradigm Research Manifesto describes:

> A much closer relationship than that which is usual between the researcher and the researched: significant knowledge of persons is generated primarily through reciprocal encounter between subject and researcher, for whom research is a mutual activity involving co-ownership and shared power with respect both to the process and to the product of the research.... The shared language and praxis of subject and researcher create 'the world' to be studied. (Reason, 1994, p 489)

The research is conducted in accordance with participatory action research principles, which have entailed a management structure involving a range of people with direct experience of the effects of the Troubles. There are ethical considerations related to entering this field of research that confirmed the desirability of this approach. One of the most devastating after-effects of trauma is the sense of disempowerment that it can bring. Working according to a principle of partnership is an attempt to avoid further disempowerment of those whose lives and experience we set out to research and document. We identified the need to deal responsibly with the vulnerabilities of those whose experiences they seek to portray or understand.

Attempting to democratise the research process by involving individuals from the researched population was one of the strategies employed in order to attempt to address this issue. For example, this entailed involving participants in the project management and in monitoring the ethical aspects of research practices; in analysis by discussion and by reviewing our findings and analysis. It also entailed a detailed process of providing transcripts to all interviewees, discussion and agreeing of transcripts, collaboration with interviewees on issues such as anonymity, and presentation of findings.

The exception to this regime has been the research in South Africa, where distance from the field has limited the level of participation of interviewees in the study. However, transcripts of tapes were sent for their review, as with other interviewees, and a number of interviewees have become involved in subsequent research events.

Levels of participation

I was uncomfortable with seeing my fellow citizens, friends and those who welcomed me into their community as merely containers of data from which the data must be extracted as efficiently as possible. If for no other reason than a wish to avoid the humiliation of getting it so badly wrong, I wished to set up structures whereby I could be accountable – at least formally – to the people who were being researched, while the research was ongoing.

The research on segregation was conducted under the auspices of Templegrove Action Research Ltd (TAR), a limited company without share capital and a recognised charity (Northern Ireland does not have a charities register). A group of people from community leaders both sides of the sectarian divide, who had been involved in dialogue about segregation, formed the board of directors. They were the grant holders for the research and the employers of research staff. I sought and obtained secondment from the university on the basis of paying the cost of my replacement out of the grant, and acted as the full-time executive director of the project. When the project was complete, the board voted to transfer the remaining assets and equipment to a new board, composed of the group of people I had called together who had been bereaved or injured in the Troubles. The name of the company was changed to The Cost of the Troubles Study Ltd (COTTS). In the latter stages of the work on segregation, I had designed and fund-raised for a study of the effects of the Troubles on the population. As before, COTTS was the grant holder, and employer of the project staff. Again, I was seconded from the university, to whom my salary was paid for the duration of the study, to act as director of the company and the study. Later studies were conducted under similar arrangements, with the board of the organisation being drawn from the population being studied. (A study of young people presented difficulties for this method of working, since one cannot be a company director under the age of 18. However, various surrogates were found, representatives of children's advocacy organisations, older young people and so on.)

There was an issue in my relationship with other board members about differentials in levels of knowledge about research and about the running of the project, and consequently about my accountability. While some board members had held similar positions in other organisations, others had never acted in that capacity before. Similarly, they knew varying amounts about research, but in most cases, I had more knowledge and information about the research in hand than any of them; that is, in both TAR and COTTS, all aspects of the project, including project design, fieldwork, staffing, data analysis, dissemination, as well as the routine aspects of staffing and finance. Board members were sometimes frustrated by the amount of routine business involved in running an organisation, and were more interested in the 'meat' of the study. Both qualitative and quantitative research methods were used in all of the studies, in order to maximise credibility and thus the policy impact. However, few board members were familiar with statistical methods, and it was necessary to find straightforward ways of explaining sampling, generalisability of research findings and other such concepts.

Since the research results were likely to be of more than academic interest, collaborative relationships with local policy makers and service deliverers were also developed from the inception of each project. A research advisory group was established for each project, and representatives of donors, policy makers, and service providers were invited to participate in that group, which monitored the research design, piloting, fieldwork and other data collection, analysis and documentation and dissemination.

The board members were broadly representative of the population being researched in terms of religious and gender balance. Indeed, a few board members were also interviewed or surveyed as part of the fieldwork. For the most part, however, their role was to ensure that the research took account of the interests of the population in all its diversity. On reflection, both the TAR and COTTS board members participated intensely in the study, and took this duty very seriously. However, the divided nature of the society, together with the diversity of the board, meant that internal conflicts in the board also absorbed time and energy. The broad representativeness of the board made this inevitable at that stage of Northern Ireland's history, and there is some evidence that the experience of board members working together on the board eventually facilitated more positive interactions beyond the board.

In retrospect, this method of working – of giving actual power over the research project to those who are being researched – had undoubted advantages. The credibility of the research with the population was enhanced; the researchers were immersed in the field and were provided with many insights into the issues they were studying; yet it was very labour intensive for the researchers. Such an approach requires additional resources in terms of the skills and time of the researcher in order to be feasible. Other approaches such as those described in Chapters One and Four of this book provide worthy comparators. A separate set of procedures was used in obtaining informed consent of participants.

Consent

Standard protocols of informed consent were used in both interview and survey research. However, in addition, interviewees were provided with transcripts and allowed to review their input and remove any parts that, on reflection, they did not wish included. On occasion, particularly in relation to the research with young people, the researcher advised an interviewee to withdraw a statement, or anonymise an interview where safety or confidentiality were likely to be compromised. Having given consent to being interviewed, filmed or otherwise represented, participants usually exert no further control over the manner in which the footage, soundtrack or data is deployed. This material may be used again, usually without consultation with those who generated it, when documentary media material is being compiled, or in further research. The interviewee (or the 'subject') does not usually exert much influence on the angle of the journalist or the analysis of researcher. In all of these studies, the board served as proxies for participants, and the advisory group monitored the data analysis, received and discussed preliminary reports, and read and commented on drafts of final reports. For participants, consent for participation was regarded as an ongoing negotiation, with the point of no return being a particular publication or, in the case of the film, the final edit.

A further issue arose in consent to the archiving of the data at the end of the study. Here, interviewees were approached individually and asked to instruct researchers whether or not to archive their data in the Linenhall Library political collection, whether to anonymise it before doing so, and what length, if any, embargo should be placed on it. A small number of participants wished all data relating to them to be destroyed, and their wishes were implemented. Survey data, being anonymous, was less problematic: it is archived in a number of places and available to other researchers. The decisions made by the board here are normally made by researchers alone or by ethics committees who do not have responsibility. The board made the decisions about the research process and about archiving, not out of any formal liability, which was limited by our company structure, but out of a consciousness of their role as proxies for the research participants, their knowledge from their own personal experience of what it is like to be bereaved or injured or otherwise affected by the conflict, and their duty to anticipate objections or sensitivities. As researchers, we constantly consulted the board on the approach we were using, asked them to anticipate how it might be received, and problem-solved with them on finding better ways of carrying out the research, with due regard to the vulnerabilities and circumstances of those we were researching.

Research design and data collection

A further cohort of people participated in the field surveys in both the TAR and COTTS studies. In the case of TAR, two surveys, each of an enclave community, were conducted. In the case of COTTS, a Northern Ireland-wide survey was conducted. In both cases, interviewer-administered questionnaires were used; self-completion questionnaires were ruled out because of the sensitivity of the subject matter and the potential for the subject area to arouse distress or suspicion in participants. The guidance from our board was that we had an ethical responsibility to ensure that participants who might be distressed or apprehensive by the subject matter of the survey were provided with information about our identity and intent, and information about relevant support services by the survey team. Leaflets that provided information on support services were prepared and distributed to survey participants. Publicity on TAR and COTTS preceded each survey, so that information about the study and its purpose, the identity of the researchers and the proposed use of the results was in the public domain and available to survey participants.

The TAR surveys were small, contained in one community, and elicited information about life in enclave communities. The researchers conducted much of the fieldwork directly. In the COTTS survey, it was necessary to recruit and train a field force. Special training was provided for survey interviewers, and they were given information on the location and remit of supportive services so that they could refer participants to the appropriate source of help should the need arise. Survey interviewers on the COTTS study reported spending much longer on interviews than the scheduled time, since some participants were keen to talk about their experiences. For security and quality control reasons, we kept track of interviewers. Some would 'go missing', only to be found hours later having listened to a very sad tale from a participant. Some of these stories collected by survey interviewers were moving, sad and emotionally demanding to listen to. As a result, regular group debriefing meetings were established for the field force, and these proved to be useful in supporting the field force, but also provided a useful additional quality control mechanism, and additional qualitative data.

In the TAR study, a public hearing was also organised, to elicit experiences of being in the minority in the city, and to create public discourse about the issue of minority–majority relations. The Guildhall was booked, a panel of judges selected, the event was advertised, and support was offered to groups and individuals to come forward and give evidence. The proceedings were documented and the report presented to a number of bodies including the city council (Smyth, 1996c).

The conduct of the in-depth interviews presented a further set of challenges. First, there was a demand for interviews. People telephoned the research office, volunteering to be interviewed: they wanted to talk. Many said that they had not spoken about their experiences before, and reported feeling better after doing so to the interviewer. Word travelled among families and friends that we were interviewing, and new recruits came forward. We interviewed everyone who wished to be interviewed. However, some of these interviews we would not have sought out, since we tried to achieve a spread across gender, age, religion and location, and some of our volunteers were not in categories that assisted us with our spread.

Impact on the researchers

All of the interviews were conducted by either Marie Therese Fay, the full-time research officer, or by me. Many of the stories that we listened to were heartbreaking, horrifying and traumatic. Often we were in awe at the capacity of interviewees to survive such tragic and traumatic experiences. After many interviews, we would find ourselves thinking about the interviewee for days. We made regular times to discuss our experiences with one another. We found ourselves helping people with simple issues, wanting to help other people but not knowing how. We confronted our own helplessness in the face of daily doses of human tragedy and misery. It became important to establish clear boundaries around our role, and although we continued to perform services for people, we recognised the danger of becoming too involved in service provision at the expense of our research role. We also recognised that in some ways, our performance of services for interviewees was designed to meet, not their needs, but our own need to help people in order to avoid facing our own helplessness.

On reflection, both of us experienced strong emotional reactions to the in-depth interviews. Both of us became angry at the inaction of politicians, political parties, government for allowing the interviewees to suffer, and for not doing more. We shouted at the television; we overworked; we did not sleep well. Sometimes we cried with interviewees, and sometimes we waited till the interview was over, and cried later. We had truly entered the world of the victims of Northern Ireland's Troubles. We were to some extent, in technical terms, traumatised by our fieldwork. In human terms, our hearts were broken. The poem at the beginning of this chapter was written out of that experience, and poses the question: would it be better if we did not feel this way? Ultimately, I concluded that no human being could meet, listen and respond to the people we met, listened and responded to without being deeply affected. Sleep disturbance, grief, anger and preoccupation with our interviewees were welcome, if uncomfortable, signs of our humanity. Our relationship to our board members shifted as a result of our fieldwork. We knew more, understood more.

Data ownership

Some of the data collected, such as the list of those killed in the conflict, was compiled from a number of sources. The database of deaths contained data on the name, address, age, gender, religion of those killed, the address at which they were killed and the identity of the perpetrating organisation. The COTTS board took the view that the information was sensitive and should not be made generally available, since it could exacerbate tension or grievance. To date, we have not released the personal data on deaths, although we have analysed the database statistically (see Fay et al, 1999). At the end of the project, the board appointed three trustees to manage these data, and to whom any decision making about access to the data could be referred. These arrangements would be unacceptable to some researchers, who regard research data that they have gathered as their exclusive property. However, when the data relates to such sensitive matters that impact so profoundly on the lives of others, as a researcher, I wish to be advised and informed by those with expertise in those issues. The unfortunate experience of many families caught up in the Northern Ireland conflict is one of having no control whatsoever over footage of their family member's funeral, or of photographs of gruesome injuries or circumstances. These arrangements were intended as an antidote to that powerlessness and lack of control, as a mechanism to try to ensure that the project did not replicate some of the practices of the media, which relatives found upsetting and distressing. It is noteworthy that the board has not prevented the researchers using the data for any purpose, although they have, on occasion, refused requests from other organisations for access to it.

Liability

The high levels of lay participation in these projects gives rise to the issue of liability for ethical or legal breaches that might occur in the course of the work. Arguably, the researcher alone cannot be liable, if he or she is being guided or directed by a board of management. In the case of the work presented here, the formal structure of the organisation (a company limited by guarantee, with no share capital) served to legally clarify the issue of liability. Board members and the company as a whole limited their legal and financial liability by company registration. However, the issue of ethical liability is more complex and not so easily resolved. Responsibility for particular decisions might vary, and the ethical responsibility must surely fall on those who took the decision, so all board members are 'jointly joined' in ethical responsibility. For the most part, decisions made were consensual, and this eased the potential difficulties about liability.

Analysis, write up and dissemination

Written reports were prepared and drafts circulated to board members. However, in many instances, these were not read carefully, or indeed at all, as the work of the project progressed and the researchers' relationship with the board and advisory group members developed. At the point when reports were being prepared, almost all the issues arising from the research had already been discussed with board and advisory group members, and an analysis evolved through these discussions that fed back into the research and data collection. This in turn would inform subsequent discussions with the board and advisory group. Board members were familiar with the overall content and direction of reports without reading them because of their participation in these discussions. In both studies, this process was invaluable. My proximity to the data was increased, my perspective improved, and my understandings and conclusions were tested and broadened by those with personal expertise and lived experience of the subject area.

Dissemination of results of the studies was the subject of much discussion on both the TAR and COTTS projects. The goal of making the study results as accessible as possible to a large number of people required creativity in designing the dissemination strategy. In the case of the COTTS study, the results and outputs of the study were to be used to raise public awareness of the human suffering caused by political violence, so the dissemination methods had to reach a broad public audience, as well as policy makers and service providers. In both studies, a variety of outputs were produced (see Smyth, 1996a, 1996b, 1996d, 1996e, 1998, 2001), to meet this need. Exhibitions were compiled, using excerpts from interviews, photographs, and graphs and charts from the survey results. Professional videos were made, and interviewees agreed to be interviewed on camera. The videos were designed to be used for a number of purposes, including training of service providers on the needs of those affected by the Northern Ireland conflict. We produced academic publications, alongside journalistic writing for local print media, and books of edited transcripts, personal accounts from interviewees of their experiences (see Smyth, 1996f; Smyth and Fay, 2000). All publications, films, exhibitions and reports were launched, and all participants invited to these occasions. In both TAR and COTTS, efforts were made to place the project outputs in prominent public positions, so the Guildhall in Derry Londonderry and the Great Hall in Belfast City Hall were chosen as venues for exhibitions. The then Secretary of State for Northern Ireland, Dr Marjorie Mowlam, opened the COTTS exhibition in the Great Hall. Such occasions were useful in raising the public profile of the work, and thereby the level of public awareness of the issues.

Evaluation: lessons learned and recommendations for future work

Accountability to the researched population

Both the main projects described in this chapter were managed by an organisation set up for that purpose and composed of directors drawn from the researched population. As a model, this is not always feasible, as was discovered when the children's research was embarked upon. Further concerns about this model relate to the amount of researchers' time and energy devoted to servicing the board and improving their participation, sometimes at the expense of the actual research. Further concerns about this model relate to the level of expertise available (for example, on finances) within certain populations. Any 'slack' or uncompleted work left by the board also falls to the researcher. In subsequent work, this model has been amended so that the board is made up by one third academics, one third voluntary sector representatives and one third drawn from the researched population. However, difficulties about levels of board participation in certain aspects of the organisation continue.

Financial management: the university and career considerations

A further set of issues relates to the relationship between the academy and this kind of research. Being on the academic staff of a university which is subject to research assessment exercises (RAE), where monies earned in research grants are counted in the university's favour, there has been a distinct lack of enthusiasm for having an organisation other than the university be the grant holder, since the money can not then be counted in the RAE. To date, no resolution to this difficulty has been found. This can adversely affect career advancement.

Support for people who participate

It is necessary to provide access to and information about support services for participants in a research field in which unmet need is likely to be uncovered. This entails researching available services and ensuring their bona fides before referring to them, or passing on their contact details. It is also important to note that many participants experience the interview itself as a supportive experience.

Healing or opening wounds

For a very small number of participants, the research was not a positive experience. In one case, an adult female was interviewed as part of COTTS, and she spoke in interview about losing a member of her immediate family in the conflict. When she went home, she told her family about her interview and about talking about the death of her family member. Thus, she broke a family taboo, since the family had never spoken about their loss. In some cases, in spite of our best efforts, sometimes participants lose or suffer as a result of their participation in our research. This must be honestly acknowledged, and proper risk assessments conducted prior to the commencement of the study, so that such risks are minimised.

Principle of least harm

The aim of research must be that it will do no harm to participants. However, as I have just described, sometimes participants do experience difficulties or suffering as a result of participation. This is a dilemma in researching traumatic fields of inquiry, where participation can be re-traumatising, or disruptive of the status quo in participants' lives. The challenge that faces the researcher is one of balancing the potential harm to participants with the potential benefit to them. Where benefit can be gained for participants, perhaps it can morally offset some of the harm, which in any event the researcher must attempt to minimise.

Since we cannot know in advance the potential psychological or social risk in such research, fully-informed consent becomes an important way of setting up a contract with participants about the potential risks and responsibilities. This is an issue that arises in other chapters of this book, on which other researchers take a different view, and which is further explored in its Conclusion.

While valuing maximum participation in research, sometimes participation is not as important, and it is quicker and more effective to revert to more orthodox divisions of labour. However, in the course of the work described here, participants' expectations of involvement were raised, and we noted that some participants came to demand more control, for example, of encounters with journalists. (Chapter Seven of this book explores these issues from a journalist's point of view, which is driven by rather different considerations than those that drive social science researchers.)

Dependence

In conducting research among vulnerable populations, the researcher has a great deal of power, which can seduce the researcher into fostering dependence in participants. Where support is offered, for example, there is a danger that the researcher, driven by the emotional impact of the research, will overstep the role of researcher to the extent where dependence is created. Critical monitoring of this issue is required in research of this kind. (This issue has already been addressed in Chapters One and Three of this book.)

Exploitation in participatory research

The potential for exploitation of the researched population is arguably greater when participatory methods are used, particularly when participants are expected to devote their leisure hours to research work. Participants may be expected to carry out unpaid work, or may have their rights ignored. However, if the potential for exploitation is greater, then the opportunity for positive empowering relationships between researchers and participants is also greater.

Working with victimhood

With the emergence of 'victim politics' in Northern Ireland (Smyth, 2000), it became clear that victimhood was a problematic state, particularly if it became static, competitive with the needs of others, and resistant to growth or change. Some of those who have suffered as a result of the Troubles have difficulty in trusting anyone from outside their immediate group. A tendency to conspiracy views and at time suspicion of outsiders and even insiders can verge on paranoia. This requires researchers to work towards gaining the trust of individuals and communities – not on a one-off basis, but by making themselves accountable in ways that do not compromise the standard of the research, and which can in fact improve it. Research must also be transparent, open and accessible to local people; in such communities where there is such suspicion or past negative experience of researchers or the media, transparency and openness are of paramount importance.

Payment of South African participants

The poverty of South African participants in the study on young people raised a number of ethical issues, one of which was the issue of payment. Some participants asked for payment, yet paying for data is taboo for most researchers. A compromise was reached where participants were compensated for any out-of-pocket expenses; they were also given food at interview, and a donation was made to a local organisation that worked in their community. In this way, the value of their participation was respected, without unduly warping the data collection by introducing payment of some participants.

Impact of the research process on the researchers

Earlier, the impact of the COTTS research on the two researchers was described, and since then, a number of studies have examined the impact of working in the field of victimhood on human services workers. Interviewer workloads require careful monitoring, so that interviewers are not over-exposed, and debriefing and support should be built into the research design. Stress management strategies were introduced in COTTS, although with hindsight, earlier introduction of these measures was called for. However, these measures may not be sufficient to entirely prevent impact on the researcher, since it is the researcher's identification with those she is researching that causes the impact, and this identification is a central part of the connection between researcher and researched.

The boundary between participant and researcher has become, in my experience, permeable and fluid as the working relationship between participant and researcher increases in depth and breadth. This deepening and broadening will inevitably follow if meaningful ways of equalising the power differential between them are found. This chapter has described my limited experience of attempting to find ways of including participants in the governance of the research. The methods used here have undoubted benefits, while presenting the researcher with a new set of problems. However, the essence of the research process itself is problem solving and identifying new and creative solutions to hoary old problems. To gain and retain the privilege of being admitted into those lives and experiences is worthy of the most creative and sophisticated research practice we can develop in order to ensure that the coming together of researcher and researched is of mutual benefit.

References

Fay, M.T., Morrissey, M. and Smyth, M. (1999) *Northern Ireland's Troubles: The human costs*, London: Pluto.

Feldman, A. (1991) *Formations of violence: The narrative of the body and political terror in Northern Ireland*, Chicago, IL: University of Chicago Press.

Knox, C. (2001) 'Establishing research legitimacy in the contested political ground of contemporary Northern Ireland', *Qualitative Research*, vol 1, no 2, pp 205-22.

Nordstrom, C. and Robben, A. (1996) *Fieldwork under fire: Contemporary studies of violence and survival*, Berkeley, CA: University of California Press.

Reason, P. (ed) (1994) *Participation in human inquiry*, London: Sage Publications.

Reason, P. and Rowan, J. (1981) *Human inquiry: A sourcebook of new paradigm research*, Chichester: John Wiley & Sons.

Roberts, H. (ed) (1981) *Doing feminist research*, London: Routledge Kegan Paul.

Smyth, M. (1995) *Sectarian division and area planning: A commentary on the Derry Area Plan 2011*, Derry Londonderry: Templegrove Action Research.

Smyth, M. (1996a) *Life in two enclave areas in Northern Ireland. A field survey in Derry Londonderry after the cease-fires*, Derry Londonderry: Templegrove Action Research.

Smyth, M. (1996b) *Three conference papers on aspects of sectarian division: Researching sectarianism; Borders within border: material and ideological aspects of sectarian division; Limitations on the capacity for citizenship in Post-Cease-fires Northern Ireland,* Derry Londonderry: Templegrove Action Research.

Smyth, M. (1996c) *A report of a public hearing on the experiences of minorities in Derry Londonderry,* Derry Londonderry: Templegrove Action Research.

Smyth, M. (1996d) *Two policy papers: Policing and sectarian division (with Ruth Moore); Urban regeneration and sectarian division,* Derry Londonderry: Templegrove Action Research.

Smyth, M. (1996e) *A report of a series of public discussion on aspects of sectarian division in Derry Londonderry, held in the period December 1994-June 1995,* Derry Londonderry: Templegrove Action Research

Smyth, M. (1996f) *Hemmed in and hacking it: Life in two enclave areas in Northern Ireland:Words and images from The Fountain and Gobnascale,* Derry Londonderry: Guildhall Press.

Smyth, M. (1998) *Half the battle: Understanding the impact of the Troubles conflict on children and young people in Northern Ireland,* Derry Londonderry: INCORE/ United Nations University and the University of Ulster.

Smyth, M. (2000) 'The role of victims in the Northern Ireland peace process', in A. Guelke and M. Cox (eds) *A farewell to arms: From war to peace in Northern Ireland,* Manchester: Manchester University Press, pp 118-35.

Smyth, M. (2001) *Two reports on children and young people and the Troubles in Northern Ireland: Young people's lives in local communities and building the future conference,* June 2000, Belfast: Institute for Conflict Research.

Smyth, M. (2004: forthcoming) 'Insider/outsider issues in research on Africa', in M. Smyth and G. Robinson (eds) *Researching ethnic conflict in Africa,* Tokyo: United Nations University Press.

Smyth, M. and Darby, J. (2001) 'Does research make any difference? The case of Northern Ireland', in M. Smyth and G. Robinson (eds) *Researching violently divided societies: Ethical and methodological issues,* Tokyo/London: United Nations University Press/Pluto, pp 34-54.

Smyth, M. and Fay, M.T. (2000) *Personal accounts of Northern Ireland's Troubles: Public chaos, private loss,* London: Pluto.

Van Manen, M. (1990) *Researching lived experience: Human science for an active sensitive pedagogy,* Ontario: Althouse.

Whyte, J. (1983) 'Is research on the Northern Ireland problem worth while?', Inaugural Lecture, Queen's University Belfast, 18 January.

Whyte, J. (1990) *Interpreting Northern Ireland,* Oxford: Clarendon.

Appendix

This set of principles came out of the discussion among participants at the Quality in Human Inquiry Conference in Bath in 1995 and are included here with acknowledgements to the creativity of that group. They have not been developed, made theoretical or sophisticated, and scarcely edited. They come, as it were, direct from the stimulating discussion of a group of scholar/practitioners deeply concerned about the nature of participation in human inquiry.

When do the (action) researcher's good intentions slide into colonial smothering?

1   When there is no dialogue about what the problem is and what questions are to be asked.
2   When there is no passionate conflict at some point in the action/inquiry about what is at stake in defining the theory and practice.
3   When the whole process is too efficient.
4   When the researcher is naive about power (does not recognise that s/he is inevitably involved in power relations on multiple levels as are the other participants).
5   When the initiating researcher(s) romanticise/idealise the 'subjects' (other participants).
6   When the initiators don't test whether their 'good' intentions are in fact good from others' points of view. (When they don't untangle researcher's intentions from others'.)
7   When the initiating researchers do not develop trust with other participants.
8   When they don't take the time to develop a relationship, to inter-act with respect, and/or to confront unrealistic expectations.
9   When the researchers cannot suspend their plan in the humility of unknowing and experience the miracle of learning something truly new.
10 When the researcher works unawares within the myth of victory rather than aware with the rune of ruin.
11 When you are not 'naturally' there, with an honesty and plausibility that can make you an insider, even in your absence, rather than merely a short-term outsider.
12 When the research is treated as an individual affair, rather than a group and communal affair.
13 When you don't (repeatedly) work through feedback and representations of the results with the subjects.
14 When you are not sensitive from moment to moment not to create dependency.
15 When you don't appreciate the interweaving of complex, inter-level, inter-categorical systems and the playing of multiple roles with the re-discovering of the simple primary, secondary, and tertiary issues at stake.

NINE

Conducting longitudinal epidemiological research in children

John Henderson

Introduction

The increasing recognition that events during pregnancy and early infancy have a bearing on future health and disease through later life (Barker et al, 1993) has led to the development of longitudinal, epidemiological studies beginning in early life to study the antecedents of important public health outcomes. The case for such studies has been further enhanced by developments in human genetics stemming from the human genome project and leading to advances in both knowledge of genetic influences on human health and disease and technology that facilitates high throughput and cost-effective analysis of human DNA. The study that will be described in this chapter – the Avon Longitudinal Study of Parents and Children (ALSPAC; full details, including design, study protocols, response rates and publications are available at www.alspac.bris.ac.uk) – was designed to study the interactions between genetic susceptibilities and environmental exposures on children's health and well-being, including health, disease, developmental, educational, psychological and social outcomes. What is described here is an example of a large, population-based, longitudinal birth cohort that was recruited specifically for the purposes of non-therapeutic, epidemiological research. The study is described, including methods of data collection, and an example given of a physical measurement that was deemed necessary to accurately characterise a particular health outcome (in this case asthma) but which was associated with administration of a pharmacological agent to healthy children with consequent risks. The regulatory framework on which this study was based is also described, as are the practical considerations of carrying out the physical testing, including parent and child interactions, understanding and satisfaction.

The Avon Longitudinal Study of Parents and Children (ALSPAC)

The study arose as a consequence of a meeting of the World Health Organisation (Europe) in 1985, at which a decision was made to develop a longitudinal survey strategy that could be used to determine what were the current problems in child health and development, and how they may be prevented. On the basis of this decision, a multi-centre European study was designed: the European Longitudinal Study of Pregnancy and Childhood (ELSPAC). The Avon Longitudinal Study of Parents and Children has developed and substantially extended the ELSPAC protocol while remaining an integral component of the European project. The primary aim of these studies is to understand the ways in which the physical and social environments interact, over time, with genetic inheritance to affect children's health, behaviour and development. To this end, the study has developed methods of data collection to provide as complete and accurate a description as possible of the environmental exposures to which each child was subjected during pregnancy and early childhood, to collect and store genetic information on all study participants, and to characterise outcomes of interest, using quantitative measures where possible.

The study is based in a geographically defined area, consisting of that part of the former county of Avon (UK) that was also within the then South West Regional Health Authority. Pregnant women who were resident in Avon and whose expected date of delivery was between 1 April 1991 and 31 December 1992 were recruited to the study. It was estimated that more than 80% of the eligible population agreed to participate in the study and 14,541 mothers were enrolled. They gave birth to over 14,000 children of whom 13,971 survived to the age of 12 months and who have been subsequently followed up, together with the mothers and their partners.

Data collection

The principal methods of data collection have been self-completion questionnaires, collection and retention of biological samples, including genetic material (DNA and cell lines) and physical measurements of the children. Questionnaires were given to the mothers at four times during pregnancy and, following delivery of the child, separate questionnaires concerning the mother, her partner and the child were sent at frequent and regular intervals amounting to approximately two detailed questionnaires each year. These contained questions repeated over time relating to parents' and children's health and well-being and about their physical and social environments. Such information included exposures to the foetus during pregnancy such as maternal cigarette smoking, nutrition and medication use. After the child was born, information was collected on diet, exposure to tobacco smoke in the home, types of heating, cooking and ventilation in the home, presence of damp and moulds in the home environment and, to assess the effects of the outdoor environment, the addresses of the children have been carefully mapped and can be closely linked to census data to provide indices of deprivation as well as sources of pollution including heavy traffic, common landfill sites and industrial plants. Health questions pertaining to the child include details of common symptoms asked annually from the age of six months after birth, accidents, contact with health professionals, including hospital admissions, and treatments given, including prescribed, over-the-counter and alternative medications. Questions are also asked about the child's relationships with parents and others, social integration and friendships, developmental progress and schooling.

Measurements, testing and assessments

From the age of seven years onwards, a series of physical measurements were planned and implemented. These included assessments of physical growth, neurological and psychological development, vision and hearing and specific measurements relating to particular disease outcomes. Examples of this last category include skin-prick testing to look for evidence of allergies to common environmental exposures, skin examination to look for evidence of eczema and lung function testing as part of an assessment of asthma. In addition, blood samples have been taken to extract and store genetic material for future genetic testing and to address specific research questions using measurements of blood constituents. The general design of the physical measurement activities is based around a half-day attendance by the child and a parent, during which a number of different measurements are performed. To date, children have attended annual measurement sessions from the ages of seven to 11 years.

Genetic and biological samples

For the ALSPAC study to fulfil its primary aim of relating environment to genetic inheritance, it was necessary to establish a source of DNA from the children and their families that could be used for the detection of variations in genes that had been discovered to be associated with particular childhood outcomes. The outcomes in which ALSPAC is interested are generally complex, polygenic conditions in which no single genetic or environmental determinant can be found and which usually give rise to heterogeneous expression or a spectrum of effects depending on the magnitude of influence of specific exposures or genetic determinants and their interactions. Therefore, a decision was made at an early stage not to make available results of genetic testing to the individuals concerned as the effects of genetic variations that were being examined could not be predicted and, therefore, their significance was uncertain. The same principles have been applied to some physical measurements also, where values outside the 'normal' range drawn from an unselected population have uncertain relevance to the health of that individual. The data are thus protected by sophisticated data management processes that do not directly link information about individuals, including genetic information, to any personal identifiers, such as name, date of birth or place of residence and by rules of confidentiality relating to the distribution of data and access to the data for the purposes of analysis and scientific publication (see discussion later in this chapter on the regulatory framework). Blood was obtained from the placenta soon after delivery and a further sample was drawn at the age of seven years for the extraction of DNA. Written consent was obtained from the primary carer of the child for the extraction and storage of DNA and for its future use in analyses of genetic variations that would be linked anonymously to data obtained from other sources in ALSPAC; questionnaires, physical measurements, and so on. The recognition that the store of DNA was a finite resource and the pressures of the pace of genetic discoveries has led to the establishment of immortalised cell lines from the children and their parents, thus providing a secure, long-term source of genetic material from this population.

Participation

From the general descriptions above, it can be appreciated that participation in ALSPAC is a substantial undertaking for a child and family. However, response rates have been maintained at a high level for the majority of the life of this study. This has been achieved through a number of mechanisms designed to keep the study population involved in and informed about the study. Newsletters are sent approximately twice a year to families and all children enrolled in the study receive a birthday card. Results of research based on the study are widely disseminated through the local and national media, with stories highlighted in the family newsletter.

Children as active participants

From the age of seven years, children have been increasingly involved in active participation by being sent their own questionnaires. The maintenance of a high profile of the study in Avon, the high proportion of the eligible population enrolled and continuing to participate in the study, and support from public bodies and businesses in the Avon area have all contributed to an ownership culture on the part of the Avon population. It is highly likely that this includes children also, there being a certain cachet associated with being one of the study participants, although whether this pertains through adolescence remains to be determined (see Chapter Three of this book).

Studying asthma in ALSPAC: the problem

Asthma is one of the most common chronic health problems of children in the UK and similar industrialised countries (ISAAC Steering Committee, 1998). There is good epidemiological evidence that the prevalence of asthma has increased dramatically in these countries over recent decades (Burr et al, 1989; Ninan and Russell, 1992; Anderson et al, 1994; Omran and Russell, 1996;

Downs et al, 2001), but, despite extensive research, the cause of this increase remains obscure. It is recognised that asthma is a complex, polygenic disease that arises due to environmental pressures on genetically susceptible individuals. Therefore, large longitudinal studies with detailed information from before birth are well placed to attempt to unravel the complex interactions between genes and environment in the expression of asthma in children.

One of the principal problems of investigating asthma in epidemiological studies of this nature is that of definition. There is no universally agreed definition of asthma and recognition of the condition is usually based on a combination of clinical features. However, these may be diverse and variable in individuals over time and between individuals in the same disease population (Martinez et al, 1995). Therefore, it was deemed necessary, in the context of this study, to complement historical questionnaire data, such as wheezing history, with objective measurements based on the pathophysiology of asthma; hence the decision to perform a bronchial challenge procedure. This is based on the premise that, in response to a variety of physical or chemical stimuli, the airways of children with asthma will constrict or narrow at a lower stimulus than those of healthy subjects. Methacholine chemical challenge was chosen on the grounds of freedom from unpleasant side effects, predictability of the time course of response, reversibility with standard therapeutic agents, and lack of late effects several hours after the challenge procedure was completed. Despite extensive anecdotal experience of methacholine challenge in children, there was a dearth of published information on its safety profile, including an estimate of the true incidence of any adverse events. The latter point was seen as being of critical importance in the context of a study for which the participants would receive no material clinical benefit. Therefore, a risk assessment was undertaken on the basis of theoretical risks associated with the known chemical and pharmacological properties of methacholine. The major risk identified was the intended effect of provoking bronchoconstriction. Therefore, children at particular risk of adverse effects would be those most at risk of severe bronchoconstriction, particularly children with asthma. In addition, the occurrence of a recent respiratory tract infection was known to be associated with increased sensitivity to bronchoconstriction agents. Therefore, children were not tested within three weeks of a viral respiratory infection.

Children with known asthma presented two problems to devising the protocol for this test: they were at increased risk of a severe response and they were usually on asthma medications that could influence the response to methacholine, and hence invalidate the results. The approach taken was to test all children who reported asthma on a pre-screening questionnaire in the presence of a qualified physician. Asthma medications were withheld for up to 48 hours before the day of testing and parents were advised to bring the child's regular treatments for administration directly after the test was completed. A reversal medication (salbutamol) was available in the testing room and was routinely given to all children, whether they had asthma or not, who had a response to methacholine – a decrement of 20% of their baseline respiratory function.

A further consideration that needed to be addressed before this study commenced was the formulation of methacholine to be used. The chemical was available as a single-patient use kit for testing an individual subject in a clinical setting but was prohibitively expensive in this formulation to contemplate its use in a large population sample. One company produced medical-grade methacholine for use in bronchial responsiveness testing but discontinued production soon after the study actually started. Therefore, it was purchased from a commercial chemical company. There was then a protracted process of seeking approval for its use in human subjects. This did not come under pharmaceutical regulatory control, as it had no intended therapeutic purpose but study subjects needed to be safeguarded in precisely the same way as if they had participated in a therapeutic trial of a new drug. The problem was addressed by seeking cover for negligent harm through the insurers of the university in which the research was carried out. The methacholine was delivered to the hospital pharmacy department and made up into batches that were sterilised and frozen for single use. In practice, a vial of methacholine was diluted to several concentrations for testing and used within a single testing session. Before release to the testing staff, each batch of methacholine was subjected to stringent pharmaceutical and microbiological quality control procedures in the hospital pharmacy.

The regulatory framework

Once the protocol for testing had been finalised by the scientific staff responsible for the bronchial responsiveness testing, it was necessary to put this study forward for approval by a number of regulatory bodies. The Avon Longitudinal Study of Parents and Children is notable for having a robust internal regulatory framework that works in parallel with statutory regulatory bodies, such as the local research ethics committees. Thus, the project to measure bronchial responsiveness was first approved by the ALSPAC Scientific Advisory Committee, which examined the scientific validity, feasibility and desirability of this proposal. In addition, external scientific peer review was involved at the stage of seeking funds to support the staff that would carry out the testing. The proposal was also reviewed by the ALSPAC Ethics and Law Committee (Mumford, 1999), an advisory body that comprised academic members, including representatives of the Faculties of Law and Social Sciences, University of Bristol, who were independent of the ALSPAC study, and lay representatives, including two parents of children in the study. Following approval by the internal regulatory bodies within ALSPAC, the project was put forward to the local research ethics committees (LRECs) of the three NHS hospital trusts within Avon. The internal bodies considered the specific project in isolation whereas the hospital research ethics committees considered this project as a component of the half-day testing session (Focus@8) that was carried out on children after their eighth birthday. This session was to comprise the bronchial responsiveness testing alongside a number of psychological and developmental tests but no other physical measurements (these having been completed the previous year).

There is no doubt that the issues raised by this proposed testing were contentious. A non-therapeutic pharmacological agent would be given to healthy children. There would be no direct benefit to the individual being tested, even if the test demonstrated unexpectedly high bronchial responsiveness it was not specific for a clinical diagnosis of asthma and test results were therefore not relayed to the primary care physician. A response to methacholine would be associated with some discomfort; tight chest and wheezing, and, although this could be relieved by medication, this would require the child to have an otherwise unnecessary medical intervention. There was a risk of severe bronchoconstriction in an unspecified proportion of the population. So what were the benefits? This study provides a unique opportunity to investigate the aetiology of asthma in a way that has not been possible in the past. Advances in the genetics of asthma required well-characterised populations to make sense of the actions of candidate genes and studies of the size of ALSPAC were necessary to examine interactions between genes and environment due to statistical limitations of smaller studies. Therefore, the benefits to the study population were that 'their' study would potentially make another important contribution to scientific understanding and the sense of altruism associated with that knowledge.

Ethical review

The study was approved in principle by all ethics regulatory bodies with one alteration imposed by one of the three hospital LRECs: that all testers of children in this session should have appropriate basic life support training. This was adopted and training was provided to the research staff. Much of the discussion about the project, rather than focusing on the risk assessment, was based around information to parents and participants to ensure that they were fully informed before giving written consent to this test. Before coming to the measurement session of Focus@8, families were sent an information leaflet that detailed all the tests that were being carried out in that session. There was considerable difficulty in wording the prior information about the bronchial responsiveness testing. There was awareness that most of the other tests to be completed within the session were comparatively non-contentious, at least in terms of their physical invasiveness, consisting of psychological testing and interviews. The study team wished to give parents and children sufficient information to know what to expect when coming to Focus@8 but to avoid alarming words, such as "breathing a chemical" that may have had the effect of discouraging attendance of the whole session, thereby jeopardising other important elements of ALSPAC's work, particularly in terms of psychosocial outcome measures. Inherent in the approach to ethics committees was the understanding that informed, written consent would be obtained on the day of testing by the tester and with the opportunity for the parent and child to ask questions before the measurement commenced. However, there was a tension between giving too much information in advance without the opportunity to put it into context and to give too little so that families were unprepared on the day and may have felt rushed or pressurised into consenting by the fact that they had attended the Focus@8 session and by implication were consenting to all the tests within that session. The information sheets that were approved and finally used in the study are included in the Appendix of this chapter.

The testing session

It was estimated that approximately 9,000-10,000 children would be available to attend Focus@8, where the lung function test was administered. Around 7,500 of these children were eventually seen during the Focus@8 session and, of this population, over 95% took part in the lung measurement session[1]. Analyses of wheezing illness in the population had suggested that just over 20% of the population had asthma and/or wheezing at each annual questionnaire assessment. This equated to the proportion reporting asthma prior to the test and approximated the proportion demonstrating a positive bronchial challenge test. Therefore, it would appear that a broadly similar proportion of children with asthma attended the session compared with the expected population prevalence. Children with asthma might be judged to have most to gain from participation but it was clear that there would be no direct benefit in knowing the bronchial responsiveness of an individual child. It could equally be argued that such children also had most to lose as they were more likely to experience adverse effects of the test, including acute wheezing with which they were familiar due to their underlying disease. A number of parents of children with asthma also took the opportunity of asking the physician on duty about their child's condition or its management. General advice about asthma was given but specific questions about an individual child's treatment or management were referred back to the family's primary-care practitioner. Mumford (1999) has discussed the general approach taken by the ALSPAC Ethics and Law Committee with regard to the feedback of information to participants and in maintaining the balance between information and anonymity.

About two thirds of the eligible children who completed baseline lung function measurements also completed a bronchial responsiveness test. The majority of those who did not were prevented from doing so by either technical difficulties with the test or because of exclusion criteria: recent viral respiratory infection or recent asthma attack. After full explanation on the day of testing, few subjects elected not to consent or participate in this session. Of course, this excludes those who did not attend the entire session due to concerns about this particular test. The majority of questions asked were in relation to methacholine (including the risk of adverse effects): What is it for? What are its actions?

No serious acute, adverse events occurred in testing over 5,000 children with methacholine in this study. Approximately one-fifth of these children received a single dose of salbutamol to reverse the bronchoconstriction brought about by the test. Of these, the vast majority were free of symptoms and the medication was given as per protocol only. A few children experienced some chest tightness and one child required a second dose of salbutamol for continued chest discomfort. All these children had lung function measured before leaving the session and it had returned to within 10% of baseline values in every case. The feedback following this session was generally favourable and many children wrote to state that they had enjoyed it. In part, this may have been related to the contrast between the activities in the lung testing session and the tasks completed in the parallel sessions but there has not been a systematic study of attitudes and these comments are based on anecdotal evidence only. However in a related study of ethical protection of participants in longitudinal, epidemiological research that included ALSPAC study subjects, 17 of 63 children interviewed reported experiences of this session and only four of this group had adverse comments ("didn't like the taste"; "waste of breath"), including one who reported it to be the worst part of Focus@8. The remaining children were neutral (seven) or had positive comments (six), such as finding it fun or enjoying the experience (personal communication with Dr T.A. Goodenough).

A very small number of parental complaints were handled by the lead investigator, the most serious of which was one mother's belief that the administration of methacholine had precipitated a significant chest problem in her child. There was no evidence that the child had responded adversely during the session or had deranged lung function prior to going home. However, it is impossible to know if this was a true adverse event or a coincidental occurrence of a chest infection in a child who was tested during the prodromal phase of an illness. This was the only potentially serious event that was reported.

The investigators were concerned during the study about the possibility for coercion brought about by families attending the session without sufficient prior information about what it entailed. A small survey was carried out to address parents' perceptions of the test based on the information they had received before coming to Focus@8 and how these matched their experiences on the day. The results of this survey are demonstrated in Table 9.1 (page 174). These show that parents were generally satisfied with the amount of information given and their experiences were equivalent to or better than expected. However, it is clear that advanced written information satisfied a smaller proportion of parents compared with face to face explanation on the day of testing.

What was learned?

- Regulators, parents and investigators have understandable anxieties about the administration of pharmacological agents in the context of non-therapeutic research in children.
- Despite anecdotal evidence and personal experience that methacholine had been used without serious adverse incident in large numbers of children

worldwide, there was little published evidence on which to base this contention when devising information for parents.

- Although there are clear regulatory frameworks for therapeutic research and the use of unlicensed medications on a trial basis, these may not extend to non-therapeutic agents (according to the regulatory framework that existed at the time of writing[2]).
- Despite knowledge of potential risks, a large number of study participants, including those with lung disease, were prepared to take part in a non-therapeutic study with no direct or implied benefit to them. It would be of interest to compare this with the response rate to a similar request in a naive population that had not invested considerable energies already in the maintenance of a large, high-profile study.

Reflections on the study

The ethical issues raised by this study were primarily oriented to avoiding doing harm to participants (non-maleficence) and the autonomy of the study participants; that is, the children taking part. In terms of the regulatory process and ethical protection of participants, it was the former of these that came to the fore in discussions with ethics committees. One of the principal difficulties in this regard was the lack of experience of performing these tests on such a large scale and the lack of hard evidence on which to base personal reassurances about the safety of the test. In this context, the occurrence of any serious adverse event was unacceptable, both in terms of the primary concern for the safety of the children involved in the study and in the wider context of the ALSPAC study itself. From the perspective of a researcher within this project, I was aware of the potential for adverse events to destabilise the whole study that had been painstakingly built up over many years by colleagues. This risk applied not only to the actual occurrence of adverse events but also to the perceptions of participant families that their children may have been put at undue risk. As a doctor whose primary concern is the health and welfare of children, the primary duty of the lead investigator was to the safety, well-being and to some extent enjoyment of children participating in the study. However, as a scientific participant in ALSPAC, there was also a duty to scientific progress, the collection of the highest quality data and the integrity of the study. The study was carried out in the context of the increasing burden of asthma in children and the considerable potential of ALSPAC to address fundamentally important questions about its aetiology. However, there were clear scientific pitfalls inherent in relying solely on self-reported information to define the condition. This raised issues about the use of data that had been collected already at considerable time and energy costs to the study participants and the ALSPAC scientific staff, as well as the financial investment of several public and private institutions. Therefore, the investigators were satisfied that there was a strong scientific justification for this study, so long as the welfare of the study children could be reasonably assured. Ideally, the latter aspect could have been best addressed by performing the tests in a clinical area with immediate access to emergency medical help or by having a clinician present at all times during testing. The first of these options was neither practicable nor would it have provided an appropriate environment for the testing session. Great efforts were made to avoid confusing these tests, of ostensibly healthy children, with clinical testing, which is focused on discriminating between health and disease but remains primarily disease rather than health-orientated. The resources of the study were insufficient to support a dedicated clinician for this study; indeed this need was rejected by the study's funding agency. Therefore, a compromise was to identify 'high-risk' individuals and to schedule sessions for their testing when the principal investigator/clinician could be present. The inevitable consequence of this was an inequality (or potential inequality) in the attendant resources available depending on whether a child had asthma, the disease under investigation, or not. In the event, this did not become an issue but does illuminate the possibility, albeit subtle, of a conflict of interests on the part of the investigator.

The second ethical concern that was raised at the outset of this study was that of the autonomy of subjects (see also Chapter Three of this book). This was not peculiar to the study described but permeated the entire ALSPAC study and has been a subject of much debate at various points in the evolution of this project. The issues relate primarily to whom one regards as the participants. As with all studies of young children, the consent to participation in this study was obtained from the principal carer, in this case the mother. The mother subsequently provided information to the study on the understanding that this would be non-identifiable but could be linked to other information about her child. Therefore, 'ownership' of this information was invested in a third party without the consent of the person to whom such information pertained. In the case of the studies described here, written consent was obtained from the mother of the child but a test was never carried out against the child's will, even with parental consent. Children of this age are generally well able to express their free will but are only beginning to develop a sophisticated understanding of causes and consequences of actions, at least to the level expected of a competent adult making informed choices about medical treatment, for instance. The resolution of some of the issues raised by the question of ownership is likely to be led by the development of children's consent to the continuation of participation in the study and to the retention of biological samples, particularly those that contain personal genetic information.

In the final analysis, who benefits from a study of this kind? The study subjects, through their continued and long-term involvement, are undoubtedly affected by being a member of the study cohort. Whether this is a benefit is a moot point but the feedback received from study children consistently suggests that they have enjoyed their experiences. Child-centred activities, such as a 'Discovery Club', have sought to involve children and to teach them about aspects of themselves that are of direct relevance to their participation in the study, so there is educational benefit and possibly even health benefits accruing from this population's awareness of health-related issues. Less tangible benefits include the altruistic notions of helping others and benefiting society in general through what is discovered during the course of the study.

The benefits to patients with common diseases are unlikely to evolve rapidly. The ALSPAC study has already demonstrated new and important associations between environmental exposures and childhood outcomes. Some of these have strong grounds for believing a causal relationship exists and, where the exposure is amenable to manipulation, these may lead to intervention studies. However, there is a long experience of lifestyle exposures, even those that have strong epidemiological associations with disease, being resistant to change. Therefore, the optimism of the scientist that his discoveries will change the world must be tempered by reality. Even patients with the disease that was being studied here garnered no direct benefit from their involvement. To the individual with asthma, knowledge of his or her bronchial responsiveness is of little or no consequence, aside from academic interest. It could be argued that active steps were taken to remove the benefit that may have been perceived in having access to an 'asthma specialist' through attendance of the Focus@8 clinic but it was stressed throughout that this was a research study and not a medical clinic. Any parent who had specific questions about the treatment of their child was referred back to their primary physician.

A major beneficiary is, of course, the researcher. As well as providing employment for research staff, the study had direct and tangible benefits to the researchers in terms of intellectual fulfilment, standing in the academic community through publication and dissemination of results arising from the study and thereby, indirectly, to career advancement. In this paradigm is perhaps embraced the true 'gift relationship' between the subject and the investigator.

Conclusions

In conclusion, this study raised a number of issues that are pertinent to longitudinal, epidemiological studies of children, of which there are many existing cohorts and a number of new cohorts are planned as the research benefits of this scientific approach are increasingly realised. At the outset of such studies, the mother is the participant recruited during pregnancy and the focus of early studies to establish environmental conditions of the foetus, such as tobacco smoke exposure due to maternal smoking. However, the subject of interest of these questions is a third party who is clearly not in a position to give consent of any sort, far less informed. After birth and for the first few years of life, the parent must be relied upon to give proxy consent on behalf of their child for the collection of information and, perhaps more contentiously for the collection and retention of biological samples including DNA, that relate to the health and well-being of that child. In this respect, the principles of ethical protection are not different from those that govern other aspects of research involving children (BPA, 1992; Sauer et al, 2002; Geller et al, 2003) and other groups unable to give direct, informed consent to participation. However, the longitudinal nature of the study means that, at some point, the onus will shift away from parental consent to first person consent by the child. The decision then needs to be taken to apply such consent to (a) information that has been collected previously and stored, perhaps in anonymised form, and (b) to future data collection, including physical and psychological examinations. Clearly the latter cannot be carried out without at least implicit consent on behalf of the child.

The shift from third party to first party consent cannot be viewed, except insofar as legal precedent dictates, as a defined point in time and it seems inappropriate, in the context of non-therapeutic research, to rely on case law that has its basis in therapeutic decision making. The process should probably be seen as one of gradual evolution with increasing involvement of the child in decision making about participation in the study but the principal axis of formal consent procedures will revolve around the carer (usually mother) and child until the latter reaches the age of majority. The point at which the child's consent would override the wishes of a parent or carer, particularly in the case of a child wishing to participate in something to which their guardian had objected has been widely debated in the context of this study but has not arisen as a practical problem. In practice, the majority of carer-child participants have a common view of participation/non-participation in individual components or in the study as a whole, although the extent to which the child is influenced by his or her carer is clearly an important factor here. When there has been dissent, it has usually arisen in the context of a child not wishing to do something to which his carer has consented, in which case the child's wishes have always been respected. This pragmatic approach has evolved for the protection of participants (children) in a situation in which they can be seen to derive no direct benefit, in contrast to clinical therapeutic decisions such as restraining a child for a blood test, and in which there is a necessity on the part of the investigators to maintain the trust and goodwill of the participants to ensure their future involvement in the study.

The beneficiaries of this type of research study may not be immediately apparent. From a clinical perspective, there was no tangible benefit to the children who took part, although there may be 'hidden' benefits that arise as a consequence of greater awareness of health-related issues among the participants. This must be balanced against a theoretical risk of raising anxiety about an aspect of health that may not have been in the subject or family's consciousness. Such a consequence could have potential implications on clinical services by stimulating questioning on the basis of greater perceived knowledge of a condition. However, this in itself could be viewed as a beneficial outcome for participants by empowering them to seek more information on their own health and state of well-being. The researchers benefited in a number of ways alluded to in this chapter. This benefit arises as a direct result of a gift-relationship on the part of the participants to the investigators. However, this is no different from other forms of research, in which the investigator may gain direct and tangible benefits, but these must be offset against the benefits to society as a whole and to specific groups within that society, such as sufferers of a disease. Without the altruistic participation of members of society in medical research, there would be severe limitations on medical advances that benefit that society. In the context of longitudinal, epidemiological research, such benefits may take a considerable time to emerge, often through indirect routes such as intervention studies based on the discovery of epidemiological associations. However, current society has benefited from the contribution of past generations and participation in research of this nature can be seen as an investment in an ongoing process that is intended to lead to the advancement of society. Therefore, a utilitarian argument can be put that it is a duty of society members to contribute in this way. The benefits of contribution must then be balanced against the risks involved. It is the duty of researchers to minimise the risks in proportion to the individual and societal benefits gained and to inform study participants of the nature of such risks. When children or other vulnerable groups are concerned, extra precautions must be taken to protect their interests but we will continue to rely on their parents or carers as the principal guardians of their best interests when seeking consent to their participation in therapeutic and non-therapeutic research. When such research has a longitudinal component, provision must be made to seek consent from the participants themselves for continued use of personal information that has been given on their behalf.

Acknowledgement

I would like to thank all the members of the large ALSPAC team who have made and continue to make this study possible. In particular, I owe a debt of gratitude to the lung function team who carried out the tests with such dedication and attention to detail. However, without the children and their families who took part there would be no ALSPAC study and I am indebted to their outstanding contribution. The Medical Research Council funded the study of respiratory function described in this chapter.

Notes

[1] General response rates to questionnaire surveys in the ALSPAC study have been around 80% of the eligible population at each annual sweep.

[2] Changes in the regulation of non-therapeutic medical research are likely to be forthcoming.

References

Anderson, H.R., Butland, B.K. and Strachan, D.P. (1994) 'Trends in prevalence and severity of childhood asthma', *British Medical Journal*, vol 308, pp 1600-4.

Barker, D.J., Gluckman, P.D., Godfrey, K.M., Harding, J.E., Owens, J.A. and Robinson, J.S. (1993) 'Fetal nutrition and cardiovascular disease in adult life', *Lancet*, vol 341, no 8850, pp 938-41.

BPA (British Paediatric Association) (1992) *Guidelines for the ethical conduct of research using children*, London: BPA.

Burr, M.L., Butland, B.K., King, S. and Vaughan-Williams, E. (1989) 'Changes in asthma prevalence: two surveys 15 years apart', *Archives of Diseases in Childhood*, vol 64, pp 1452-64.

Downs, S.H., Marks, G.B., Sporik, R., Belosouva, E.G., Car, N.G. and Peat, J.K. (2001) 'Continued increase in the prevalence of asthma and atopy', *Archives of Diseases in Childhood*, vol 84, pp 20-3.

Geller, G., Tambor, E.S., Bernhardt, B.A., Fraser, G., Wissow, L.S. (2003) 'Informed consent for enrolling minors in genetic susceptibility research: a qualitative study of at-risk children's and parents' views about children's role in decision-making', *Journal of Adolescent Health*, vol 32, pp 260-71.

ISAAC Steering Committee (1998) 'Worldwide variations in the prevalence of asthma symptoms: the International Study of Asthma and Allergy in Childhood (ISAAC)', *European Respiratory Journal*, vol 12, pp 315-35.

Martinez, F.D., Wright, A.L., Taussig, L.M., Holberg, C.J., Halonen, M. and Morgan, W.J. (1995) 'Asthma and wheezing in the first six years of life', *New England Journal of Medicine*, vol 332, no 3, pp 133-8.

Mumford, S.E. (1999) 'Children of the 90s: ethical guidance for a longitudinal study', *Archives of Diseases in Childhood*, vol 81, pp F146-51.

Ninan, T.K. and Russell, G. (1992) 'Respiratory symptoms and atopy in Aberdeen schoolchildren: evidence from two surveys 25 years apart', *British Medical Journal*, vol 304, pp 873-5.

Omran, M. and Russell, G. (1996) 'Continuing increase in respiratory symptoms and atopy in Aberdeen schoolchildren', *British Medical Journal*, vol 312, p 34.

Sauer, P.J., Ethics Working Group, CESP (Confederation of European Specialists in Paediatrics) (2002) 'Research in children. A report of the Ethics Working Group of the CESP', *European Journal of Paediatrics*, vol 161, pp 1-5.

Appendix

Parent information given prior to methacholine bronchial responsiveness testing

This session has been designed to help explain why some children suffer from asthma. The observations will not diagnose asthma, but will measure lung function and airway responsiveness in both children who have breathing problems and those who do not. We hope this will determine the important factors involved in the development of childhood asthma. The session is divided into two parts:

Part 1: Lung function

Your child will be asked to blow into a spirometer (measuring tube), so that we can measure their lung function (the amount of air the lungs can hold). They will be asked to repeat this a few times so that we may make an accurate measurement.

Part 2: Bronchial challenge

The majority of children will then be asked to take part in a bronchial challenge, so that we may determine how responsive their airways (bronchi) are. This involves the child inhaling a few puffs of a substance called methacholine. Methacholine is a chemical agent which is similar to the body's naturally produced chemical, acetylcholine, and has the same mechanism of action, causing a temporary narrowing of the airways, thereby affecting lung function. We test whether the inhaled methacholine has had this effect by measuring lung function again to see if there is any change. This process is repeated using increasing doses of methacholine until either all of the doses have been given, or we see a decrease in lung function of 20%. A child whose lung function decreases by 20% is said to have responded to methacholine challenge. We expect 10-15% of children to show such a response. In general, children with asthma and lung disease respond to a lower dose of methacholine than other children, but some children who do not have asthma may demonstrate a response, even if they never have chest problems. Therefore, this is not a test for asthma, but increased responsiveness is one of the components of asthma.

Is the methacholine challenge safe?

Methacholine challenge is safe in children. The amount of methacholine used is very small, even when children have every dose. In thousands of methacholine challenges in children carried out using identical methods to ours, no unexpected serious reactions have occurred. It is administered directly to the lungs and the dose is not sufficient to cause general effects to the rest of the body. The reaction we can expect is a drop in lung function due to tightening of the bronchi and this is what we measure. Although we are trying to provoke this response, we take a number of precautions to ensure this is not likely to be severe. The amount of bronchial narrowing at which we stop (a 20% fall from baseline) is not likely to cause any symptoms at all in the majority of children who respond. Evidence suggests that symptoms do not occur until lung function has fallen to 60-70% of normal. We do not do the test within three weeks of a respiratory tract infection to avoid the period when bronchial responsiveness may be increased following the infection.

The action of methacholine is known to gradually wear off over about 90 minutes and the airways will return to their previous state. However, as a precaution we give Ventolin, which counteracts the effects of methacholine, to all children who have a response to the challenge, even if they feel well. If children do have symptoms of chest tightness or wheezing, these symptoms will be relieved by Ventolin. The duration of action of a single dose of Ventolin is longer than that of methacholine so it protects the bronchi from narrowing until the methacholine has worn off.

As an added precaution, if a child has a history of asthma, we will arrange to see them at a Focus@8 session with a doctor present.

A small group of children, within a particular range of lung function, will not take part in the methacholine bronchial challenge, but instead will be given Ventolin only to see if their lung function increases compared with their normal lung function.

Table 9.1: Survey of parental opinions of pre-test information[a] given out prior to the bronchial responsiveness session (n=129)

Question	Yes	No	Incomplete/don't know	Comments
Was the breathing session as you expected?	112 (86.8%)	13 (10.1%)	0/4 (3.1%)	Three of incomplete responses 'Didn't know what to expect'.
Were you given sufficient information on the breathing session?				
a) before visiting Focus@8	86 (66.7%)	33 (25.6%)	5/5 (7.8%)	
b) within the breathing session	126 (97.7%)	1 (0.8%)	2/0 (1.5%)	
Did you find the 'What happens at Focus@8' leaflet helpful with regard to the breathing session?	96 (74.4%)	11 (8.5%)	15/7 (17.1%)	
Did you have any questions during the breathing session that were **not** answered to your satisfaction?	6 (4.6%)	122 (94.6%)	1/0 (0.8%)	Of six responding 'Yes', only one stated that a question was asked and not satisfactorily answered, others gave no further information.
Do you think your child was provided with enough information to understand what was required of them and what they would be doing during the breathing session?	126 (97.7%)	2 (1.5%)	1/0 (0.8%)	

Note: [a] Information was sent in advance to parents specifically about the test described in this chapter. They also received more general information about the session of which this test was a component in a separate leaflet, *What happens at Focus@8*. Further information and a chance to ask questions were provided on the day of testing prior to written consent being obtained.

TEN

Speaking truth to power: experiencing critical research

Phil Scraton

Introduction

This chapter affirms the centrality of the relationship between the 'researcher' and the 'researched' in the context of doing critical research into the use and abuse of power in state institutions. It takes as its starting point the criticism 'from below', that mainstream social sciences' research has been implicated in maintaining the status quo, misrepresenting the lives and experiences of people marginalised and excluded by structural inequalities. It traces the theoretical underpinnings of critical research and its potential for constructing alternative accounts to those embedded in official discourse. Focusing primarily on research into the aftermath of deaths in controversial circumstances, the article reflects on the process of researching the experiences of the bereaved in seeking truth and acknowledgement. It demonstrates how a critical approach can secure the participation, collaboration and integration of research 'subjects' – people – in the development of an inclusive research process. Finally, it considers the methods of research, the responsibilities and ethical dilemmas faced by researchers and the challenges to the powerful that together comprise the process of critical research.

On 'knowing'

> Your clever academics befriend us for a few months, they come down to our site, eats our food and drinks our tea. Some of them even lives among us. Then they disappear to their nice homes and university libraries. Next thing we know they're giving lectures on us, writing books about us ... what do they know about our struggles? How can they know our pain? We live it all the time. Our persecution lasts a life-time, not just a few months. Give us the tools to say it right and we'll tell you like it is. You know what we call them on our site? Plastic gypsies. (Quoted in Scraton, 1976, p 76)

Roy Wells, then President of the National Gypsy Council, spoke these words in 1975 at the launch of an academic report into the deterioration in relations between house-dwellers and travellers. Flanked by academics and policy makers, he reminded the audience of several hundred local authority councillors and officials of what it felt like to be in the goldfish bowl of academic research, of the distance between researchers and the researched and of the experience of alienation when the control of a people's destiny lay elsewhere. He refused to be the 'token gypsy' on someone else's stage and, with good grace and great oration, he instructed the investigators and the interventionists that the diversity of cultures that comprise the travelling population was neither a curiosity for the voyeuristic gaze nor an enemy within. He was under no illusion as to the purpose of government-funded research. It would, as it always had, inform new strategies of surveillance, regulation and control. It would result in laws and policies to 'discipline' travellers in a move towards the longer-term objective of enforced assimilation.

At the time, I had worked with Irish travelling families in Liverpool for two years. As a researcher I had known the realities and difficulties of being an insider-outsider. I was on the site daily, spending more time there than most of the travelling men. Involved with the on-site traveller school, in advising on imminent evictions and in reading and writing letters for families, I was an 'insider' in terms of trust. Yet I was an outsider in every other way. I struggled with the seemingly implicit contradictions of my research. While I experienced the apparent vagaries of an ever-changing 'community' and came to some understanding of its historical and contemporary realities, I witnessed the direct impact of unremitting interpersonal and institutionalised racism.

I visited the West Midlands where, during a technically unlawful eviction, three children had been burned to death as a trailer (caravan) had been ripped from its jacks. The moment when I met with the family will never leave me. Writing from jail, Johnny 'Pops' Connors (1973, p 167) illustrates the experience of being an Irish Traveller in mid 1970s West Midlands:

> [M]y wife kicked black and blue by the police in her own trailer three days before the baby was born; my little son very badly injured and my trailer smashed to pieces; the hospital refused to treat us; the councillors said, 'Kick them out at all costs'.

Back in Liverpool on the windswept site of urban dereliction that was Everton Brow, home to over 50 Irish Traveller families, a leaflet was circulating the local estates. It demanded that the local authority evict the "Irish tinkers", the "dirty parasites", threatening "Get the tinkers out or else". Within months, in Warrington, a leading councillor called for a 'final solution' to the 'gypsy problem'. Given the genocide directed against Roma in the Holocaust, the comment was calculated to instil fear within the local travelling population. Gypsies, classified as genetic asocials by the Nazis, have remained the ultimate, collective illustration of 'otherness'. Even their mass deaths have been erased, their suffering "largely absent from discussions of the Holocaust, as they are absent from the monuments which memorialise it" (Clendinnen, 1998, pp 10-11).

In this climate of hate, Howard Becker's portrayal of 'outsider' is literal. There is no adoption of or adaptation to a chosen life-style, no room for a negotiated acceptance. The daily reality of life on Everton Brow was local authority harassment, local community attacks and police brutality. Evictions happened at first light and the self-styled, private hire bailiffs were undiscriminating and unremitting in their use of force. While men and women defended their homes and families, their children screamed in fear. There were no case studies, ethical guidelines or briefing papers to advise the fledgling researcher on her/his place and role in such circumstances. Academic conferences were as distant in their analyses of such events as were their contributors from the action.

Writing on the hidden history of aboriginal oppression in Australia, Henry Reynolds recalls meeting two young aboriginal girls sitting on a dirty mattress on a prison cell floor surrounded by shards of glass. They had a bucket for defecation and the air was stale with the stench of urine. Both girls, one bleeding, stood before Reynolds, ashamed. They had sworn at their teacher and been imprisoned for a day. He was shocked by the arbitrary and "grossly disproportionate" punishment. Yet it was rationalised "within the parameters of what was thought normal on the island". Reynolds (1999, pp 7-8) concludes:

> [I]t seemed so utterly out of place in the modern Australia I knew about ... if such manifest injustice could flourish in 1968, whatever had been done in the past? If this could be done to children, whatever punishments were meted out to adults? Why didn't I know? Why hadn't I been told?

Throughout my first research project, I too struggled with questions. What kind of men would recklessly evict travellers, killing their children in the process? What kind of state, supposedly an advanced, inclusive, democratic state, would sanction such acts of brutality? What kind of an investigative and inquisitorial system would deliver verdicts of accidental death? Alongside these was Henry Reynolds' question. Gypsies and travellers had endured violent repression for generations. Why weren't we told? Why didn't I know? As Reynolds argues, social, cultural and political representation is not happenstance. It reflects a "system of presuppositions and principles that constitute an elite consensus, a system so powerful as to be internalised largely without awareness" (Herman and Chomsky, 1988, p 302). Alternative discourses are rooted in challenging the purposeful, propagandist constructions of what is published and taught as 'official history'. Through personal exploration and the revelation of *context*, and as a process of reinterpretation and understanding, 'knowing' is an antidote to the official suppression of truth and the denial of responsibility.

Establishing a critical research agenda

> Critical social research does not take the apparent social structure, social processes, or accepted history for granted. It tries to dig deep beneath the surface of appearances. It asks how social systems really work, how ideology or history conceals the processes which oppress and control people … [it] directs attention to the processes and institutions which legitimise knowledge … [it] involves a critique of 'scientific' knowledge which sustains [oppressive structures]. (Harvey, 1990, p 6)

Lee Harvey's critique of the positivist and phenomenological perspectives within sociological research proposes a critical perspective "delving beneath ostensive and dominant conceptual frames, in order to reveal the underlying practices, their historical specificity and structural manifestations" (Harvey, 1990, p 4). It owes much to Wright Mills' searing attack on mainstream social science 30 years earlier. Wright Mills (1959, p 20) stood "opposed to social science as a set of bureaucratic techniques which inhibit social enquiry by 'methodological pretensions', which congest such work by obscurantist conceptions, or which trivialise it by concern with minor problems unconnected with publicly relevant issues". State-sponsored academic research could not be considered independent, rigorous or value-free. According to Wright Mills (1959, p 193), social scientists were hired for their utility; as "technicians" who accepted "problems and aims" defined by the powerful, who were ideologically compromised by the promotion of "their prestige and authority".

In contrast, the "sociological imagination", critically self-reflective of personal context and understanding of "the intersections of biography and history", operates between the "personal troubles of milieu" and "the public issues of social structure" (Wright Mills, 1959, pp 7-8). Personal troubles arise from the unique experiences of 'self', the direct associations of interpersonal relations. Yet public issues "transcend these local environments of the individual" being derived in the "larger structure of social and historical life" (Wright Mills, 1959, p 8). For Wright Mills, to have an awareness of the social structure and the intricate connections of institutional arrangements and to be "capable of tracing such linkages among a great variety of milieux" is "to possess the sociological imagination" (Wright Mills, 1959, p 11).

Wright Mills' critique challenged the structural functionalist orthodoxy that dominated post war sociology. Within the academy it dispelled the assumptions, never shared on the streets and in the neighbourhoods that attracted the attention of research, that 'society' was a stable, integrated and smoothly functioning entity. It rejected the depiction of state institutions and large-scale corporations as consensual, meritocratic operations reflecting a plurality of respectful competing interest groups. In the US of the 1960s, however, the struggle against Deep South apartheid, the growth of the civil rights movement, the antagonism of large-scale corporation bosses towards unions, the anti-Vietnam

War movement and the rise of second-wave feminism reminded academics and politicians alike that they lived in anything but a consensual society.

As Howard Becker (1967, p 240) famously demanded his academic colleagues to reveal their "personal and political sympathies", thus disclosing "whose side are we on", Alvin Gouldner (1969) portrayed sociology as in "crisis". Consistent with Becker, Gouldner considered that value-freedom was a deception. Issues of structure, power and legitimacy had been deliberately evaded by academics operating as social engineers or welfare technicians financially and intellectually in hock to the status quo rather than social investigators researching the contexts and consequences of structural inequalities. In expressing deepening concern over social voyeurism, Gouldner (1973) argued that academics, including Becker, were drawn to "dangerous" neighbourhoods to observe "wayward" lifestyles and functioned as "zoo-keepers of deviance". He called for a reflexive sociology contextualising contemporary social and cultural relations in their material history and their political-economic present. Only then could the issues of power, legitimacy and authority be understood and analysed.

In acknowledging powerlessness, particularly the extent to which the ideological construction of outsider status is internalised and accepted rather than rejected and resisted, this debate provided the foundation for a critical approach. Social research, whatever its specific focus, has to engage with the material world, its history, its ideologies, its political economy, its institutional arrangements and its structural relations. To fully grasp and interpret social action, interaction and reaction, critical analyses require the inter-weaving of the 'personal', the 'social' and the 'structural'. Knowledge, and its processes of definition, acquisition and transmission, cannot be separated from the determinants of "existing sets of social relations" (Harvey, 1990, p 2). The challenge for "a critical methodology is to provide knowledge which engages the prevailing social structures ... oppressive structures [such as] those based on class, gender and race" (Harvey, 1990, p 2).

The underlying 'premise' of critical analysis is "that 'knowledge', including the formalized 'domain assumptions' and boundaries of academic disciplines is neither value-free nor value-neutral" but "is derived and reproduced, historically and contemporaneously, in the structural relations of inequality and oppression that characterise established social orders" (Chadwick and Scraton, 2001, p 72). Yet the critiques of mainstream social science theories are only part of the story. Within the political management processes of advanced democratic societies, official discourse confers legitimacy on power, thus underpinning the exercise of authority. For Foucault (1980, p 131), each society operates a deeply institutionalised 'regime of truth'. It comprises:

> the types of disclosure which it accepts and makes function as true; the mechanisms and instances which enable one to distinguish true and false statements, the means by which each is sanctioned; the techniques and procedures accorded value in the acquisition of truth; the status of those who are charged with saying what counts as true.

Just as information is manufactured through the professional conventions and industrial processes of the mass media, so truth is produced through the political processes of government. While not totally *determining*, the "production of truth and the exercise of power are inextricably interwoven" (Scraton, 2002a, p 28). As Foucault (1980, p 94) concludes, power "never ceases its interrogation, its inquisition, its registration of truth". It "institutionalises, professionalises and rewards its pursuit". In this context, the discourses of academic and state institutions, employing constructs such as 'state security' and 'public interest', combine to produce formally sanctioned knowledge. For Cohen (1985, p 196), the "logic and language of control" provides state institutions and their professional agents with an unrivalled, and often uncontestable, "power to classify". It is in their "methodologies, techniques and functioning" that "established bodies of knowledge" consolidate. Yet it is a process of legitimacy derived in, and supportive of, "the determining contexts of material power relations" (Scraton, 2002a, p 29).

Critical social analysis sets an oppositional agenda. It seeks out, records and champions the 'view from below' ensuring that the voices and experiences of those marginalised by institutionalised state practices are heard and represented. Through in-depth, contextual analysis critical social research unlocks the potential of turning 'cases' into issues (Sivanandan, 1990). This is the transcendence of local environments to include the "larger structure of social and historical life" envisioned by Wright Mills (1959, p 8) in his discussion of personal troubles and public issues. It is the application of the sociological imagination "to change the world, not only to study it" (Stanley, 1990, p 15).

Breaking the silence

> Intellectuals who keep silent about what they know, who ignore the crimes that matter by moral standards, are even more morally culpable when society is free and open. They can speak freely but choose not to. (Cohen, 2001, p 286)

In disclosing and analysing the "underlying mechanisms that account for social relations", a significant dimension of critical social research is its stimulation of "dramatic social change from grassroots level" (Neuman, 1994, p 67). It challenges the portrayal of the marginalised, the excluded and the oppressed as helpless or hopeless victims of circumstance. It recognises the collective strength and formidable articulation of people galvanised to resistance by the insensitivity, recklessness and neglect of state institutions and corporate bodies. In his in-depth study of state killings in Northern Ireland, Bill Rolston (2000, p xv) notes how the state "degraded the ideal of human rights over three decades". Yet campaigners, many of whom had suffered loss, "struggled to uphold the ideal in the most hostile of environments". As a consequence, "private ills were transformed into public issues" and "individual experience became a spur to political action" (Potton, 2000, p 319).

In circumstances where individuals or communities experience the brunt of poverty, racism, sexism, homophobia or ageism, it is difficult for the social investigator not to be partisan, not to 'take sides'. Yet, with a few notable exceptions, academics remain silent when oppression within liberal democratic states is institutionalised. Research that focuses on serious civil disorder, the differential policing and regulation of communities and the use of state-legitimised force and negligence by those in authority, is conceived, formulated and realised in volatile circumstances. Its agenda, a priori, is political. Interviewing people in the immediate aftermath of arrest, bereavement, court cases and so on, brings the researcher face-to-face with raw emotion. It is not feasible, in the heat of such moments, to be free of moral judgement or political conviction. But the researcher's experiences, values and commitment are not necessarily inhibitions to fact-finding, bearing witness or truth telling. If anything, critical research offers analyses of great integrity and honesty. For, rather than claiming some mythical 'value-neutrality', or sanitised, controlled environment, critical social researchers position their work, identify themselves and define 'relevance'.

In April 1979, Blair Peach, a New Zealand teacher, was brutally killed by members of the Metropolitan Police Special Patrol Group as he walked home with friends from an anti-fascist demonstration. Two months later, Jimmy Kelly, a 54-year-old unemployed man in ill health, died on the charge-room floor of a Liverpool police station following arrest by several Merseyside Police Officers. The cases received unprecedented media attention galvanising friends and relatives of people who had died in custody to form INQUEST: United Campaigns for Justice. As a founder member, I began a long association with INQUEST, researching and publishing on deaths in controversial and contested circumstances. What soon emerged from a systematic analysis of these cases (see Scraton and Chadwick, 1987a, 1987b) was the

> yawning gap between official discourse, inquiries or [inquest] verdicts and alternative accounts provided by bereaved families, [prison] regime survivors, rights lawyers, community workers and critical researchers. (Scraton, 2002b, p 112)

Inevitably, however, researching deaths in controversial circumstances, particularly those involving the police, prisons, young offenders' institutions and special hospitals, presented political as well as methodological and ethical challenges.

As academic departments depend on local and central government to commission 'independent' research and evaluation there is often concern, usually indirectly expressed, that critical research could jeopardise lucrative and regular contracts and consultancies. An inherent problem in researching the powerful from the standpoint or experiences of the powerless is the discretionary use of institutional power to inhibit, or prohibit, access (see Berrington et al, 2003). Associated with such inhibition is the selective commissioning or appropriation of knowledge through which particular academic perspectives are ascribed credible status by the powerful in the context of a prevailing 'politics of truth'.

In denying funding to critical work, in challenging its methodological rigour, pressure is exerted on departments, universities, learned societies and independent research bodies to reconfigure their work. Jupp (1989, p 158) concludes that the most "serious threats" to the publication of research findings come from sponsors and influential gatekeepers "who have the power to protect their interests". Yet 'mainstream' social research adopts a "most dangerous relationship to power: the categories and classifications, the labels and diagnoses ... being both stigmatizing and pejorative" (Hudson, 2000, p 177). As our early work on deaths in custody (Scraton and Chadwick 1987b) concluded, the negative imagery and established ideologies "deeply institutionalised in the British state", and supported by narrowly defined academic research, provided the "ready justification for the marginalisation of identifiable groups". It amounted to

> [a] process of categorisation which suggests that the 'violent', the 'dangerous', the 'political extremist', the 'alien', the 'inadequate', the 'mentally ill', contribute to their own deaths by their pathological condition or personal choice. (Scraton and Chadwick, 1987b, p 233)

The primary methodological challenge of the deaths in custody research concerned access to state institutions and their personnel and to significant documentary material. Prisons, police stations and special institutions are walled institutions. As so many miscarriages of justice cases have shown, lack of disclosure of vital information is a serious inhibition to justice through the courts. Critical researchers have no access to primary locations or sources. Thus, their work requires close relationships with the bereaved and their lawyers, accessing statements through court disclosure to families. It also requires thorough court observation and availability of transcripts. The Hillsborough Project reflected a decade's successful research and publication regarding deaths in controversial circumstances.

The Hillsborough Project

> This wasn't a surge. It was like a vice getting tighter and tighter. I turned Adam round to me. He was obviously in distress ... my actual words were, "My lovely son is dying", and I begged him [the police officer] to help me and he didn't do a thing. I started punching the fence in the hope I could punch it down. No-one opened that gate. Right at the beginning when I was begging the officer to open the gate, if he had opened it, I could have got Adam out. I know that because I was there. (Eddie Spearritt, personal communication, February 1990)

Eddie Spearritt's son, Adam, died at Hillsborough. His painful testimony of the final minutes before he and Adam lost consciousness is part of a harrowing story told in full by Eddie and his wife, Janet (Scraton, 1999, 2000). Eddie also gave this account at the subsequent inquests. It constitutes precisely the 'view from below' at the heart of critical analysis. It is 'bearing witness', 'storytelling'; the words "I know that because I was there" resonated around the courtroom, demanding the audience's full attention.

On 15 April 1989, a severe crush on the terraces at Hillsborough football stadium, Sheffield, resulted in the deaths of 96 men, women and children. Over 400 were physically injured and thousands more traumatised. It occurred in a carnival atmosphere, the screams of the dying drowned out by the excited roar of the crowd as the two teams, Liverpool and Nottingham Forest, took to the pitch and the FA Cup semi-final kicked-off. Six minutes later the referee stopped the match as fans were compressed against the high perimeter fences. There was no escape from the pens. Pens like cattle pens. A crush barrier collapsed at the front of one of two central pens taking down a mass of tangled bodies. Fans frantically tried to scale the fences to escape. The police presumed crowd trouble rather than serious over-crowding. As unconscious fans were dragged through two small gates onto the pitch, the obvious question was already being asked: how could this happen in a stadium designated suitable for such an important match?

While fans used advertising hoardings as makeshift stretchers, the South Yorkshire Police match commander informed FA officials that Liverpool fans had broken into the stadium causing an 'inrush' onto the back of already full pens. Police alleged that Liverpool fans were drunk, violent and ticketless. Together these comments coloured all that followed. In an unprecedented move, the coroner ordered blood alcohol levels be taken from all who died, including children. When the bereaved arrived to identify loved ones, they were interrogated about the behaviour and drinking habits of the deceased. The Prime Minister, Margaret Thatcher, was informed that a "tanked-up mob" had forced entry into the stadium (Bernard Ingham, press secretary, personal communication). Within days, *The Sun* newspaper devoted its front page to the headlines:

THE TRUTH. SOME FANS PICKED THE POCKETS OF VICTIMS; SOME FANS URINATED ON BRAVE COPS; SOME FANS BEAT UP PC GIVING THE KISS OF LIFE.

The story was attributed to police sources.

These serious allegations were made as a Home Office Inquiry under Lord Justice Taylor began its work. They contradicted the fans' version of events, including statements by doctors and nurses who tended the dying. It was evident from CCTV footage that there had been an earlier crush *outside* the stadium as fans arrived at the turnstiles half an hour before kick-off. This was caused by a well-known bottleneck and deficient turnstiles. It soon emerged that the police opened an exit gate, under the direction of the match commander, to relieve the crush at the turnstiles. There had been no break-in. Consequently, thousands of fans walked unstewarded and unpoliced into an unfamiliar stadium, and down a 1:6 gradient tunnel. They had no way of knowing that the central pens were full yet the side pens were almost empty. Once down the tunnel, there was no way back.

Given the intensity of the published allegations and counter-allegations, Liverpool's City Council commissioned the Hillsborough Project to research the public inquiry, the inquests, the civil and criminal legal processes, the media coverage and its impact. The Hillsborough Family Support Group and the survivors group were contacted and given details of the intended research. Families and survivors requested that the research include their appalling treatment by the police and other agencies during the immediate aftermath of the disaster. Given the range of the remit it was a complex project, focusing on the treatment of the bereaved and survivors, the negative imagery and 'reputation' of Liverpool, the media representation of the region, of fans and of families and the full range of legal processes and inquiries.

Although initially commissioned for one year, the Hillsborough Project conducted primary research for five years. It published two reports (Coleman et al, 1990; Scraton et al, 1995), and the research continued without funding until 2000 and the conclusion of the private prosecution of two senior police officers (Scraton, 2000). The immediate aftermath involved in-depth interviews with the Head of South Yorkshire Police CID, the South Yorkshire Ambulance Service's Deputy Chief and Head of Operations, hospital administrators, consultants, social workers and clergy. Semi-structured interviews were held with the bereaved, survivors and witnesses. Researching the inquiries, inquests and court cases required attendance throughout, access to all transcripts and in-depth interviews with the bereaved and those survivors called as witnesses. A brief survey of all families was conducted at the conclusion of the longest inquests in legal history. Researching the negative reputation of Liverpool and Merseyside involved archival analysis, political and police records and academic studies. Media analysis included broadcast and print content and structured interviews with journalists. The police evidence was researched after finally gaining access to police statements in 1997-98. Analysis of the statements revealed they had been subjected to a systematic process of review and alteration involving a team of senior officers appointed by the Chief Constable in collaboration with the force's solicitors. The private prosecution, 11 years after the disaster, was researched through court observation, note-taking, accessing the legal submissions and court rulings, and in-depth interviews with families.

Given the combination of hostility and defensiveness emanating from the police, it was clear from an early stage that a decision had been taken at a senior level within the South Yorkshire Force to deflect responsibility from its operational planning and practice. The simple strategy was to 'blame' the fans. It was a decade before the force's Head of Management Services admitted that the climate in which officers had been instructed not to write entries in pocket-books, and their statements were reviewed and altered, was one of "backs to the wall". It was, he stated, "absolutely natural for them to defend themselves" (excerpts from original transcript in Scraton, 2000, p 192). South Yorkshire Police had privileged access to the evidence presented to the inquests and inquiries. It reflected a position of significant institutional power bolstered by the lack of transparency of the police investigation and the limited rights of disclosure afforded to the bereaved families and their lawyers. The research found that the police investigators, Lord Justice Taylor, the coroner and the Home Office were aware of the review and alteration of police statements.

The official inquiries and investigations did not consider the treatment endured by the bereaved and survivors in the immediate aftermath. Yet these experiences were central to the research. The early interviews resulted in a mass of data requiring considerable editing and cross-referencing to build a coherent and consistent account of the aftermath and the events that followed. Families were involved at all stages of the research and with the presentation of the material. Successive inquiries, official statements and court rulings provided a discourse privileged by full access and protected by the rules of disclosure. The research sought alternative accounts, from the bereaved and survivors and also from inside the police and other agencies, establishing a consistent and reliable 'view from below'.

The Dunblane research

Early in the school day on 13 March 1996, a lone gunman walked calmly and unchallenged into the Dunblane Primary School gymnasium and, using semi-automatic weapons licensed by the Central Scotland Police, he shot dead 16 five- and six-year-olds and their class teacher, Gwen Mayor. A further 10 children and three teachers were injured. He fired 105 rounds in just over three minutes and then he killed himself. This cold and seemingly calculated execution of young children in the haven of school was immediately fixed in the public's collective consciousness. Dunblane is a beautiful cathedral city, no bigger than a large village, its name now permanently associated with a single act of terror.

Within an hour, the major incident plan was operational, the most seriously injured evacuated to hospital and the school cordoned off as over 300 parents and relatives waited for news. As Primary 1 parents arrived, they were escorted to a nearby hotel. Without explanation, parents of children in Primary1/13 were taken to a nearby private house and then, in minibuses, to the school staff-room. There they were held, without any information, until the afternoon. Between 1.45pm and 3.30pm, six hours after the shootings, they were led from the staff-room and informed of the deaths of their children. Until that moment, they had no knowledge of the incident, the injuries or the killings.

Eight days later a public inquiry, to be chaired by Lord Cullen, was announced. He heard oral evidence over 26 days and, six months later, he presented his report and recommendations. Much of the report, as directed by the inquiry's terms of reference, focused on the context and circumstances of the shootings, particularly the long-term controversial relationships between the gunman,

Thomas Hamilton, and the authorities. The police had investigated him on several occasions and one internal report questioned his suitability for gun and ammunition licences. Cullen also commented on the treatment of families in the immediate aftermath. He noted families' concern over "delays in being informed of the fate of their children". The situation was "entirely unacceptable, especially when combined with the distressing lack of information" (Cullen, 1996, p 17). Yet Cullen accepted the police explanation that delays were the inevitable consequence of ensuring the accuracy of information and the briefing of family liaison teams. He praised the "general quality of work which was done by the Central Scotland Police" (Cullen, 1996, p 18), giving the impression that families were satisfied with the inquiry, its scope and conduct.

For families, the key issues were, first, how Thomas Hamilton, given his known personal history, could acquire an armoury with police endorsement, and, second, what had caused them to endure such unacceptable treatment throughout the immediate aftermath? A bereaved father criticised the inquiry for its lack of clear structure, overly legalistic language and its failure to hear evidence from the Procurators Fiscal regarding their earlier reticence in prosecuting Hamilton (personal interview, June 1998). Subsequently, Mick North (2000), whose daughter Sophie was killed, noted Cullen's further omissions: the "link" between Hamilton and Dunblane, particularly his "problems" with the town and its authorities; the failure to call witnesses to explore that link; the decision not to call successive Central Scotland Chief Constables; the lack of open discussion of Hamilton's alleged Masonic connections; the partial examination of discrepancies and deficiencies in the gun-licensing process; the serious inconsistencies in evidence between police witnesses and parents, and their social workers.

North (2000, p 197) concludes that had Cullen adopted a "ruthless determination to establish the truth", police officers "who'd distorted the truth ought to have been recalled". According to another bereaved father, the police evidence amounted to a "concerted attempt to make out we had not been left waiting for news of our children as long as we had" (personal interview, June 1998). Another bereaved relative was "stunned" as the police "just stood there and lied on oath" (personal interview, June 1998). In contrast, a family's social worker was "subjected to tougher cross-examination", regarding the verification of times, than that directed towards police officers (personal interview, June 1998). As social workers supported the families' version of events and police officers were not required to explain the clear discrepancies in their evidence, "it was us who were made to feel that we were the ones who were lying" (bereaved mother, personal interview, June 1998).

Lord Cullen placed the crucial internal police report on Thomas Hamilton under a 100 years' non-disclosure order. Following a campaign initiated by the bereaved families, the ban appeared to be lifted in March 2003 by the Lord Advocate under pressure from the Scottish Parliament. It transpired that 106 documents had been subject to the order and the four that were released were 'edited' versions of the originals. Serious issues concerning the historical context and immediate circumstances of the Dunblane shootings remain unresolved, compounded by the lack of disclosure and limitations on evidence.

Establishing new agendas

Each project used taped, semi-structured interviews to enable personal stories to be told and relived. Storytelling, however, cannot be restricted by the 'structure' of interviews. When people do 'memory work', they reflect as well as remember, occasionally making connections for the first time. Often the unexpected, the profoundly personal, is revealed. So vast was the scope of primary research, in the numbers of participants and the length of interviews, that the process of extracting and abridging the core elements of each testimony was onerous. In these circumstances, it was vital that selection of data did not result in its distortion. Extracts, their use and publication, were discussed with participants to ensure nothing was taken out of context or meanings changed. This consultation included exploration of the potential implications of publication. At each stage of the process they retained the right of withdrawal.

Despite the different contexts and circumstances of the tragedies, the Hillsborough and Dunblane research, alongside in-depth interviews with families bereaved by the Lockerbie and *Marchioness* disasters (see Davis and Scraton, 1997, 1999), revealed marked similarities and consistencies. In each case, powerful political and economic interests, with much to lose, were implicated. In the immediate aftermath, procedures were dominated by inter-agency conflict, particularly concerning the operational role and priorities of the police. As in the deaths in custody research, the bereaved complained of insensitive and unacceptable treatment by the authorities. This involved poor communications, absence of reliable information, misinformation, lack of humanity in handling the process of body identification, inadequate provision for receiving and interviewing the bereaved and inappropriate procedures of inquiry. The concern voiced across all projects and cases was that families were, at best, marginalised and ignored and, at worst, excluded and abused.

Marginalisation and exclusion extended beyond the immediate aftermath to the processes of inquiry, investigation and inquests or fatal accident inquiries (Scotland). As discussed earlier, lack of disclosure and/or selective presentation of evidence combined with inaccessible medico-legal processes and discourses inhibiting understanding and restricting participation. Yet, as major 'public interest' cases, the families found themselves thrown into the international media spotlight. With deflection of blame and denial of liability foremost in the legal strategies of those in authority, the bereaved were impelled into defending their campaigns for greater transparency and protecting the reputations of their loved ones. It was in this volatile and occasionally vituperative climate that the researchers operated, regularly providing procedural explanations and personal support to distressed families and survivors.

With the consent and participation of bereaved families, the researchers successfully applied to the Economic and Social Research Council (ESRC) for funding to hold a series of eight international research seminars. The series examined all aspects of the aftermath of disasters and other controversial deaths, including deaths of civilians in Northern Ireland. It brought together family group representatives, campaigners, lawyers, journalists, academics, emergency service workers, counsellors and social workers. The core group (comprising the initial researchers and family participants) set the agenda, established the focus of each seminar and invited outside participants. They shared lead roles in seminar presentations. Two bereaved participants (Partington, 1996; North, 2000) had previously published significant personal accounts. The seminars provided a unique forum for discussion of this work, incorporating and promoting its content and analysis. In evaluating the seminars, the bereaved and survivors were unanimous regarding the personal benefits of their involvement. One bereaved mother stated that

> research into disaster cannot claim academic integrity if it fails to place at its centre the experiences of the immediate victims and their families. This, for me, is the only credible starting place.

A bereaved father noted that the bereaved and survivors "are rarely consulted about how they were treated. Not only does this diminish, even nullify, the value of such [research] reports, but also means that valuable lessons are lost". The seminars enabled the sharing of "common experiences", revealing "universal themes of insensitivity, collective indifference and distortion" by those in authority. They provided "a forum ... not simply for emotional outpourings" but one in which "victims' experiences were always given a broader context provided by those whose expertise ensured that the conclusions reached were always made objectively". A bereaved mother commented that people "who have lived through extreme experiences represent awkward questions". She felt that the seminars met these questions "head on, with courage and imagination". She continued:

> Sometimes I would feel almost euphoric on the long drive home. I suggest that was because I got my say – and a hearing. You could see it in the faces of others – they were being believed.

The significance of the seminars was well illustrated by the following statement from a bereaved sister:

> This innovative research has been an invaluable, two-way, mutual process which has enabled a rare blend of healing and scrutiny in its underlying quest for a more compassionate, more just and more honest way forward for those affected by disasters.

The long-term success of the research projects, including the subsequent range of publications and the seminars that followed, is a consequence of the close, mutual relationship between researchers and participants. It has established a foundation of shared trust and skills on which further applied research, and the dissemination of its findings, will be constructed and developed.

Speaking truth to power

> Whether the 'truth' sets you free is neither here nor there. The choice is between 'troubling recognitions' that are escapable (we can live with them) and those that are inescapable. This is not the 'positive freedom' of liberation, but the negative freedom of being given this choice. This means making *more* troubling information available to more people. Informed choice requires more raw material: statistics, reports, atlases, dictionaries, documentaries, chronicles, censuses, research, lists ... regular and accessible. (Cohen, 2001, p 296)

Critical research is concerned with disclosure at two distinct but related levels. As argued earlier, it is about the revelation of context: locating moments, events and responses within their structural determinants. Returning to Wright Mills, at this level 'personal troubles' can only be fully understood and explained in the structural relations of social and historical conditions. The second level concerns discovery of 'troubling recognitions' that have been denied, neutralised or reconstructed. The disclosure and dissemination of 'troubling information' is the responsibility of the critical researcher, whether academic or investigative journalist. Herein lie alternative discourses, building on case studies to transform personal troubles into public issues, making troubling recognitions accessible and contesting regimes of truth.

I stood with Jimmy Loveridge amidst the rubble, mud and squalor of the Everton Brow Travellers' site. The City Council was determined to evict, to use whatever force necessary to escape its statutory obligations to provide for its travelling population. Jimmy was talking about the pub on the hill. That day he'd gone in and ordered a pint of beer. No one responded: "the fella just looked straight through me". Naively I asked, "Did he have a 'No Gypsies' sign on the door?" Jimmy smiled wryly and responded, "No ... it wouldn't be lawful". There was a pause; then he added, "He's got the sign in his head". When politicians talk of tackling 'social exclusion' and academics promote 'social capital', they seem oblivious to the experiences of 'outsiders', of what it takes to deal daily with the dimensions of 'otherness'. One moment 'otherness' means invisibility, the next it is the full-on physical force of state intervention: harassment, eviction, injury and even death. One moment the attitudinal racism of interpersonal conflict, the next the institutionalised racism of state policies and practices.

For those policies and practices to be formulated and enacted, they require not only institutional authority but also the legitimacy of academic 'knowledge' and professional discourses. In vocational training, applied research and much vaunted 'evidence-based' evaluations, the objective is to establish regimes of truth represented as objective, scientific and value free. Take the disciplines/ professions most influential in processing the cases discussed above: medicine and the law. Each claims to be dedicated solely to the 'common good': medicine for care and cure; law for rights and justice. Yet they are connected implicitly to maintaining and reproducing the status quo. The 'due processes' of legal or medical inquiry rarely confront powerful political-economic interests. These are core elements within regimes of truth. Despite considerable obstacles, not all doctors, lawyers and academics accept the set professional agendas: they form alliances with campaign and support groups to encourage and validate the 'view from below'.

Critical research is often questioned regarding its objectivity and validity. The assumption being that because it sets out to expose 'troubling recognitions', with the intention of 'righting wrongs' or promoting socio-legal reforms, its objectivity is essentially skewed. Certainly there are ethical dilemmas. Discipline-based ethical codes provide guidelines detailing researchers' responsibilities towards research participants. They prioritise safeguards to protect the physical, social and psychological 'best interests' of the researched who should not be adversely affected by their participation. The impact of the research process, however, cannot always be predicted. While guaranteeing privacy or anonymity, neither of which are afforded legal privilege, revisiting deeply sensitive issues is always an emotional, and often painful, experience. In encouraging people to recall and reflect, researchers have to be prepared for unexpected disclosures and, occasionally, personal discoveries brought on through participation. Disclosure and discovery are not necessarily empowering and can emphasise vulnerability. This is particularly significant when powerlessness is institutionalised (for example, research into imprisonment, mental health, bereavement, childhood). Critical researchers should be accountable for handling a process that requests traumatised participants to relive their suffering. As the research seminars show, personal support cannot be restricted to conducting a sensitive interview. The more substantive and enduring needs of participants must be identified and prioritised.

All qualitative research is predicated on establishing personal, moral and political relationships of trust between the researcher and the researched. In-depth research sets out to achieve maximum openness in these relationships. In addressing vulnerability, however, there are ethical imperatives. Consent should be freely given and based on full and accessible information regarding the purpose, funding, objectives, presentation and publication of the research. Anonymity and confidentiality should be guaranteed unless participants agree otherwise. The right to withdrawal and the right to deny permission to publish should be established at all stages of the research. Findings should be discussed fully with participants and any further use of data, by other researchers or through submission to archives, should receive consent. The decision to disseminate and publish findings carries with it a responsibility regarding the 'facts' as found and the risks faced by participants whose accounts enter the public domain. The personal, social and institutional implications of publication, particularly regarding media and official responses, require informed discussion between researchers and participants.

As this chapter demonstrates, however, guarantees and safeguards cannot be applied equally to all participants. The powerless are afforded greater protection, including confidentiality, than the powerful. Institutions and their officers are called to account, while the bereaved and survivors give their testimonies. Thus ethical codes are adjusted in the face of power and its institutional relations. Each project discussed in this chapter reveals the difficulties associated with addressing conflicting interests between powerful state institutions, their officials, and the relatively powerless. Given the structural determining contexts of power, guarantees of confidentiality, privacy and revision cannot be offered to those who represent and protect the interests of corporate bodies or state institutions. A form of 'public interest' defence, more often attributed to investigative journalism, should apply to critical research into alleged abuses of power.

Informing official representatives of the purpose of the research, and the possible consequences of participation, is not always achievable or desirable. Beyond this lies the difficult and often dangerous terrain of covert research. Full participant observation has been defended methodologically on the basis that those being researched will not be influenced by their knowledge of their participation in the research. In critical work covert research is used as a means of accessing powerful and inherently secretive institutions and their operations. If disclosure is formally denied or partially granted, there are no other means of gaining uninhibited access. Put another way, the 'public interest' ends justify means, which, in ethical terms, violate the principles of securing informed consent from all participants.

Clearly, critical research can (and does) subject the researcher to levels of personal and professional commitment which carry serious consequences. Working on controversial cases brings suspicion, hostility and, occasionally, vilification, as those in authority defend their corner. It also leaves the researcher open to accusations of 'over-identification' with their 'research subjects', of 'idealising' the 'view from below', of distorting the analysis in pursuit of political agendas and of exploiting the 'vulnerable' to build academic reputation. In publishing critical accounts and making them accessible to a wide audience, the libel laws are weighted heavily in favour of powerful interests which have the resources at their disposal to initiate proceedings at the drop of a name. Within the academy, anonymised peer review polices and regulates the funding and publication of critical social research. I have experienced directly and personally the impact of each of these inhibitions, including informal approaches to my employers and the censoring of primary research reports. The most profound personal impact, however, is derived in bearing witness to the depths of people's pain and suffering and the consequences on their lives of the uphill struggle for truth, justice and acknowledgement. Yet this is where the foundation of critical research is laid. Hearing, recording and contextualising these testimonies, ensuring that they are afforded the credibility they are due, are the prerequisites to answering the questions with which this chapter opened.

In confronting 'inescapable', 'troubling recognitions', in delving beneath the spin, manipulation and deceit of official discourse and in pursuing alternative accounts, critical social research is concerned with speaking truth to power. Turning cases into issues, it creates platforms for significant societal change. Its protagonists and defenders, however, are unlikely to recruit support for this mission in the corridors of power or the cloisters of the academy. Yet, critical social research has a broader agenda. Providing the 'raw material' that is the stock-in-trade of alternative accounts, and stimulating informed debate and active participation, recasts research as a form of resistance. In this sense, it is a necessary prerequisite and healthy manifestation of democratic societies.

Acknowledgements

Many thanks to my former co-workers at the Centre for Studies in Crime and Social Justice, Edge Hill University College. I have worked with Kathryn Chadwick on deaths in custody for two decades. More recently, Eileen Berrington, Howard Davis, Hazel Hartley and Ann Jemphrey have contributed significantly to our collective endeavour in the Disaster Analysis Research Group. The work of the ESRC Seminar Group has been a unique and remarkable experience for all involved. Thanks particularly to Liz Capewell, Julie Fallon, Mick North, Marian Partington, Eddie Spearritt and Isabel Wilson. As usual, I owe much to Deena Haydon, her considerable research experience, personal support and academic critique. Our collective work, however, could not advance without the unselfish and often painful participation of the bereaved and survivors.

References

Becker, H. (1967) 'Whose side are we on?', *Social Problems*, Winter, pp 239-47.

Berrington, E., Jemphrey, A. and Scraton, P. (2003) 'Silencing the "view from below": the institutional regulation of critical research', in S. Tombs and D. Whyte (eds) *Researching the crimes of the powerful: Scrutinising states and corporations*, New York: Peter Lang.

Chadwick, K. and Scraton, P. (2001) 'Critical research', in E. McLaughlin and J. Muncie (eds) *The Sage dictionary of criminology*, London: Sage Publications, pp 72-4.

Clendinnen, I. (1998) *Reading the Holocaust*, Melbourne: Text Publishing.

Cohen, S. (1985) *Visions of social control*, Cambridge: Polity.

Cohen, S. (2001) *States of denial: Knowing about atrocities and suffering*, Cambridge: Polity.

Coleman, S., Jemphrey, A., Scraton, P. and Skidmore, P. (1990) *Hillsborough and after: The Liverpool experience*, Liverpool: Liverpool City Council.

Connors, J. (1973) 'Seven weeks of childhood: an autobiography', in J. Sandford (ed) *Gypsies*, London: Secker and Warburg, pp 117-78.

The Hon Lord Cullen (1996) *The public inquiry into the shootings at Dunblane Primary School on 13 March 1996*, Cm 3386, Edinburgh: The Stationery Office.

Davis, H. and Scraton, P. (1997) *Beyond disaster: Identifying and resolving inter-agency conflict in the aftermath of disasters*, London: CSCSJ Report for the Home Office.

Davis, H. and Scraton, P. (1999) 'Institutionalised conflict and the subordination of "loss" in the immediate aftermath of UK mass fatality disasters', *Journal of Contingencies and Crisis Management*, vol 7, no 2, pp 86-97.

Foucault, M. (1980) *Power/Knowledge: Selected interviews and other writings 1972-1977*, C. Gordon (ed), Brighton: Harvester Wheatsheaf.

Gouldner, A.W. (1969) *The coming crisis of Western sociology*, London: HEB Paperbacks.

Gouldner, A.W. (1973) *For sociology: Renewal and critique in sociology today*, Harmondsworth: Penguin.

Harvey, L. (1990) *Critical social research*, London: Sage Publications.

Herman, E.S. and Chomsky, N. (1988) *Manufacturing consent: The political economy of the mass media*, New York, NY: Pantheon.

Hudson, B. (2000) 'Critical reflection as research methodology', in V. Jupp, P. Davies and P. Francis (eds) *Doing criminological research*, London: Sage Publications, pp 175-92.

Jupp, V.R. (1989) *Methods of criminological research*, London: Allen & Unwin.

Neuman, W. (1994) *Social research methods: Qualitative and quantitative approaches*, Boston, MA: Allyn and Bacon.

North, M. (2000) *Dunblane: Never forget*, Edinburgh: Mainstream.

Partington, M. (1995) 'Salvaging the sacred', *Guardian Weekend*, 18 May.

Reynolds, H. (1999) *Why weren't we told? A personal search for the truth about our history*, Melbourne: Viking.

Rolston, B. (2000) *Unfinished business: State killings and the quest for truth*, Belfast: Beyond the Pale Publications.

Scraton, P. (1976) 'Images of deviance and the politics of assimilation', Unpublished MA Thesis, University of Liverpool.

Scraton, P. (1999) 'The lost afternoon', *The Observer Review*, 11 April.

Scraton, P. (2000) *Hillsborough: The truth*, Edinburgh: Mainstream.

Scraton, P. (2002a) 'Defining "power" and challenging "knowledge": critical knowledge as resistance in the UK', in K. Carrington and R. Hogg (eds) *Critical criminology: Issues, debates, challenges*, Cullompton: Willan Publishing.

Scraton, P. (2002b) 'Lost lives, hidden voices: "truth" and controversial deaths', *Race and Class*, vol 44, no 1, pp 107-18.

Scraton, P. and Chadwick, K. (1987a) *In the arms of the law: Coroners' inquests and deaths in custody*, London: Pluto.

Scraton, P. and Chadwick, K. (1987b) 'Speaking ill of the dead: institutionalised responses to deaths in custody', in P. Scraton (ed) *Law, order and the authoritarian state: Readings in critical criminology*, Milton Keynes: Open University Press, pp 212-36.

Scraton, P., Jemphrey, A. and Coleman, S. (1995) *No last rights: The denial of justice and the promotion of myth in the aftermath of the Hillsborough Disaster*, Oxford: LCC/Alden Press.

Sivanandan, A. (1990) *Communities of resistance: Writings on black struggles for socialism*, London: Verso.

Stanley, L. (1990) *Feminist praxis*, London: Routledge.

Wright Mills, C. (1959) *The sociological imagination*, New York, NY: Oxford University Press.

ELEVEN

Domestic violence and research ethics

The Domestic Violence Research Group, University of Bristol
Hilary Abrahams (HA), Gill Hague (GH), Ellen Malos (EM),
Melanie McCarry (MM), Tais Silva (TS) and Emma Williamson (EW)

Introduction

The Domestic Violence Research Group (DVRG) in the School for Policy Studies at the University of Bristol – re-launched as the Violence Against Women Research Group in September 2004 – conducts national, international and local studies of domestic violence and of other forms of violence against women. It also offers wide-ranging consultancy, teaching and training on the issue and works, broadly speaking, from an activist perspective. The group works alongside Women's Aid, the principal national organisation working with abused women and their children, and has links throughout the activist movement, in both this country and abroad. Our principles derive from our long history of involvement with feminism and from an understanding of violence against women as a manifestation of inequality in society between men and women.

This chapter evolved from an edited Round Table discussion about the ethics and sensitivities involved in researching domestic violence and other forms of violence against women with a group of researchers associated with the DVRG. We met together and held tape-recorded discussions about the relevant research issues, chosen by the facilitator in consultation with other contributors, and our views about the relationships we have with research participants and research governance. The resulting piece of writing was edited collectively in a lengthy process to which all participants contributed, and which included detailed individual editing, circulation of drafts, group editing, discussions and further meetings. The result is therefore a form of collaborative writing, although individual participants have maintained their own voices where sections of the discussion are included.

We chose this method of collaboration in order to illustrate the importance of researchers collectively discussing and identifying ethical dilemmas that emerge in the course of the research process. It was also relevant that all of the researchers involved in this chapter research around what could be deemed a 'sensitive' research area. Research about violence against women raises additional ethical concerns relating to confidentiality, informed consent, and notions of risk and/ or harm. It is these key issues, in addition to the context of power within the research relationship, which form the content of this chapter.

The discussion also offers an inter-disciplinary perspective. The authors of the chapter have conducted research in the areas of health, education, housing, mental health services, the voluntary sector, social services, and in relation to perpetrators of abuse. As has been discussed in a number of the previous chapters and within the introduction to this book, the guidance given to researchers across these areas frequently differs. Precisely because the authors of this chapter have *diverse* experiences of these research governance frameworks, the following discussion should prove useful to a range of researchers addressing ethics in research.

The contributors were:

- Hilary Abrahams, currently researching supported housing for women and children experiencing domestic violence, after conducting a studentship[1] with the Women's Aid Federation of England as the community sector partner. Her PhD research investigated the structures, models and climate of support offered in domestic violence refuges to women and children experiencing abuse.
- Tais Silva is a psychologist and researcher from Brazil and who is currently conducting a PhD with the DVRG on domestic violence and its medicalisation in Brazil.
- Melanie McCarry currently holds a Post-Doctoral Research Fellowship in the School for Policy Studies at the University of Bristol on domestic violence and has recently completed her PhD on young people, domestic violence and concepts of masculinity.
- Emma Williamson has conducted various research projects in the Centre for Ethics in Medicine and researched domestic violence and health for her PhD. She has written a book on this issue (Williamson, 2000).
- Ellen Malos and Gill Hague are the joint founders (in 1990) and co-ordinators of the DVRG and have conducted a large number of research projects and produced many publications on domestic violence.

Why ethics?

The approach taken within this chapter enabled the participating researchers to reflect not only on key ethical issues in research ethics such as governance, informed consent, confidentiality, and anonymity, but also on their own use of ethics within a variety of research projects. What became apparent early in those discussions was an acknowledgement of the symbiosis between the ethics (morality) of the researcher, and the application of those ethics within the research process. Words such as humanness, fairness, dignity, equality and respect, were used to describe the ideal researcher–participant relationship. Underlying the motivations of the researchers to conduct 'good' research, which was scientifically rigorous, was a desire to conduct that research in a way which both included and protected participants. This highlighted a difficult ethical dilemma that runs through the various themed discussions that have been included in this chapter. The authors of the chapter used the opportunity to question whether or not they had a responsibility to protect participants and whether including participants throughout the research process was a fair and justified expectation. In addition, they considered how practical approaches could be improved in order to address equality issues within research such as ethnicity, sexuality, disability, nationality, and religion.

Alongside the desire to produce ethical and good research was also concern about the role of ethical research governance in this area. A number of fears emerged, both practical and ideological, about the role and purpose of the governance process. Some of these issues are addressed explicitly within this chapter but it is important to acknowledge the unease which notions of externally enforced governance elicit. These fears stemmed largely from a lack of discussion within contemporary social sciences about the philosophical foundations on which research governance decisions are made. For example, we discussed whether a utilitarian or deontological (rights-based) approach to governance was appropriate in our particular research about violence against women. We were also cautious of the medical model of research governance, a position which stemmed, at least partly, from our experiences of submitting non-medical research to a predominately medical committee format. These issues are apparent in a number of the previous chapters in this book and further add credence to the need to consider ethical governance in a transparent and holistic (rather than prescriptive and legalistic) way.

Consent

Consent is an important aspect of ethical protection within all research. The notion of participant consent is intended in most non-therapeutic research contexts to safeguard the autonomy of participants and was enshrined in the Declaration of Helsinki (WMA, 1964). Although the research governance frameworks (and thus the relative practical requirements) differ across disciplinary divides, the notion of consent is apparent within all research (with the minor exception, in terms of prevalence, of covert research). The authors of this chapter raised concerns about what could be deemed to constitute 'informed' consent especially within the context of vulnerable participants such as women who have escaped domestic violence. In addition, questions were asked about whether participants can ever fully give informed consent to research participation when they (and the researchers) may not know at the outset what the impact of participation might be on their emotional and psychological well-being. The following is an excerpt from the round table discussion that addressed these issues.

GH: "I think that there is a responsibility to try and make it as clear as possible to the respondents, to have very clearly presented supporting materials that you would share with them first. To talk about consent and confidentiality issues in language which is appropriate, particularly where you might be dealing with people whose first language isn't English or who don't read things that are written down. So to be as sure as you possibly can that they have understood, you have to take a bit of time and be as sensitive and careful as possible. Also to check back with them if you are going to use what they say, if you are going to anonymously quote them you would still try and find them again and check back to make sure that was OK. Do it more than once maybe to make sure. In the Domestic Violence Research Group, we traditionally haven't got signed things because we have often felt that it was almost useless to do so and can be very difficult for women experiencing abuse, to commit a possibly incriminating or public signature to paper. But obviously from now on we will have to do it because all researchers must. But we have always been very careful to make sure that the person seems to understand at least what is happening and what the research is and what might happen as a result, and that takes time. You have got to give time when you are doing an interview, not just get her to quickly sign it without really knowing about it."

EM: "Yes, there is a problem with signed forms isn't there, where women are worried about their disclosure and their identity, and then they would prefer not to sign something and that maybe creates a problem?"

HA: "That is going to create a lot of difficulties because quite a few women in my sample did not want to sign anything. They were very happy to talk with me, and they made it clear they wanted to, but definitely did not want to put anything in writing. Picking up on a point that you [EM] mentioned, you check that a woman has given formal consent at the beginning, but you don't know what sort of can of worms you are going to open up halfway through the meeting. I think in terms of the ethics of that, you have got to be prepared. A part of you is listening very attentively and is thinking, 'Hang-on, this isn't right!', and you have got to stop and say to the person, 'Do you want to say this?' 'Do you clearly understand what this may lead to?' Especially when it is something like, for example, harm to somebody else, drug abuse, something that is endangering the security of the refuge or anywhere else. I think that it is our responsibility to take care of this, because women may not fully appreciate the consequences of what they are saying and they are happy talking to you, so it is your duty of care to them to point it out. I mean, I did warn people at the start that if any issues around self-harm, or harm to others, or child protection came up while we were talking, that I would have to take some sort of action, but that I would first discuss it with them. But there are other things that may arise during the interviews that you have got to stop and discuss with them before they go on, because of this duty of care."

TS: "I also think that the idea of getting written consent as a universal and fundamental procedure in research does not take into consideration issues of class. It assumes that all participants are able to read or write. From my experience both as a psychologist and a researcher, I would say that in Brazil many illiterate women, who cannot either read or write, would find it humiliating and threatening having to sign a form in order to be interviewed."

A number of issues are raised here in relation to consent. The first is a practical issue in that the requirement to obtain written informed consent may not always be possible for a variety of reasons; for example, participants might be illiterate, they may fear a loss of anonymity by committing to a written document, or there may be language constraints, exacerbated by funding and time restrictions. These difficulties may make the translation of formal consent forms problematic, and the length of time for which consent is valid is also an issue. While it is acknowledged that obtaining written consent is 'accepted practice', the primary concern for the researchers involved in this discussion centred round participants' fears of surveillance, particularly in the context of vulnerable social groups. If, for instance, a competent participant wishes to take part in the research process but does not consent to give written permission, should that research take place? If no written contract exists what other safeguards exist to ensure the validity of the research process and the safety of the participant? Where there is a lack of external approval of research practices, these decisions are made by individual researchers on an ad hoc basis. Increasingly, however, concerns about (legal) liability within academic institutions make it difficult for researchers to deviate from so-called 'accepted' practice of written consent, even when this occurs with the (verbal) consent of the participant.

Power is also apparent when discussing the responsibilities of researchers to protect research participants in terms of potential incrimination and the unforeseen consequences of research participation. Consent traditionally represents a contractual agreement whereby researchers and participants agree to enter the research relationship (Alderson and Goodey, 1998). The discussion presented earlier undermines the ability of the researcher to abdicate responsibility to the participant on the basis of that contract. The reasons why this might be necessary are alluded to when it is questioned whether researchers can always adequately explain the purpose of the research in a manner accessible to the participant. This acknowledgement of the power inherent in the researcher role is important in this context because the notion of a consent contract presupposes the transference of elements of that power from the researcher to the participant.

Considering this point from another perspective, portraying participants as in need of protection would, particularly within a medical setting, be tantamount to paternalism. While in a therapeutic setting paternalism has been challenged as unethical (Beauchamp and Childress, 2001), in a non-therapeutic research context the situation is somewhat more complex. The researchers quoted earlier are questioning whether (a) we can adequately inform participants about the consequences (risk/harm) of participation, and (b), if we cannot adequately inform them, where do our own responsibilities begin and end both within research interactions and across the research process as a whole? It could be argued within a governance framework that such research should not take place if the risks and potential harms of research cannot be adequately quantified, but within social research such risks are frequently unquantifiable (BSA, 2002[2]). The implications of this may mean that such research cannot ever take place.

It is also relevant to examine whether participants may have a right to engage in informed risk taking, and that, provided the limits of the researcher's ability to know and predict risk are explained to the participant, they have the right to decide in the light of the best available knowledge. Anything else, it could be argued, would be paternalistic.

These issues were developed further in the round table discussion in relation to proxy consent, particularly in research with children where the concepts of autonomy and beneficence may come into conflict.

Proxy consent and participant protection

MM: "A central issue for me was that of consent in relation to working with young people. For example, if I had asked the parents for consent and there was violence in the home, there is every likelihood that the parents would not want their child to participate. So, the question remains: how then do you get to interview children where this is going on in their home? So it is problematic about who has ultimate responsibility and control. In my research, I wanted the young people to have the final say in whether they participated or not, but I had to go through the numerous gate keepers before the young people's voices could be heard. Additionally, when it came down to it, no one actually asked if I had been police checked, for instance, or what questions I was asking them or what I was going to do with the information, or how it was going to be used, or where it was going to be used."

GH: "Yes, that is a really cogent point. When we did our children and school research, we did jump through a lot of hoops. We had to provide training and support for teachers if they wanted it, contacts and support for the pupils if required. We had to provide all sorts of additional things."

EM: "We had to send our questionnaires for detailed vetting."

GH: "Yes, we did send out questionnaires, didn't we? And were refused by quite a lot of the schools because they thought it was too sensitive and we had to provide all sorts of things as safeguards, which was good."

EM: "We didn't do police checks, though, did we?"

GH: "No we didn't, but it wasn't quite such a big issue at that time, police checks, child protection, checking for paedophiles, a couple of years ago when we did it, as it has become now."

Two important issues arise here. The first is whether, within social research of this nature, a case can be made that proxy consent from parents can be omitted where the inclusion of such a requirement would undermine the scientific validity of the research process (McCarry, 2004: forthcoming). Certainly within non-therapeutic medical research, the principle of autonomy is paramount, particularly in relation to children (WMA, 1964). Likewise, proxy consent is also required through guidance (British Medical Association, 2001). Within a therapeutic model, however, children would be allowed to consent to participation in treatment (although not able to refuse) (Huxtable, 2000).

The parameters of 'proxy' are also questioned in this discussion in relation to the role of schools and teachers when making decisions on behalf of parents and/or children and young people. At present, there is no national guidance from the Department for Education and Skills (DfES) on the gate-keeping responsibilities of local education authorities. Individual head teachers, who may or may not have experience of research, have the discretion to make such decisions independently. This is incongruent with research practice within medicine where governance is decided centrally and/or through local research ethics committees.

Second, the issue of proxy consent and gate keeping were briefly linked in this discussion to issues of child protection. There is concern expressed that the child protection function of police checks are not being used adequately, yet an ideological gate-keeping role is currently in force, albeit in an ad hoc fashion. Again it is important that researchers consider these issues, particularly in the social sciences where the implementation of more stringent research governance procedures are imminent. In addition, the current discrepancies between different locations of research (schools, hospitals, and so on) are likely to be challenged by the implementation of the government's current Green Paper, *Every child matters* (DfES, 2004).

The problems of gate keeping also emerged within the round table discussion when talking about accessing competent adult research participants through specific agencies.

HA: "Some of the refuges that I approached had had unfortunate experiences with researchers and each of them separately put their own screening process in place. You could argue that that wasn't empowering women by not allowing them to choose if they wanted to participate or not. But the groups felt that they had been used and exploited and they weren't prepared to take part in any further research without thorough checks. So they were very thorough in vetting me and I was quite happy with that. But it seems very sad that there is this ethical problem where researchers may exploit and damage women."

EW: "Can you say a little bit more about the screening processes that they used?"

HA: "Sure. Although Women's Aid nationally had publicised why the research needed to be done, I had to obtain individual agreement from each of the refuges that wanted to work with me. They wanted to know exactly the purpose of the research, what I was going to be asking, what I was going to do with the information, and they wanted to meet me personally, because that is part of building the trust and the rapport and knowing that they would be able to work with me. As I was saying about how you get on with other people, they have got to feel that you are OK from that point of view. So there was a personal vetting and a vetting of the ethics and morality of what I was doing, that it was going to benefit women in general, and that they were going to get full feedback on the research and contribute to the research results. So, openness and honesty were what they were looking for, but it was quite a thorough process and I was content that it should be that way."

While it might be obvious that what we do as individual researchers has an impact on the ability of other researchers to conduct research, the practical implications of bad, and potentially unethical, research are outlined in this extract. This is a very important reason why the wider discussion about ethics and research must be an inclusive process crossing academically defined disciplinary divides, and why a more transparent process that includes ethical considerations is crucial.

It is also worth considering how the experiences described in Chapter Five of this book may differ from those described here, whereby it was a research ethics committee (REC) which suspended approval to conduct the research within a medical setting. In the description earlier, individual refuges are making judgements on the basis of the individual researchers' motivations, reasons for wanting to conduct the research, and their qualifications and/or experiences. Similarly, many decisions about research within schools are being made on the basis of individual gate keepers.

In Sarah Nelson's case (Chapter Five of this book), her experience as a social researcher was undermined by the accusation that her lack of clinical qualifications made her unqualified to continue the work. In the refuge example outlined earlier, it is not on the basis of academic or clinical qualifications that the researcher is being judged, but instead on her previous research and other experiences. On the basis of these discrepancies, we need to examine the existence of power within the gate-keeping and governance frameworks not just between researchers and participants, but between researchers and those by whom they are governed.

The DVRG talked in detail in the round table discussion about 'duty of care'. This, a compromise between participants taking responsibility for participation and paternalism on the part of the researcher, was a useful way in which to consider the responsibilities of the researcher.

Powerful groups and a duty of care

The issues of power and responsibilities were touched on earlier in terms of informed consent. It became apparent in further discussions that there was considerable unease and inconsistency in the way researchers approached powerful and vulnerable groups in terms of differing responsibilities within the research interaction.

> *EW:* "Do we still have the same duty of care? If it's a powerful or less powerful group, is it the same?"

> *MM:* "I think there are various levels and responsibilities depending on which group of people you are researching and their positions of 'power'. If you are trying to investigate a powerful group or an abusive group, you have to be aware that the way you deal with them is fundamentally different to the way that you work with a disempowered group or people who have decisions taken for them."

> *TS:* "I think we always have to keep in mind the idea of 'duty of care'. At the same time, I totally agree with MM when she says that the ways you deal with powerful and less powerful groups are quite different. Going back to what I said before, if you are dealing with a group whose voice has been silenced, for example an ethnic minority, I think it is fundamental to have their feedback throughout – during the research process, the transcription, in the analysis, and even by consulting participants about how the research will be delivered. But if you are dealing with more powerful groups, I think there are other ways of bringing their feedback into the research process. In my research, I did not give policy makers the chance of changing their interviews, as I would have done with women survivors of violence."

> *GH:* "And trying out different methods for different groups of respondents to deal with whatever the different power dynamics are, but without prejudging the research results. I know that another point is our interviewing strategy, for example. Where the woman is experiencing domestic violence, we would ask her if she would like a copy of her interview or tape or to change it or edit or just keep it or whatever. She often might say no, but we

offer that possibility. With a service provider or a statutory agency, we have a different strategy because you don't need to do that, and we might not do it, or not so much, I don't think, with an abuser either. But I would have thought, where we are interviewing an abuser, we would still have a duty to do so, as for anyone else, in a professional way and would try to get full consent and interview respectfully."

The way in which this group of researchers approaches differences in power of respondents is useful in identifying the ways in which participants engage with the research process. For example, there is a suggestion that less powerful respondents and service-users should be better incorporated within the whole of the research process. This would include participant group representation in the planning and dissemination stages as well as feedback of transcripts to individual participants, and rests on the commitment of the research group in question to raising the voices of otherwise silenced groups and to working within an activist framework with women who have experienced domestic violence. With professional and/or more powerful respondents, this incorporation is not deemed as necessary, partly because the power a respondent has influences their individual and collective ability to challenge that research and the potential implications of it. In addition, it is worth considering how other researchers approach the issue of feedback and dissemination. Within epidemiological research, for example, participants will not normally be given individual feedback about the results of their involvement. This is sometimes due to anonymisation. It is still good practice, however, to ensure that research participants in all disciplines are given general feedback in relation to the research outcomes. It is pertinent, however, to ask why? Generally it is considered polite to ensure that participants who are recruited in order to improve knowledge are given the opportunity to engage with that knowledge themselves. This raises additional questions about the way in which research is ordinarily disseminated. It could be argued, for example, that if researchers were better at communicating with participants about their work, such measures and discussions about inclusion would be unnecessary. In terms of policy research and development, it is now considered good practice to involve – and seek the views of – service-users.

The round table discussion about the inclusion of participants in the complete research process extended to participants being given the opportunity to comment on and be critical of that process.

Participant inclusion

HA: "I started off getting informal feedback, which was that the interviews were very, very helpful and that, as EM mentioned earlier, people enjoyed talking to me. Even if it was painful to look back, they could see where they had got to, and it was somebody outside the refuge who was sitting and listening to them and giving them their whole attention for a period of time. Following discussions with the collective, I actually went for written feedback in my last refuge and that was really amazing, because I got a very high response rate from women and workers. It was all supposed to be anonymous, but the residents signed their names and put little notes saying 'Thank you'; that was wonderful. And I actually picked out three quotes that I thought were key points in this process. Two women said 'We felt important and useful again', so it was actually bolstering their self-esteem and self-confidence that somebody was listening and using what they were saying. One of them said that she enjoyed the chance to get her views across to others, and some of her views were highly critical but she was able to say what she wanted to say which maybe she didn't want to say in the refuge setting. And the last quote was from a woman who said 'I hope it helped others; the interview made me decide to be positive and to think of myself and what I want to do in the future'. So it wasn't just a looking back; it was actually a springboard forward for her as an individual. And I am pleased that I did the written feedback and the fact that it actually showed that it was doing a lot of good for them, that they felt happy about it."

GH: "Yes, exactly. Like we've always said that it should try to be about empowerment. We hope that our research is a little bit empowering for the participants at the best. What we always hope will happen, rather than the research just being an exercise that all the parties go through, or even something that would disempower the person and make them feel worse than they had before. But of course we shouldn't kid ourselves that that is the case in instances when it probably isn't. We can imagine we are being more empowering and 'right on' than we are."

MM: "Like HA, the feedback I got from the young people was overwhelmingly positive, and they all said they really appreciated the opportunity to talk and to be asked to talk and to be involved in it. At the end of all the interviews, I asked the young people to be consultants and asked what they could suggest to make this better for the next group, for future interviews. They gave me feedback in that way. But because I was going through an institution to get to them and, because it was anonymous (I wasn't taking full names or addresses), it was very difficult for me to get any more formalised feedback from them or to them. So, when it is anonymised, it can be a bit more complicated if you are wanting to follow up."

GH: "I'm sure our principle is to involve participants at all stages of the research but in fact we almost never do it as regards the analysis. We would like to do it. But it is very difficult to work out how to do it. There is also that other thing about the women being involved, together with researchers, in designing research from the beginning, rather than just being interviewed about something designed by someone else. About the designing of the research, things might come through Women's Aid and at least there is a little bit of input that way perhaps from survivors ... but, again, it's very difficult."

MM: "I think there is a bit of a contradiction: we have a commitment to be empowering and to break down the hierarchy of research but I think ultimately we are the ones that have the research training so you do not want to assume that people can or want to be more involved."

EM: "Well you would say, 'Would you like to do this?' One of the problems is surely that the kind of research funding which we get doesn't permit us to experiment with those kinds of things very much because we are mostly doing something which is very short in terms of time. We work flat out getting the stuff together and producing it. We don't really have the means to do more. It would take longer if you wanted to really and truly involve women or respondents in the process of producing the final piece of work."

HA: "I think when you have got a longer period to do the work in, there is a chance to do that. I took my research back to the Women's Aid conference and the participating refuges. I did the analysis, because that is my expertise, but they are the ones with the knowledge. I took it back and said, 'This is what it looks like to me and this is what I am thinking about. How does that resonate with your experiences?' I think the feedback we had at conference and what I got from the refuges said, 'Yes, that clicks, that is it'. And they then went on and suggested other things, so that they were adding more depth from their knowledge to what I was doing. So although they didn't sit down and transcribe the tapes, or actually go through them, they were involved in the practical aspects of the analysis and I think they added a lot to it. But I would agree if I was doing a quick project, I couldn't possibly do that."

GH: "In the Abused Women's Perspectives research, we attempted to involve survivors all the way through. The study was advised by an advisory group consisting mainly of domestic violence survivors who were professionals, and was also formally advised by a local steering group of domestic violence survivors who weren't professionals, but were women from a local council estate. And we fed it back several times at Women's Aid refuges and Women's Aid conferences and held a variety of workshops for survivors at different stages of the research to comment on the research, to give their views on it and to put forward ideas on what should be included. We also involved survivors' groups formally in the dissemination process."

This final section on inclusion includes some innovative ways of incorporating the views of research participants throughout the research process. This included liasing with representative, advocacy or activist groups (for example Women's

Aid); feeding back to participants and gate keepers; supporting advisory groups which include participant representation; consulting service-users and research participants about the content and direction of the research; and individual feedback and involvement from the participants themselves. How and when this inclusion takes place was debated, particularly in relation to the skills and expertise that researchers and participants bring to the research interaction and process. This discussion illustrates, however, the ways in which researchers learn from and depend to a large extend on the inclusion of participants' perspectives throughout the research process and not just in relation to actual research participation. From the perspective of these researchers, this inclusion is a positive and central element of their work. In relation to governance, it also suggests that any governance framework needs to incorporate all aspects of the relationship between participants and researchers and not just that which occurs within the research interaction.

Conclusion

This chapter has addressed a number of ethical issues that arise in the course of conducting research. Although focused on social science research in the area of violence against women, the issues raised are transferable across a number of subject and disciplinary boundaries. In particular, many researchers will identify with the fears and concerns raised in this chapter. From the potential impact of externally enforced governance, to the relationship between researchers and powerful respondents, this chapter identifies those factors that, from the researcher's perspective, influence their interactions with research participants. The chapter has also considered the positive and negative impact of practice on the conduct of ethical research. Proxy consent, for example, raises contradictions about the rationale for doing research and the need to protect vulnerable participants. This chapter has illustrated that the route through these contradictions needs to be based on the realities of individual projects, the integrity of individual researchers, and a wider discussion about the purposes, role and governance of research in society. The authors acknowledge that participants and researchers are not homogenous groups. Yet there are similarities within those groups in relation to the way in which they experience research and research ethics.

This chapter began with a consideration of consent. The discussion has moved from one of individual autonomy within the research contract to one of wider social inclusion within the research community. Researchers bring valuable skills to that community, as do research participants.

The following is the final extract from the round table discussion we conducted. Put very simply, we asked "If you knew then what you know now, would you do it differently?"

> *EW*: "If you had known then what you know now, how would you have done it differently? Certainly after I had finished my own research, I think

that, although it was very important for me to understand the process of interviewing women and understanding their experiences of health in relation to their experience of domestic violence, looking at it afterwards, I did question whether or not I actually needed to ask that question. I think it helped me to analyse the other data much more clearly, the fact that I had … so I think it added quite a lot, but in terms of what it cost those participants to take part, I could have gone to archive material. I could have done it in a different way, and I think that is certainly something that I took away from my research. I would have found another way to access those experiences of violence without asking the women to actually go through it."

MM: "What I would like to have done differently is meet with the young people first before we did the interview. The groups that worked best, and by that I mean they were most forthcoming in what they were saying, were the ones where we had a chat before it and they got to know more about me: me as a person; me as a researcher; the politics of the research; why I was doing it; and what I was doing with it. Basically, just trying to reduce the hierarchical relationship by giving them more information about the research and me. However, this was not to lull them into any kind of false sense of what they were there to do. They were all very aware of what they were there to do and, as soon as the tape recorder went on, it changed. But I think if I had had a longer time to speak with them first, it would have made it less daunting and easier for all of us."

HA: "Yes. I think I would go along with that. I wish I had put a lot more effort into building the trust and rapport in the self-contained refuge I went to. I am not saying knocking on doors, but, you know, invited them to come and meet me and talk to me. I was trying to be unobtrusive and not get in the way. But I think it would have made better research if I had put a bit more effort into trying to break down the barriers of self-contained accommodation. So, similar to MM, I would like to have built up those first."

GH: "Those first projects that EM and I were engaged in, I think we designed the methodology in this respect really well and we have got bits in the reports that we wrote then about evolving our methodology that we might want to use here. We really thought about it a lot and we did it in a very good way and we took on these issues very purposefully and recorded them. But now, because of all the pressure of work, we have got six things going on at the same time and the pressures from above, a lot of that is becoming almost overwhelming and relentless, so sometimes the sensitive way of doing the research with women suffers. The other thing is that we both had a real commitment to doing research, not only to breaking down power differentials between the researcher and the researched person, but also breaking down power differentials within research teams. So that it wasn't the case that a couple of people directed it, and the research assistants went out and did it. We never wanted it to be like that and we always tried not to have it like that. But now we are being forced into that situation really, and that means that we are having to retract from some of this. We can't do anything about it and I know it is going to become more like that in universities in the future. So I feel that we try as hard as we can to hang on to that kind of stuff but we have kind of lost it a bit because of pressures from the institution. But we have to try to hang on to something about the integrity and humanness of it. What I would like to emphasise is the humanness of the endeavour of research. It is not just a mechanistic thing: it is a deeply human interaction and that is what we have to hang on to."

This final discussion was particularly honest, and underlies the reason for writing this chapter in the collective way in which it was done and, in the end, the basic humanity of the research endeavour. By taking the time to discuss research ethics among colleagues, in an open and transparent way, each of the authors learnt more about research ethics and was encouraged to continue the development of innovative ways of approaching the research relationship. As a result, we would encourage other researchers to undertake this exercise – preferably before external governance is imposed upon us.

Notes

[1] A CASE studentship involves collaboration between a university department and a statutory, voluntary, or business partner organisation. The CASE student would be expected to work with the external organisation in order to define and develop research questions relevant to the work of that organisation. Following the publication of interim reports, the student would be expected to theoretically expand the work in order to fulfil the requirements of a PhD. This collaborative process may also contain political and other activist considerations, which have to be carefully negotiated.

[2] The British Sociological Association (BSA) acknowledges this dilemma by highlighting the need for researchers to be aware of the potential emotional impact on participants of any social research.

References

Alderson, P. and Goodey, C. (1998) 'Theories of consent', *British Medical Journal*, vol 317, pp 1313-15.

Beauchamp, T.L. and Childress, J.F. (2001) *Principles of biomedical ethics* (5th edn), London: Oxford University Press.

British Medical Association (2001) *Consent, rights and choices in health care for children and young people*, London: BMJ Books.

BSA (British Sociological Association) (2002) *Statement of ethical practice for the British Sociological Association*, London: BSA.

DfES (Department for Education and Skills) (2004) *Every child matters*, London: The Stationery Office.

Huxtable, R. (2000) 'Re M (medical treatment: consent). Time to remove the "flak jacket"?', *Child and Family Law Quarterly*, vol 12, no 1, pp 83-8.

McCarry, M. (2004: forthcoming) 'Ethical considerations when conducting social research on domestic violence with young people', in T. Skinner, M. Hester and E. Malos (eds) *Researching women and violence: Creating evidence for change*, Devon: Willan Publishing.

Williamson, E. (2000) *Domestic violence and health: The response of the medical profession*, Bristol: The Policy Press.

WMA (World Medical Association) (1964, amended 1989) *Declaration of Helsinki*, Hong Kong: WMA.

Conclusion

Marie Smyth and Emma Williamson

This edited collection has examined the relationship between researchers and those they research from an ethical perspective. From the first chapter written by the Strategies for Living Project, it is demonstrated that the very terms 'researcher' and 'participant' create a distinction that is not always present in real life. Participants and service-users can be researchers and, as acknowledged in Chapter Eight, researchers can also be participants. By seeking to conduct research that addresses the relationship between researchers and participants, a number of contributors have demonstrated how the distinction between those involved in the research process can be broken down, challenged and as a result, more reflexive research can be accomplished. But why is that important?

A number of methods of inclusion have been described in this book including the use of service-user researchers, reference groups, stakeholder boards of directors and consultative feedback methods. An examination of these methods demonstrates how the nature of the relationship between the researcher and participant impacts directly on the methodological and epistemological characteristics of the research itself. Within disciplines where positivistic and strict notions of epistemological and methodological rigour exist (for example, within epidemiological research outlined in Chapter Nine by John Henderson), the strict differentiation between researchers and participants (subjects) remains. That is not to say, however, that such research is less inclusive or ethical. Such research undergoes rigorous ethical governance processes where lay representation is mandatory, whereas such rigour in ethical review is largely absent in the social sciences in general, for example.

By looking at governance and control across the disciplinary divide, this collection illustrates discrepancies in the current system. This is most apparent in direct comparison between specific chapters. For example, Nelson (Chapter Five) explores the problems that can occur in the governance process when certain groups in society are not represented on research ethics committees. This was also an issue for the Strategies for Living Project (Chapter One), although those fears proved unfounded, and for Cameron et al (Chapter Six). Other researchers did not encounter this problem, not because the subject of their work was less of an emotional risk to participants, but because the location of the research was different, and they did not have to submit to a third-party ethical review process such as that experienced by Nelson, Henderson and others in this volume. For example, the Domestic Violence Research Group (Chapter Eleven) were not obliged to seek external ethical approval since their work accessed participants from within domestic violence refuges. Likewise, Rafferty, an investigative journalist, describes research in Chapter Seven which does not require ethical approval even where the subject of the research, like that described by Nelson, is child sexual abuse.

These comparisons raise a number of important questions about the way participants of research – and researchers – are differentially treated across the various disciplinary settings in which research takes place. These questions include issues of control over the initiation of research, risk assessment, fiduciary relationships and proxy consent, the role of participants in data collection, analysis and dissemination, participants' views of their various experiences as participants and on how they would wish their rights to be protected.

What we conclude here is that the answers to these questions, at present, vary according to the disciplinary context of the research. This, in turn, raises important ethical issues such as that of equity between the professions. Why should a doctor undergo a third-party review and a social scientist not? It is not entirely because the risks to participants are fundamentally different in each field, but because the historical evolution of research governance and the ideological platform on which it stands is not a level one. There are a number of reasons for this.

First, government research governance through the research ethics committee (REC) system serves a number of purposes of which participants' protection is only one. An equally important function is to manage the liability of government departments in which research might take place.

Second, ethical codes differ and priorities vary. For example, a journalist such as Rafferty in Chapter Seven might prioritise the publication of a story in the public interest over the rights of an individual interviewee. Conversely, in service-user research, the inclusion and involvement of participants in the process might be the overriding aim and objective (Chapters One and Four).

Third, even where there is a formal ethical determination by a governance mechanism, professional conflicts of interests can and do arise, particularly if a piece of research is perceived as challenging the authority of that profession (Chapter Five).

Participant involvement in knowledge decisions makes the assumption that participants want to be involved. In the chapters by the Domestic Violence Research Group (Chapter Eleven) and that by Smyth (Chapter Eight), it is clear that those who hold the knowledge and experiences being investigated by the research process have a vested interest in that subject being studied, whether that is women who have experienced domestic violence, or citizens living in a conflict-torn community. However, addressing the construction of knowledge with participants raises further questions about epistemological and methodological approaches. Scraton addresses this point in Chapter Ten. He challenges whether traditional research methods enable us to truly include participants in a research process where researchers ultimately speak on participants' behalf.

A number of specific ethical issues and dilemmas faced by participants and researchers were raised within individual chapters. These included researcher safety; payment to participants; the governance process; responsibility;

accountability; and liability. Underlying these issues and the ethical dilemmas inherent within them contributors described how they juggled the often conflicting demands of the principles of participant anonymity, confidentiality, consent and proxy consent.

Anonymity and confidentiality

There was surprising synergy across the various chapters about the ethical principles of anonymity and confidentiality. This included the importance of protecting 'sources' as discussed by Rafferty in Chapter Seven. All of the contributors acknowledged the importance of confidentiality in protecting participants, and the dilemmas faced when the limits of confidentiality are breached; for example, where child protection (Chapter Eleven) or harm to vulnerable participants became an issue (Chapter One). The primary concern about confidentiality referred to the relationship between researchers and services, where service evaluation was the aim of the project (Chapter Five). It was also raised in Chapter Six (Cameron et al), when discussing the inclusion of family members in research with older people with dementia. The issues of confidentiality discussed here related primarily to the boundaries of individual autonomy.

Improving ethical practice in relation to anonymity and confidentiality involves the resolution of practical dilemmas in all the various disciplines. Better dissemination of information on good (and bad) practice in research in general would improve the ability of researchers to make good ethical research decisions. This may require that ethical training and support (such as that described in Chapter One) is made available for researchers, where they have access to information on solutions to ethical dilemmas, and the opportunity to discuss and comment on ethical decisions they have to make. It is important that participants' views are included in this process. This is in order to avoid paternalism where researchers might act in order to protect participants without proper consultation or involvement of participants.

Consent and proxy consent

There was agreement across the majority of the chapters that individual participants' consent to participation should always be sought. This is standard procedure, although there is some variation when verbal or written consent is obtained. Some researchers (Chapters Five and Eleven) questioned whether written consent was always appropriate. There were situations where the issue of consent became more problematic for researchers. The relationship between initial informed consent-giving and on-going consent throughout the research process is one such situation. Where the involvement of participants was as active researchers (Chapters One and Four), the input of service-users and participants was continuous, thus implying the continued consent of those taking part. In other examples of research, the contact between researchers and participants was in the form of a one-off meeting. For example within the epidemiological research discussed in Chapter Nine, consent was given for the data to be collected, with the bulk of the research process being taken up with the analysis of that data. Consent issues were also complex in the longitudinal research described in Chapter Six, there were several contact points between researchers and participants over the course of the project.

In terms of risk and potential harm, some researchers, including the journalist Jean Rafferty (Chapter Seven), raised questions about whether participants (respondents) could be prepared for the impact of participation. In the case of some research areas such as domestic violence (Chapter Eleven), sexual abuse (Chapter Five), armed conflict (Chapter Eight), ethnic discrimination (Chapter Ten), dementia (Chapter Six), and cancer and ill-health (Chapter Two), the emotional impact on both participants and researchers of recounting or hearing traumatic personal experiences was acknowledged by researchers in relation to the ability of participants to give properly-informed consent. The majority of contributors to this book believed that the researcher had some responsibility to address this problem, either by warning participants about the potential impact prior to taking part, or by ensuring that additional support was available to participants after the initial contact took place.

The analysis of information that is exchanged varied between those researchers who gave respondents the ability to comment on the analysis and those who did not. The analysis process itself is discussed later in this conclusion. The way consent is sought will impact on the ability of participants to withdraw from research at a later date. The consent process, as outlined within the governance guidance to health researchers, should include information about what happens to information during the analysis and dissemination phases of the research process.

The issue of proxy consent was also addressed in a number of chapters where research with potentially vulnerable populations was examined. Research with children (Chapters Three, Nine and Eleven), mental health service-users (Chapters One and Five), people with learning disabilities (Chapter Four) and with older people with dementia (Chapter Six) raised issues of proxy consent, and its viability over time. These chapters discussed the problems of obtaining consent by proxy and the ethics of including participants who could not give informed consent. Researchers also questioned the difference it made if participants' inability to give consent was due to competence or legal definitions of competence. For example, within Chapter Six, Cameron et al discuss how a small number of the older people in their research were suffering from, or began suffering from, forms of dementia. In their case, the competence of participants to give consent fluctuated during the course of the research, making it difficult to maintain fully-informed consent. Where this arose, other family members were included in the research both as proxy consent givers and as participants. Within the research described by Tarleton et al (Chapter Four), the non-competence of the participants was challenged, as was the need for proxy consent in some cases. The impact of proxy consent on the confidentiality of participants is substantial, and the methodological impact of proxy consent was also addressed in Chapter Eleven. There, concern was raised that parents who were violent and abusive might be more prone to refuse to give consent for their young people to discuss such issues, thus biasing and undermining the research itself.

Whether subject to external ethical review or not, researchers reported how they took advice from colleagues and discussed the potential ethical problems which would result from the various options. As with other ethical dilemmas that were identified in the various chapters, the inclusion of participant representatives was a good way to identify the impact of the decisions made. For example, the authors of Chapter Four describe in detail the importance of approaching participants with respect for their autonomy irrespective of whether that status was legally binding.

Different perspectives

These ethical issues underpin the parameters of the relationship that exists between those who collect and those who provide the information that creates knowledge. It is our assertion, from the diverse descriptions contained in this book, that before we can adequately address professional guidance and governance within research, that all stakeholders' perspectives need to be acknowledged.

This book was written primarily as a result of concerns expressed by the editors about the way in which ethical guidelines for researchers were being devised. This book has placed as central the experience of research from researcher and participants' perspectives. Researchers from different disciplines have described how they approach the ethics of that relationship, thus illustrating how the ethical problems facing health and social researchers, journalists and medics are fundamentally the same, or at least have substantial commonalities. Basic human values of respect and humanity underpin good ethical governance, as several authors point out. Whether these values will emerge so clearly and so prominently, if research participants are excluded from the discussion, is a key question.

As we begin to introduce stricter ethical guidance within the social sciences, it is therefore crucial that we put right the omission of participants from the debate. This book, we hope, has begun that process. The boundaries between research, science and evaluation are beginning to change as more interdisciplinary work is conducted, where service-users are consulted, and where action orientated research is taking place. The breaking down of distinctions between types of researchers also compounds the blurring of these distinctions. Increasingly, university-based academic researchers are conducting service evaluation either independently or in collaboration with service providers. Similarly, scientists are encouraged to engage with the public, through the media, to communicate scientific issues and how they impact on wider society. Distinctions within research itself become less evident. Certainly, the comparisons within this book illustrate how service-users (Chapters One and Four), health researchers (Chapter Five), social scientists (Chapter Eleven) and journalists (Chapter Seven) are engaged in similar work.

Changes are occurring in the institutions where research takes place, and it is argued here that good governance must include the perspective of all those with a vested interest in that process including participants. Innovative forms of inclusive research methods, such as those described by contributors to this book, can provide a useful starting point for setting the conditions necessary to begin addressing broader governance questions in a way which includes, rather than excludes, participants and respondents.

Finally, the issues addressed in this book go beyond the governance of individual researchers or projects. Fundamental questions are raised by all of the authors about the concept of knowledge and its purpose. There are a range of motivations which drive researchers to conduct research: to advance medical knowledge; to test drug safety; to gauge public opinion; to understand more about social issues and problems; to uncover corruption and skulduggery; or to advance an academic career. The products of research similarly vary: knowledge which will improve health services, or voice given to silenced 'victims' of acts of inhumanity; or understanding the motivation of those who carry out such acts, so that understanding can lead to change. For those who contribute their time and cooperation as research participants to this process, and for those who conduct it, there are costs and benefits. Individual risks and costs are balanced against benefits to wider society, the distress caused to the individual 'victim' of abuse in an interview can be off-set by the potential benefit such as improved services to other 'victims'. Researchers, too, benefit, whether they be a medical researcher, a sociologist, or a journalist. This volume offers a reflection on the equity of these cost/benefit analyses as embedded within the power relations which inevitably exist between those who do the researching and those who are researched, those who have, create, and have access to, the knowledge created by the research process.

The final chapter (Eleven) in this collection consisted of an edited round table discussion conducted by a group of researchers. We would ask that readers of this book consider engaging in such a discussion, where ethical issues and practical dilemmas faced in their own work are explored. Whether in an academic, media, medical, or service-provider setting, this will help to ensure that the foundations on which research is based are ethically sound.

Index

skills for research 82-3
support for 79, 83-4
Pilgrim, D. 98, 99
police
  checks for domestic violence
    researchers 200, 201
  deaths in custody 181, 182
  Dunblane inquiry 185-6
  harassment of gypsies 176, 177
  Hillsborough evidence 183-5
  miscarriages of justice 181
Policy Studies Association 14*n*
Political Science Association 14*n*
Post Traumatic Stress Disorder 139
power relations
  critical research view of 181-2, 190-1
  in domestic violence research 199-
    200, 203-4
  in investigative journalism
    editorial power 129-31
    and interviewee 123-4
  and knowledge 4, 5, 6, 181-2, 216
  people with learning difficulties as
    researchers 74, 79, 84, 85
Press Complaints Commission 133, 134
Presswise 11
Preston, Peter 133
protection *see* ethical protection
proxy consent 214-15
  child participants 3, 57-60, 64, 67, 69,
    160, 168-9
  domestic violence issues 200-3, 215
  dementia sufferers 107, 108
psychiatric services *see* childhood sexual
    abuse survivors; service-user-led
    research
psychotic patients: exclusion from
    research 92
public audience
  critical research 190-1
  investigative journalism 123
  Northern Ireland survey 150
public hearings
  Northern Ireland survey 147-8
  see also official inquiries
public interest considerations
  critical research 191
  investigative journalism 126-8

R

racism towards gypsies 176-7, 189
Rafferty, Jean 7, 12-13
randomisation concept 37

randomised controlled trial participation
  35-51
  focus groups 37-8, 53-4
  informed consent 36-7, 50
  participants' understanding of
    concepts 37
  subjective influences 43-4
  and voluntariness of participation
    42-4
  methodology 37-9
    data analysis 39
    negative feedback on hypotheses
      38-9
  research findings 39-42
    altruism as motivation 48-9
    concept of choice 40-2
    process of choosing to participate
      44-6
    risk of participation 46-7
    self-interest as motivation 47-8
    voluntariness and freedom of choice
      42-6
Reason, P. 142-3
recovered (false) memory debate 93,
  98-9
RECs *see* Research Ethics Committee
  system
reflexive subjectivity 141
regimes of truth 179-80, 190
regulation of research *see* ethical
  review/governance process
research: nature of 3, 5-6, 216
research advisory groups
  domestic violence research 206
  Northern Ireland study 145, 146
  people with learning difficulties 75-8,
    77-8
research advocates 3
research companies in Northern Ireland
  144-5, 149, 151
Research Ethics Committee (REC)
  system 8-9, 21, 35
  Beyond Trauma project dispute 91, 92,
    94-6
  composition
    dominance of medical professionals
      29-30, 94, 101-2, 211
    guidelines extend range of members
      101
  extent of remit 100-1, 212
  and old age and dying study 106, 108
  and randomised controlled trial
    participation 37, 38
  service-user-led research 29-32, 33

V

Van Manen, M. 142
'victim politics' 153
'view from below' *see* critical research
Violence Against Women Research
    Group 195
voluntary sector: representation on
    RECs 101
'vulnerable' individuals 3
  creating dependency 152
  and critical research 190, 191-2
  domestic violence survivors 197,
    203-4
  ethical responsibility 13, 213
  and informed consent 36, 51*n*
  see also childhood sexual abuse
    survivors; old people

W

W, Claire (abuse survivor) 134, 135
Walmsley, J. 73, 75, 83
Ward, L. 75
Waters, Rachel 21
Watson, Alan 132
Watson, Barbara 125-6
Watson, Diane 131-3
Watson, Margaret 131-3
Wells, Roy 176
Wells, Stephanie 21
Whyte, J. 139-40
Williams, Val 74, 81, 82-6
Williamson, Emma (EW) 196, 202, 203,
    207-8
women *see* childhood sexual abuse
    survivors; domestic violence research
Women's Aid 195, 202, 206
World Medical Association *see*
    Declaration of Helsinki
Wright Mills, C. 178, 180, 189
Wright, Sarah 21

Y

young people
  and domestic violence 200-3, 205,
    208, 215
  impact of Troubles on 141
  militarisation in Middle East and
    South Africa 141, 153
  see also Avon Longitudinal Study;
    childhood sexual abuse survivors

Discursive analytical strategies
Understanding Foucault, Koselleck, Laclau, Luhmann
Niels Åkerstrøm Andersen, Department of Management, Politics and Philosophy, Copenhagen Business School, Denmark

This exciting and innovative book fills a gap in the growing area of discourse analysis within the social sciences. It provides the analytical tools with which students and their teachers can understand the complex and often conflicting discourses across a range of social science disciplines. Students will find the clear exposition of the theories and strategies supported by an easy-to-digest, easy-to-read layout, which includes summaries and boxed examples highlighting the relevance of analytical strategies to social and policy research.

Paperback £16.99 US$29.95 ISBN 1 86134 439 2
Hardback £45.00 US$59.95 ISBN 1 86134 440 6
240 x 172mm 160 pages January 2003
INSPECTION COPY AVAILABLE

An exploration of guidelines for the ethical conduct of research carried out by mental health service users and survivors [tbc]
Alison Faulkner, Independent Survivor Research

This report provides invaluable guidance to researchers, trainers in research skills and interviewers working from the perspective of mental health service users and survivors. There are helpful hints and suggestions, as well as quotations and ideas reflecting the experiences of those who were consulted for the development of the guidelines.

Paperback £9.95 US$16.95 ISBN: 1 86134 641 7
297 x 210mm 48pp tbc November 2004
Published in association with the Joseph Rowntree Foundation

Talking about care
Two sides to the story
Liz Forbat, Centre for Research on Families and Relationships, University of Edinburgh

Despite its familiarity, the realities of care are both complex and contested. This book offers a unique approach to scrutinising the co-existence of both care *and* abuse in relationships. It demonstrates ways of increasing critical reflexivity when working with people involved in difficult care relationships. *Talking about care* is an important resource for practitioners, trainees and academics in health and social care who want to critically examine the way that care is talked about. It explores new territory by addressing both *practice and theoretical issues*, drawing particular attention to the *utility of discourse analysis* in practice.

Hardback £45.00 US$69.95 ISBN 1 86134 621 2

234 x 156mm 224 tbc pages January 2005

Love, hate and welfare
Psychosocial approaches to policy and practice
Lynn Froggett, Department of Social Work, University of Central Lancashire

"... highly erudite, thought-provoking and an exhilarating read." *Journal of Social Policy*

This book presents a psychosocial examination of the changing relationships between users of services, professionals and managers in the post-war welfare state. It challenges the current emphasis on consumer rights by linking social responsibility to its psychosocial roots and breaks new ground in theorising the links between the intimate day-to-day experiences of care and the development of social policy.

Paperback £17.99 US$28.95 ISBN 1 86134 343 4

Hardback £45.00 US$69.95 ISBN 1 86134 344 2

234 x 156mm 216 pages October 2002

INSPECTION COPY AVAILABLE

To order further copies of this publication or any other Policy Press titles please contact:

In the UK and Europe:
Marston Book Services, PO Box 269, Abingdon, Oxon, OX14 4YN, UK
Tel: +44 (0)1235 465500
Fax: +44 (0)1235 465556
Email: direct.orders@marston.co.uk

In the USA and Canada:
ISBS, 920 NE 58th Street, Suite 300, Portland, OR 97213-3786, USA
Tel: +1 800 944 6190 (toll free)
Fax: +1 503 280 8832
Email: info@isbs.com

In Australia and New Zealand:
DA Information Services, 648 Whitehorse Road Mitcham, Victoria 3132, Australia
Tel: +61 (3) 9210 7777
Fax: +61 (3) 9210 7788
E-mail: service@dadirect.com.au

Further information about all of our titles can be found on our website:

www.policypress.org.uk